Inventory Management and Purchasing

Tales and Techniques From the Automotive Aftermarket

By

Pete Kornafel

ISBN: 1-4140-5910-8 (e-book)
ISBN: 1-4140-5909-4 (Paperback)
ISBN: 1-4140-5908-6 (Dust Jacket)

Library of Congress Control Number: 2003099932

This book is printed on acid free paper.

Printed in the United States of America
Bloomington, IN

First Edition

1stBooks - rev. 05/03/05

"A fool and his inventory are never parted."[1]

"An approximate answer to the right question is much more valuable than an exact answer to the wrong question."[2]

[1] William B. Miller and Vicki L. Schenk. All I Need to Know about Manufacturing I Learned at Joe's Garage. Bayrock Press, 2001.
[2] Quote from John Tukey in David Salsburg's The Lady Tasting Tea, Henry Holt and Company, 2002.

Acknowledgements

My first acknowledgement is to Anders Herlitz.

In the early 1970's, Hatch Grinding Company was a very rapidly growing auto parts distributor, managing an expanding inventory of about 35,000 items with stock cards and a lot of inventory clerks. About that time computer systems became affordable for small businesses, and we desperately needed one for inventory management. We placed the first order in Denver for IBM's System/3 when it was announced in 1973.

Anders was an IBM software developer specializing in inventory. He wrote the IBM Field Developed Program, INVEN/3, for distributor inventory management.

Hatch placed an early order for INVEN/3, and I met Anders at the first training class held by IBM on this product. We implemented it rapidly. For several years, Hatch had the inventory with the most SKUs of any of the INVEN/3 users, so Anders used our database to benchmark processing times. We became good friends.

In 1980 Anders decided to leave IBM. I became his partner, and we formed E3 Associates. Anders wrote several key enhancements to IBM's package. We tested them at Hatch, and sold them to INVEN users. After a couple of years E3 was established and Anders bought me out with a handsome return on my original investment. E3 went on to dominate the market for inventory management software, and sold many major companies, including Ace Hardware, Victoria's Secret, CVS Drugs, Advance Auto, Pep Boys Auto Parts, Fleming, and many others. E3 was acquired by JDA in 2001.

I learned how to apply inventory management mathematics from Anders. His techniques helped us grow Hatch Grinding 30 fold in sales and profits over 20 years. Much of the math in this book came from him, while he was at IBM and E3.

I also wish to acknowledge Dr. Glenn Staats. Glenn owned Cooperative Computing, Inc., a specialist in computer systems for automotive stores and distributors. They are now known as Activant Solutions.

Martin Fromm made the Automotive Warehouse Distributors Association into a major force in our industry, and our affiliation with AWDA made Hatch a much better company. Lou Zuanich, and Chuck Udell let me teach the Inventory Management workshop for more than 20 years. Anders and Glenn each helped me as instructors several times. Recently, Kris Walker and Braxton O'Neal have instructed the AWDA workshop. I learned more from all of them.

All the students who attended the workshop over 20 years also broadened my experience in automotive inventory management. My forehead has a flat spot, from hitting it with my hand whenever one of them made a profound observation and I said, "Why didn't I think of that." Many examples are from them...

I wish to thank General Parts, Inc. Raleigh, NC, for permission to use their internal data for examples.

Braxton O'Neal and Jody Pritzl provided extensive and valuable editing and additions to this book.

Louise Veasman, my assistant for almost 20 years, also provided an extensive edit of this book. She always helped me look my best, and she improved this manuscript a lot, too.

Jay Dahl kept Hatch's computer systems running smoothly for many years, and provided excellent software for our company.

Mike Riess, John Krasovich, Dede Geary, Rena Bond, Randy Onorato, and Kathy Dowell all worked in various positions in inventory management and purchasing at Hatch Grinding, and I learned a lot from all of them.

Finally, I am most indebted to Annie, my wife of 36 years. We were partners in business at Hatch Grinding for 25 of those 36 years. We figured out how to live together and love each other full time. Today you would say we have been married 24 x 7 for 36 years. She tolerated the time this took, and her help made this book much better.

Any errors, however, are mine...

Table of Contents

Table of Figures

To the Reader
Did you choose to be a Buyer?

I've had the pleasure of working with hundreds of buyers and inventory managers in the automotive aftermarket.

I always ask. No one has ever told me that as a child, growing up, they wanted to become a buyer for an automotive parts distributor. Nor have many told me they spent a big part of their formal education studying statistics, logistics, forecasting, negotiating skills, and other key topics to train themselves to be a buyer or inventory manager.

A few of my acquaintances chose to become buyers or inventory managers, but most of us arrived at the job of managing inventory not by our own choice. Most of us learned our skills "on the job". Usually, that meant practicing with someone else's money. In my case, as a business owner, it meant practicing with my own money. The mistakes of buying too much were still in inventory and visible to all. It was harder to see the impact of the mistakes of not buying enough, and giving poor service.

I believe almost everyone connected with managing a distribution inventory will find ideas of value in this book. I hope that is true for you.

About the organization of this book

This book is organized from the ground up. All the basic "building blocks" are discussed first. You'll have to read a lot to get to replenishment purchasing, but that's the way your system should operate.

All my experience in inventory management convinced me that it is necessary to get all the underlying data "right" first. If you do that, then a well-designed system can largely take care of itself. Buyers will seldom have to change an item on a suggested order if the underlying data has already been entered and validated. If they do decide to change a suggested order quantity, it means they need to update the underlying data, too.

The system can drive your inventory and service levels toward your goals only if these goals are recorded and implemented at the item level. Otherwise, you have to "steer" the system continuously, and probably won't get the best results.

If you have embedded approved seasonality information into your item or category forecasts, then the system will ramp inventory up going into the season, and ramp it down near the end of the season. If you don't have this, you have to have a yellow sticky note on your calendar to remind you to manually change something at these turning points.

If you have to order $2,000 from a vendor to get prepaid freight, your system shouldn't even suggest an order until you need that amount, or until the projected lost sales of not ordering now offset the added freight expense of a small fill-in order.

If you have a service level goal (and you should), then that should drive your safety stocks. If it doesn't, only luck will bring you close to your goal.

As an aside, buyers who do not have all the right software tools will have LOTS of yellow sticky notes stuck everywhere in their office, to remind them to do all the things their software won't do on its own. They need notes about the start and end of every season for every seasonal line, and a thousand other details. It's an easy way to tell how good an inventory system is. No sticky notes in the buyer's office means the data is already recorded in the system, and the buyer doesn't have to try to remember it.

If you're an inventory manager or buyer, and you need lots of sticky notes (or "jogs" in your Outlook files, or notes in your calendar, or any other system except posting all the data to your inventory data base), then your system may not give you the right tools for optimum inventory management.

Applicability—Items with long life cycles

The techniques discussed in this book can apply to the inventory management of a wide range of hard goods.

The major exception is that these techniques will not help manage fashion items of any kind.

All of the techniques presented here presume that there is demand history for an item, and that history can be used to forecast the near future demand for that item. Fashion items do not fit this model. Other forecasting techniques must be used to estimate demand for things like the latest CDs and DVDs, or seasonal apparel, or best-seller books. These items might have a total life cycle of a few weeks or months.

Certainly some items in these categories become regular sellers over a longer period of time, and then the techniques in this book could be applied to them.

So, the critical measure is the overall life cycle of an item. The techniques in this book will not help manage items that go from introduction to obsolete in a span of weeks or months.

The life cycle for most replacement auto parts and many other items is measured in years or decades. For these items, forecasting based on demand history works well. If the item is truly seasonal, the seasonal pattern is likely to repeat in a coming year. If the item has some reasonably mild up trend or down trend over the past several years, that trend is likely to continue into the near future. If the item has a generally level, even if erratic, demand pattern, a good forecast can be based on the demand history and safety stocks can be based on the level of variability in demand and lead time.
If you have an interest in inventory management of these kinds of items, read on...

Overview
The Mission Of Purchasing and Inventory Management

David Viale[3] provides a concise summary of the mission of inventory management:

"The objective of inventory management is to replace a very expensive asset called inventory with a less expensive asset called information."

"The major reason for managing inventory is to reconcile the following potentially conflicting objectives:

1. Maximizing Customer Service
2. Maximizing Efficiency of Purchasing (and Production)
3. Minimizing Inventory Investment
4. Maximizing Profit."

In addition, Braxton O'Neal of General Parts points out that the maximum generation of gross profit depends on good customer service, to maximize order fill. That depends on the best possible use of available inventory investment dollars. So, determining the best mix of inventory is also a critical part of good inventory management.

The Profit (not the Devil) is in the Details

The process covered here manages an inventory from the bottom up. The most profitable inventory management occurs when each item and all categories of items are optimized. The best service level goal and safety stock, the best order frequency, and the best forecast will optimize the performance of the overall inventory.

This is an important distinction. If the inventory system has the right techniques and does the best job of managing all the details, then the profitability of the company will be maximized.

The overall service level and inventory turnover are measurements of the result of this process. They are what they are. The key is to optimize profitability, rather than to try to manage the turnover or service level.

---

[3] J. David Viale, Basics of Inventory Management, Crisp Learning, Copyright 1996.

Many inventory management systems attempt to drive the process from the top down. They set an overall target for inventory turnover, or an overall target for service level, and attempt to achieve those by basing item level decisions on some criteria to match the overall goals. It is not possible to implement these overall targets without compromises on individual items, and every one of those compromises reduces overall profitability. So, this book builds the management system from the item level up to the total organization.

Chapter 1 and 2 outline the shape and size of inventories in the automotive aftermarket, and give an overview of this distribution channel.

Chapter 3 starts with Best Practices for Inventory Control. You can't do a good job unless the basic data is accurate and timely.

Chapter 4 explores the issues in counting demand accurately.

Chapters 5 and 6 show ways to classify inventory and select items to be stocked at stores and distribution centers (DCs).

Chapter 7 discusses the benefit of short lead times.

Chapters 8-12 cover several models for forecasting. A forecast must be developed for every stock item where the replenishment time is more than a few days or the demand is more than a few units. Not all items are equal, and no one forecasting model can adequately cover all item behavior patterns. There are chapters on forecasting "regular", "slow", "lumpy", "trend", "seasonal", and "promotion" items. This, coupled with lead-time, replenishment frequency, vendor requirements, and some safety stock is needed to compute a stock level and order quantity for every item. Even in "pull" systems a forecast is needed for almost all items, as explained below.

Chapter 13 covers Economic Order Quantity, and when it should and should not be used.

Chapter 14 presents a method for forecasting lead times for both product lines and individual items.

Chapters 15 and 16 present formulas for computing safety stocks and a method for determining service level goals.

Chapter 17 discusses the issue of establishing Order Frequency, or Review Time for items and product lines.

Chapter 18 shows how to set up a purchasing schedule and budget.

Chapter 19 discusses the methods used to replenish store inventories.

Chapter 20 presents procedures and formulas for replenishment purchasing for distribution centers.

Chapter 21 covers Forward Buying.

Chapter 22 covers Alternate and Superseded Items.

Chapter 23 presents a process for performing stock adjustments at both stores and distribution centers.

Chapter 24 covers methods for identifying overstock and dealing with vendors on stock adjustment returns.

Chapter 25 covers areas that should be tracked, and ways to Measure Performance.

Chapter 26 presents some ideas for the logistics of multiple locations.

Chapter 27 discusses topics for supplier performance reviews.

Chapter 28 discusses the strong impact of good inventory management on gross margins.

Chapter 29 covers some Supply Chain considerations.

Chapter 30 is a short summary and a checklist.
All this is a "bottom up" process that builds the system from all the details.

About IBM's INVEN package: In the mid 1970's, Anders Herlitz, while at IBM, developed the INVEN family of inventory management packages for IBM's System/3, System/34, System/38 and AS400 computers. Our company, Hatch Grinding, was a very early user of this package. We had the largest number of items of any early INVEN user, so our files were used frequently to benchmark performance. The formulas for forecasting, safety stocks, order frequency, and replenishment purchasing are all the formulas we used at Hatch with the INVEN package. These are reproduced here with permission from IBM.

About E3 Associates: In the early 1980's Anders Herlitz left IBM. He founded E3 Associates, and I was his 50/50 partner for the first two years of its existence. E3 first created and sold enhancement packages to INVEN users. Anders bought out my interest after he got established, and E3 went on to develop TRIM and other inventory management packages. E3 was acquired by JDA in 2001. The procedures for seasonal forecasting, lead time forecasting, setting service level goals, and forward buying all were developed by E3 when Anders and I were its only two employees. These are reproduced here with permission from JDA.

Hatch used the INVEN package and the E3 enhancements continuously until 1996, when it merged with another CARQUEST member.

Chapter 1. Introduction to the Automotive Aftermarket

There are several factors that make inventory management more critical for success in the automotive aftermarket than in some other wholesale goods businesses.

- **Hundreds of Thousands of SKUs:** There are almost 40,000 unique make-model-year-engine combinations of vehicles in operation in reasonable numbers in the U.S. There are roughly 3,000 unique mechanical and electrical parts on a typical car or light truck. Many replacement parts fit a single make and only a few years or models. As a result, a typical full line automotive parts distribution center stocks about 100,000 SKUs, from a universe of many times that number of available replacement parts. A typical auto parts store stocks about 20,000 SKUs. Even large service outlets seldom stock more than 1,000 SKUs. The project of selecting which items to stock at each level in the channel requires a great deal of ongoing effort.

- **High, Fast Service Level Requirement:** Auto repair is seldom a scheduled, budgeted item for vehicle owners. An unexpected need for auto repair is usually a disruption to most households. So, most people want to take their vehicle to a convenient service provider, and have it properly repaired and returned in one day. One of the best things your repair shop can tell you is that your vehicle is "ready when promised". It requires that the repair shop quickly and accurately diagnose the vehicle and determine the needed repair. When replacement parts are required, they are usually not in the shop's inventory. They must be located and purchased quickly. The typical standard in the industry is for an auto parts store to deliver parts to a repair shop within 30 minutes. That service must be provided consistently for the shop to meet its commitment to have a vehicle ready when promised. The typical store's inventory of about 20,000 items covers only about 80% of overall demand. The remaining items must be sourced from a distribution center or manufacturer. Many distribution companies offer "will call" service or deliver to their store customers more than once a day, to meet this high service need. The best mix of inventory in the right locations is critical to meeting the vehicle owner's expectations.

1

The automotive aftermarket is almost unique in providing this level of service. You can't get a VCR, or a TV, or a refrigerator, or most other pieces of equipment repaired in one day. With a full service contract, you might get a PC repaired in one day, but the needed number of replacement parts is in the hundreds, not the hundreds of thousands.

About the Automotive Aftermarket

First, the automotive aftermarket is a huge industry. There are more than 200,000,000 vehicles in operation in the U.S. They require the full range of service from maintenance of items like oil and filters to repair of any of several thousand functional parts on each vehicle. Those two key factors—the huge number of items and the demand for quick repairs has shaped the entire industry. Here is a primer on the players in the aftermarket.

- **Vehicle Dealers.** New car dealers perform almost all of the warranty services on vehicles they sell, and about ¼ of the total maintenance and repair business. Their market share is highest for new vehicles under warranty, and drops off rapidly as vehicles age and come off warranty. Most of their needs are supplied by the vehicle original equipment (OE) manufacturer, or by their OE parts vendors. For example, Delphi Automotive supplies many original equipment parts to General Motors (and other vehicle manufacturers). Delphi also supplies parts to the Service Parts division of GM, known as AC-Delco. AC-Delco distributes these and other items to GM dealers. They also sell to aftermarket customers, who in turn supply their own stores or repair shops. New car dealers buy needed items not in their inventory from local suppliers. In 2001 there were 21,600 new car dealers in the U.S.[4]

- **Service Chains.** Goodyear, Firestone, Midas, Sears, MAACO, AAMCO, and Jiffy-Lube are examples of company owned or franchise chains of automotive service outlets. The franchisees typically get the key product categories directly from their franchiser, but they also buy lots of needed items from local suppliers. AAIA estimates there were 13,800 specialty repair

---

[4] All the statistics on the market volume and number of outlets come from the Automotive Aftermarket Industry Association (AAIA) Aftermarket Fact Book, 2002/2003 Edition, and the AAIA Mini-Monitor. Copyright 2002, AAIA.

outlets, 5,800 quick lubes, and 12,700 tire stores in the U.S. in 2001.

- **Service Stations.** I'm old enough to remember when all gas stations really were service stations. Today, most just sell munchies instead. However, there are still 95,600 "Service" stations with at least one repair bay in operation, according to AAIA. They buy almost all of their parts from local suppliers, including wholesale parts stores, car dealers and some distributors.

- **Independent Repair Shops:** According to AAIA, there are 165,300 independently owned garages and repair shops. This includes mechanical shops and collision repair shops. They buy almost all of their parts from local suppliers.

Overall, these outlets performed about $125 billion of service and repair work in 2001. This is referred to as the "do-it-for-me" or DIFM market. In addition, these outlets sold almost all of the 2001 aftermarket of $20 billion of tires.

- **Retail Parts Stores:** There are five major chains of auto parts stores whose principal customers are "do-it-yourself", or DIY consumers. The five largest chains, AutoZone, Advance, CSK, O'Reilly and Pep Boys own and operate about 8,000 stores. Wal-Mart, Target, and other discount stores have automotive departments, and, in some cases, auto service bays as well. In total, there are about 18,000 retail parts stores and automotive departments at discount and mass merchandise stores according to AAIA. The total DIY market in 2001 is about $35 billion, according to AAIA.

- **Wholesale Parts Stores / Jobbers:** There are about 21,000 auto parts "jobbers" in the U.S. These are local stores who supply repair shops, service stations, fleets and other customers in their immediate area. Roughly 1/3 of these stores are owned or controlled by their distributor. The other 2/3 are typically single location, independently owned auto parts stores.

- **"Traditional" Distributors:** Roughly 1,000 distributors supply the jobbers and some repair outlets. Our company, Hatch Grinding Company, fit in this category. The largest traditional distributors are Genuine Parts and General Parts. Genuine Parts, Inc. and one other distributor supply about 6,500 NAPA

Auto Parts stores. General Parts, Inc. is the largest of several distributors who supply almost 4,000 CARQUEST Auto Parts Stores. There are a number of other "program groups" of distributors who collaborate on marketing and group buying. The largest of these is the Alliance. These distributors supply All-Pro, AutoValue, and Bumper-to-Bumper jobber stores. PartsPlus and Federated are similar, smaller groups.

So, there are more than 300,000 various size inventories of auto parts in the U.S. That creates lots of opportunity for good and bad inventory management to show up. The requirement for very quick service to almost every customer really separates well-run companies from weak ones.

There are areas where the automotive aftermarket distribution channel is similar to other hard goods channels. Many types of hard goods flow from manufacturers to distribution centers to stores to end-users. The examples and techniques in this book can be (carefully) applied to these similar areas in other channels.

Chapter 2. The Shape of and Size of Auto Parts Inventories

Automotive replacement parts exhibit a huge range of popularity and demand potential.

At the high end of the scale are a few very high volume items like motor oil. There are 200 million cars and light trucks in the U.S. They currently get about 1.6 oil changes per year per vehicle. That translates to an annual U.S. consumption of about 1.6 billion quarts of motor oil, in a few brands and viscosities. To satisfy that demand, motor oil is available in almost every auto parts store, grocery store, drug store, mass merchandiser, wholesale club, hardware store, service station, quick lube, and all kinds of vehicle service outlets. Even with all that availability, every merchant can get great turnover on motor oil items.

At the other end of the scale are many parts that each fit a very small universe of vehicles, and rarely require replacement. For example, engine control computers are generally specific to a single make, model, year, and engine combination. In some cases the computer's software can even vary based on the vehicle's optional equipment, and each variation creates a unique item. Some of these items fit fewer than 1,000 vehicles in the U.S. An engine control computer might last 5-8 years of normal operation, so the total U.S. demand for each of many items in this category is less than 200 units per year. Scale that by almost 40,000 total wholesale and retail auto parts stores in the U.S., and the average demand is .005 units per store per year. It is hardly meaningful, but that also means that if an average auto parts store stocked one unit of one of these items, it might be a 200-year supply.

A fact of life in the automotive parts business is that there has been a huge proliferation of items, and many have very small demand potential. This has been going on since the beginning of the automobile, but the pace accelerated dramatically starting about 1980. Several factors are driving this:

- **Proliferation of makes and models.** Today, more than 500 unique make/model combinations exist for each model year. Granted, some are very similar. There are many common parts used on both a Chevrolet and a GMC pickup truck. However, there is much more variety of vehicles than ever before, and many niche market vehicles, resulting in thousands more SKUs for each model year.

- **New vehicle market shares spread out across more manufacturers.** General Motors has experienced a steady decline in market share from over 50% to less than 30% over the past 25 years. No single competitor has captured that share, but market shares for Toyota, Honda, Volkswagen, Mercedes, BMW, Nissan, Kia, and other companies have all increased. That has had the impact of reducing the number of vehicles on the road in any single make/model combination. So, there is a smaller market for replacement parts specific to all these lower volume vehicles.

- **Replacement parts fit fewer model years.** The Japanese auto manufacturers have had several key advantages over the U.S. manufacturers. They have leveraged these to gain market share. All of their advantages have increased inventory proliferation in the aftermarket.

The Japanese have had much more productivity in their vehicle development process. They compressed the development cycle for a new vehicle (from concept to production) from about 5 years to about 2-½ years. That enabled them to shorten the overall life of a vehicle platform, and introduce new models more frequently. As a benchmark, the Ford F-Series pickup had a 6 or 7-year cycle, with newly designed models in 1967, 1973 and 1980. The first Ford Taurus was on the market for 6 model years, from its introduction as a 1986 model through the 1991 model year. Engine families lasted even longer. The basic Ford "Small Block" Windsor V-8 engine was introduced in a 221 Cubic Inch V-8 in 1962, in 260 and 289 Cubic Inch versions in 1963, and as a 302 Cubic Inch engine in 1968. The 302 engine was still in production for the 1995 model Mustang.[5] A few parts fit more than 30 years of this single family of Ford engines.

By comparison, Honda produces a new Accord every 4 years. Honda introduced all new models in 1982, 1986, 1990, 1994 and 1998.[6] A new model F-Series or Taurus typically had about 50%

---

[5] History of the Windsor small block.
http://home.pon.net/hunnicutt/history_windsor.htm.

[6] Articles on model generations for various vehicles are from www.edmunds.com. The specific URL is http://www.edmunds.com/reviews/generations/articles/.

new items, while a new generation Accord typically had 70-75% new parts.

In addition, the Japanese extensively use lean production and *kaizen*. Kaizen is the practice of making continuous incremental improvements in an item to reduce its cost or improve its quality. When someone discovers an improvement to an alternator, for example, the Japanese will get it into production as quickly as possible, even if that means changing it in the middle of a vehicle cycle, or even in the middle of a model year. They generally do not require that the new item fit all the prior vehicles, so the aftermarket winds up with two unique replacement parts for one model year.

The overall result is that it takes many more replacement parts to service the Honda Accord than the Ford Pickup or Taurus, and each Honda item fits fewer vehicles.

- **Better vehicle quality has reduced aftermarket replacement rates.** The OE manufacturers, led by the Japanese vehicle companies, have made great strides in improved vehicle quality. New technology and new materials for many components has led to much longer service life for mechanical and electrical parts. A prime example is the exhaust system. Original equipment mufflers and tailpipes were made of galvanized or coated steel until about 1990 on most U.S. cars and light trucks. Starting about 1990, the OE material was switched to stainless steel. Galvanized mufflers and tailpipes rusted and failed after about three years of operation in the Northeastern states, where salt is used on the roads in the wintertime. Stainless steel mufflers and tailpipes typically last eight to ten years in that same environment. The total aftermarket unit sales for exhaust system components have had a dramatic decrease. At the same time, the increasing mix of vehicles has led to an overall increase in the number of SKUs in this category. The result is a huge decrease in unit demand per SKU.

- **Vehicle bodies last longer.** Dramatic improvements in corrosion protection and paint have led to much longer lasting vehicles. Because the bodies last longer, owners are willing to make major mechanical repairs on much older, higher mileage vehicles than ever before. This has somewhat offset the improved component quality, but increased the variety of vehicles still in service.

I always ask a taxi driver about the mileage on his taxi, as an informal market survey. The numbers have been going up steadily. My personal record is a ride in a Chevrolet Caprice taxi in Houston, in January 2002. The driver said it had 324,000 miles on it. He thought he could drive it one more year. It got an oil change weekly, and a set of brakes every month, but many items were still original.

A chart from Motor Equipment Manufacturers Association shows the average mileage of vehicles at the time they are scrapped and is very revealing.

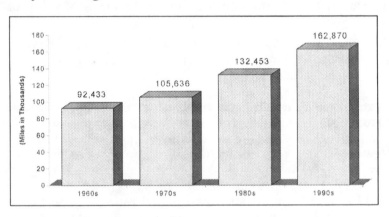

Ch 2 Fig 1. Average odometer reading of scrapped vehicles.

Model proliferation, longer vehicle service life, and factors like kaizen have resulted in a significant increase in the total universe of SKUs in the automotive aftermarket. Fewer vehicles in each model and better quality cause significantly lower replacement rates for each individual item. The overall result has been to spread the industry demand across many more items, with each item selling fewer units.

Inventory Proliferation Result

Here is a chart of the proliferation of SKUs and the flattening of demand across those items over the past 20 years.

Ranked	Auto Parts Proliferation History					
	Percent of Total Dollar Demand Covered					
Items	1986	1988	1990	1993	1996	2003
100	17%	14%	13%	12%	11%	10%
200	23%	22%	20%	19%	16%	15%
500	32%	30%	28%	27%	23%	21%
1,000	43%	40%	38%	37%	31%	25%
2,000	56%	53%	50%	50%	40%	30%
5,000	74%	71%	68%	68%	54%	50%
10,000	88%	85%	82%	81%	75%	66%
20,000	97%	94%	93%	92%	87%	79%
30,000	99%	98%	97%	96%	92%	87%
Total Stock Items	62,000	74,000	79,500	93,500	98,000	88,000
Total Items in Master File		100,000		200,000		450,000
Source - Hatch Grinding Co. Denver (1986-1996), General Parts, Denver (2003)						

Ch 2 Fig 2. Coverage of Total Demand by Top Ranked Items

This chart is based on a descending ranking of all items stocked at Hatch Grinding Company's distribution center in Denver, Colorado at various times.[7] It includes replacement parts, chemicals, lubricants, tools, supplies, and some equipment. It does not include tires, sheet metal, upholstery, or glass.

The total number of stocked SKUs increased 50% during this 15-year span. The decline from 1996 to 2003 is a result of an intentional program to stock fewer items, not a change in the overall trend. As you can see, the demand has flattened out dramatically, and across the entire spectrum of the inventory. For example, the fastest moving 2,000 parts (measured in dollar sales) covered 56% of this distribution center's total demand in 1986, but only 30% of the total by 2003. A parts store could get 88% coverage with 10,000 items in 1986, but that requires 30,000 items today.

A graph of coverage in 1986 and 2003 shows even more dramatically how many more items it takes today to give each level of coverage.

---

[7] Data on stocking items for 1986-1996 is from Hatch Grinding Co., Denver. In 1996 this company merged with General Parts, Inc. so data for 2003 is from the same facility as General Parts, Inc. Denver distribution center. Ranking for 1986-96 is by descending gross margin dollars generated by each item. Ranking for 2003 is by descending unit demand for each item. While these are different rankings, the author feels they do not distort the overall result portrayed in this chart.

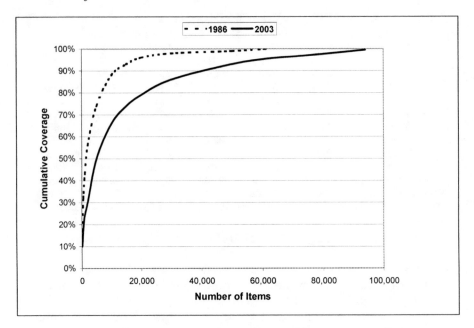

1986 **2003**

Cumulative Coverage

Number of Items

Ch 2 Fig 3. Chart of Proliferation of Automotive Items

This inventory proliferation has had a dramatic impact on the automotive aftermarket.

Consolidation has been a major activity in many industries over the past 15 years. This has happened to banks, department stores, airlines, accounting companies, and almost every other kind of business. The automotive aftermarket has had all the same general factors driving all these industries toward consolidation. But, in addition, the proliferation of the automotive aftermarket inventory has added an additional, major impact to spur even more consolidation in the auto parts industry. Here are the ways it has affected each kind of auto parts outlet.

Impact of Inventory Proliferation on The Distribution Channel

Automotive Departments—The top 500 Items: This is about the number of automotive items that a grocery, drug or hardware store is likely to carry. In 1986, they could cover about 1/3 of the total auto parts demand from this inventory width. By 2003, that level of inventory covered only about 1/5 of demand. Rather than expand these inventories as parts proliferated, many of these outlets have almost completely eliminated application parts. They still stock oil, chemicals, and a few very broad coverage items like light bulbs, but most of these outlets have stopped stocking filters, spark plugs, and other light maintenance parts.

Service Centers—The Top 1,000—2,000 Items: The industry has also experienced a full cycle of the development and then evolution of specialty repair shops. For example this inventory proliferation was one factor to spawn thousands of quick lube outlets, specializing in oil changes, wiper blades and a few other very light repairs. Even though there are many more oil filter and wiper SKUs, these specialized outlets can do enough volume to support a full inventory in these few categories of replacement parts.

For many years, the industry supported thousands of exhaust and brake specialty shops in chains like Midas, Meineke, Speedy, and others. For a long time, these specialty shops could do enough volume to support a full inventory of exhaust and brake items, and be successful with just those services. They could give very fast service to all customers for these repairs.

However, longer intervals between oil changes, and longer lasting exhaust and brake parts have reduced the overall potential of these specialty locations for their original services. As a result, there has been a huge consolidation in the quick lube business.

Almost all specialty shops have added services and broadened their overall menu to sustain their volume in the face of overall declines in their core, specialty lines. Many Quick Lubes now change belts and hoses, flush transmissions, and offer other services. Midas is a dramatic example, too. They have gone from shops doing only exhaust and brakes to their new theme "We do it". Midas stores now solicit almost every kind of repair and maintenance work in an effort to keep their shops busy.

Mass Merchandisers—The Top 2,500 to 5,000 Items: 5,000 items is about the number of items a large mass merchandiser or a very large auto service center carried in the late 1980s. It was about the number of items carried at Sears, Montgomery Ward, Wal-Mart, and other Auto Center type outlets. In 1986, this width of inventory could cover almost 3/4 of the market. By 2003, it covered less than 1/2 the total demand.

Mass merchandisers, too, have been faced with a "get in or get out" decision. They either had to greatly expand the number of items, or discontinue stocking a category completely. It doesn't make sense to stock the top 15 disc brake pads, or the top 20 shock absorbers, if these only cover a small fraction of vehicles. The individual item demand declined so that it did not justify a wider inventory in a single location. As a result, many of these companies have eliminated inventory for some or all application parts categories. The inventory at a typical Sears Auto Center of today is almost all devoted to tires, batteries, and a few chemicals and accessories. Sears will still replace your alternator, but they'll have to buy the part locally for that repair.

Some, like Wal-Mart, have expanded their automotive departments in an effort to maintain their coverage. K-Mart, on the other hand, has dropped out of automotive completely. They sold their auto departments to Penske Automotive, but Penske closed operations in early 2002. As other merchants like K-Mart dropped out, the survivors like Wal-Mart were able to gain market share to justify the larger inventory.

The result is a consolidation to fewer, bigger outlets.

Parts Stores—The top 15-20,000 parts: This is the inventory coverage of a typical local auto parts store. In the early '80's, an inventory of the right 15,000 items could cover over 90% of demand. A parts store could give good service with this level of availability on the shelf. In 1983, the median automotive wholesaler achieved 2.88 inventory turns.[8]

By 2003, even a large inventory of about 20,000 items, worth about $300,000, could still only cover about 80% of total demand. A typical auto parts store got about 2 inventory turns in 2000.[9] Today's auto parts stores need local, quick access to even broader inventories at distribution centers to give good service to all customers.

This has led to "hub stores", "superstores", and direct selling distributors.

It has also led to a steady attrition of smaller auto parts stores. Today, a small store with only 10-15,000 items just can't give enough service from its own inventory to keep customers satisfied. Thousands of smaller auto parts stores have closed or merged into larger stores over the past 15 years.

So, at the store level, too, there has been dramatic consolidation into fewer, bigger auto parts stores. Inventory proliferation, along with

---

[8] 1984 Edition, Automotive Wholesaling Financial Operation Analysis. Automotive Service Industry Association, Chicago, Illinois.
[9] CARQUEST internal reports.

the other factors driving consolidation in general, caused more consolidation in the automotive aftermarket.

The full line Distribution Center: The increase in the total number of items required a huge increase in inventory investment by all distributors. Without a gain in market share, the additional demand was not there to justify this increased investment. So, this drove another change in the shape of the distribution channel. In some cases, distributors abandoned categories, and became specialists, in an effort to gain enough market share to support larger inventories.

For full line distributors, consolidation has been the outcome. Denver is a good example of a fairly isolated metropolitan market. In 1986 Denver had about 1.5 million people, and 8 full line auto parts distributors. This included NAPA (Genuine Parts), Big-A (APS), CARQUEST (Hatch Grinding), Auto Value (Republic Automotive), Federated (Gaddie Distributing), Parts Plus (Parts Inc.), Bumper to Bumper (MAWDI), and Pronto (Lambert Automotive Warehouse). By 2003, even with population growth to over 2 million, the industry consolidated to 3 full line auto parts distributors, NAPA, CARQUEST, and Star Automotive (who acquired Republic's Denver distribution center).

Fewer, bigger outlets were the only viable answer to this huge proliferation of inventory and lower unit demand for individual items.

Chapter Summary

- Inventory proliferation has been, and will continue to be, a fact of life in the automotive aftermarket.
- More SKUs are required at every step in the channel to maintain past service levels.
- Some new techniques will be discussed later in the book that try to cope with this ongoing proliferation.
- While many other commodities have not had this dramatic proliferation of inventory, some proliferation has occurred in most hard goods categories. Some of the lessons learned in the auto parts industry will have valid application to other product channels.

Pete Kornafel

Chapter 3. Best Practices For Inventory Control

All the classic textbooks show that it takes more inventory to give better service levels. That is true, but only in an extremely well run company. It is not necessarily true for all distributors. I had the opportunity to meet and work with almost 200 auto parts distributors over 20 years in the industry workshop on Inventory Management, and it was not true for many of them.

In the automotive aftermarket, the best run companies achieved the highest service levels, and did it with less inventory than the companies that were not so well run. Not so well run companies had poorer service levels, more inventory, and smaller profit. Good customer service and good profits both begin with the very basics of good inventory control.

Glenn Staats compiled most of the items on this list of best practices for the AWDA Purchasing and Inventory Management workshop we both instructed. He referred to it as his "Axioms for Good Order Fill and Turnover". I added a few of my favorite ones, too.

1. **Accurate Inventory:** The most important practice is to have an accurate inventory. Whenever your computer thinks you have an item in stock, but it is not there, it is a lost sale waiting to happen. You won't buy any more of that item, because you think you have it, but it won't be there when you need it. Whenever you have inventory on hand but not on the computer, it is a completely wasted investment. You are unlikely to ever sell that item, especially if you give your customers an on-line way to inquire and order directly from you. You'll just keep telling them you don't have this item in stock, and they'll go elsewhere to buy it.

    Auditing inventory should be a key, ongoing task. There are three key processes:

2. **Find and audit potential errors every day:** Everyone should be charged with the responsibility of identifying items that might have inventory balance errors. There should be a way to compile that list and audit those items that same day. Every distributor and store should have someone who is responsible for doing daily inventory audits.

    Your order pickers can be a huge help. We printed the quantity to pick and the remaining balance on hand on our picking tickets. We asked the pickers to verify the remaining balance when they picked the part if the remaining balance was nine units or less. It took a negligible amount of extra time to do this, and it gave us thousands of inventory count validations every day. The pickers flagged the item for a recount if it looked like the remaining balance was wrong. They were not responsible for recounting the item, but just for identifying items where the balance looked wrong. We kept score on the errors each order picker discovered, and gave a $100 bonus each month to the picker who found the most errors in our inventory. We gained far more than that because our inventory was more accurate.

Every customer report of a shortage or overage should be recounted. If you sent the wrong item to a customer, the on hand balances are wrong for both the item you sent and the item you should have sent. Both have to be counted. If a customer reports a shortage, and your audit shows the item is still on your shelf, you feel very good about issuing an adjustment credit and correcting the on-hand balance for the item. If you have a lot of faith in your inventory accuracy and your audit shows the item was picked, you can begin to form an opinion about the quality and reliability of information from that customer. In any case, every reported discrepancy should be audited.

Your accounts payable department can help, too. We computed the value of items posted to our inventory on every inbound shipment, and compared that to the vendor's invoice. If they matched within a small tolerance, then we were pretty sure our item prices and item quantity received both matched the vendor's data. If they were not the same, then we audited both the prices and the item quantities to discover discrepancies. We would find an occasional item where the vendor changed our cost without notifying us, and items where the quantity we posted as a receipt did not match the quantity billed by the vendor. We found items where the vendor changed the quantity in a case, or shipped eaches and billed us for cases. Those items had to be audited, too.

3. **Check Receipts:** You can start a lively debate in a group of automotive distributors by asking what percentages of inbound shipments are checked in at each company. Among over 200 companies who attended the AWDA workshops, my "show of hands" survey reveals a small percentage that check in 100% of new merchandise shipments. While this should produce the most accurate inventory, it requires a significant investment of labor and generally adds one or two days to lead-time. At the other extreme, a small percentage of companies check in

nothing. They are likely to have the most trouble maintaining an accurate inventory. The majority check in a portion of shipments. Here are some tips for deciding what to check in:

- Check in every shipment where the carton or pallet counts shows a shortage or overage, or where sealed containers or shrink-wrapped pallets have been opened.
- Spot-check every vendor at some regular frequency, and keep a log of the vendor's accuracy. If you have multiple locations, you can spread this work out among locations, and share results. Make sure you "keep score" separately for each vendor's shipping point if they have multiple distribution centers.
- Check all shipments from vendors who exhibit high error rates on spot checks.
- Check in all shipments of very high cost items or items subject to pilferage. Our brake parts shipments almost always arrived short one or two 5-gallon containers of brake fluid. We finally concluded the carrier kept them for their own use, and hoped we wouldn't discover it and file a claim. That truck line got their parts from us that way for years.
- Check all shipments for a period of time with every new vendor, or whenever there is a change in a vendor's distribution points or the vendor's software or other order processing systems.
- Check in all shipments from vendors with upcoming labor contract deadlines or active labor disputes.
- Check in all shipments for a period of time before and after any vendor closes for a vacation period.
- Check in all shipments on any product line where a cycle count or annual physical inventory reveals more than an average number of errors.

4. **Cycle Counts:** We had two part time people in each distribution center who performed the daily recounts of items identified above, and then inventoried entire product lines. Our practice was to inventory a line just before we submitted our annual stock adjustment request to that vendor. That gave us the best opportunity to return exactly the items we didn't want to keep. Their job was like painting the Golden Gate Bridge. They started at one end, worked their way to the other end, and then started over. We used the calendar of planned stock adjustments, and counted every line once a year just before we did our stock adjustment on that line. There is a good discussion on Cycle

Counting by Max Muller in Essentials of Inventory Management.[10]

5. **Annual Physicals:** The normal practice for most distributors is to do a complete inventory audit once a year, typically just before their year end. This is usually a big event, and most distributors bring in their sales people, factory sales people, and other part time people or volunteers to help with this project. They have to get it done over a weekend or close and lose a day's business. I know this is very common practice, but we never believed in it. I've been to sales school, and I know that no one teaches sales people how to count accurately, especially when they would rather be doing something else. We audited our entire inventory annually, but by cycle counting one line at a time. Our people were very good at it, because that was their total job.

   Each year our auditors selected a statistical sample of about 200 items (out of almost 100,000), and they counted them at year-end. We always passed their test. They always certified our financial statements based on that small sample audit. The only time in over 20 years we did a complete inventory all at one time was when we merged our company with another CARQUEST member. They were amazed at the accuracy of our inventory, but we were not surprised.

6. **Count the Zeros:** Most items in our inventory would get to a zero balance on hand sometime during each year. A few hundred items reached a zero balance each day. I had the theory that we should count those items at that time. I thought it would be easiest and most accurate to verify a zero balance. It was also an important time, because we would tell customers were out of that item, begin to lose sales, and reorder the item. If we actually had some on the shelf, we avoided all that. I frequently asked our part time inventory auditors to do this. I told them that if they would do that, we could skip the cycle counting effort. I told them it would make their work a lot easier, as they wouldn't have to handle and count lots of very heavy inventory. They always refused. They said we were paying them to count stuff, and they felt it would be wrong if they counted nothing. So, we never did it, but I still think it would be another good way to maintain an extremely accurate inventory.

7. **An Ongoing Tally:** It is important to keep score. The inventory is the largest asset for every distributor. We had a complete inventory transaction file. We would have called it a data

---

[10] Max Muller. Essentials of Inventory Management. AMACOM, 2003.

warehouse if that term had been invented then. Each day we generated a report with extended cost of every item that had an on hand balance adjustment. We recounted all items where the adjustment was more than $50, just to be very accurate. We kept a cumulative total of up, down, and net changes. If we were accumulating an overall shortage, it was a potential security issue. We discovered one or two dishonest employees over many years. I think it was a small number because everyone in our company knew we were watching continuously (and because everyone was in our Profit Sharing plan).

8. **Good Timing:** If you do "live" counts of suspect items and cycle counts, you must have synchronization of the physical goods and the computer balances. If an inbound shipment has been put on the shelf, it has to be posted to the computer, too. If customer returns have been restocked, the credit memos have to be processed, too. If inventory balances are relieved as orders are taken, those orders have to be picked, too. If you don't synchronize the timing, your counting will introduce errors, not fix them.

   Our inventory transaction log was very valuable. Our audit crew could see whether the shipment, return, or order had been posted to the computer at the same time they were counting the item. I wish we could have equipped them with RF Wireless handheld devices, but they hadn't been invented yet. They had a computer terminal on a stock cart with a 200-foot cable. They rolled it around with them so they could look at the item transaction log at the same time they were looking at the shelf.

9. **Complete All Work Quickly:** It really helps your inventory accuracy and your customer service if you keep up with all the work.

   In our company, we had to complete processing of every order entered today, with no exceptions. Our customers expected to receive everything they ordered in that night's delivery. We had a standard of processing returns and shipments within three workdays, and systems to monitor that. I knew one auto parts distributor who would not let his warehouse crew go home until every shipment received that day had been put away. I don't think his warehouse manager ever told him they made a deal with all the truck lines to never deliver anything after 10 a.m., but I still admired them for their practice.

As you'll see in later chapters, short lead times really help your service level. Your internal time to stock a shipment is a part of the lead-time that is in your control.

10. **Complete Data:** Complete and prompt data base maintenance is important. There are always new items, price changes, and other data to be entered. Every delay is a potential loss of profit. You can't order and sell a new item until it is completely loaded into your system. You'll lose a lot of margin if you don't implement a price change exactly when it is supposed to go into effect.

   In our company we stocked about 100,000 items, but that was out of a universe of several times that. We had a part record loaded for everything a vendor had available, whether we stocked it or not. This was the only way we could accurately track lost sales, and decide whether to add an item to our inventory.

11. **Good Housekeeping:** Every well-run distributor I've ever seen was fanatic about good housekeeping. No inventory was sitting around, and everything could be found just where it was supposed to be. Floors have to be swept every day, and everyone should help dispose of trash. I've never seen a distributor with bad housekeeping, good inventory accuracy, and great customer service.

Chapter Summary

- Good inventory management begins with accurate and timely inventory data.

- Good inventory accuracy requires daily attention. Recounting items with suspected errors, cycle counts, and checking in some shipments are critical processes.

- Like all "best practices", these processes can become routine, and form the best foundation for the rest of the inventory management system.

- The best run distributors have accurate inventory, complete all work quickly, have great housekeeping, give the best customer service, and make the most money. Period.

Chapter 4. Defining Demand

All good inventory management systems begin with accurate item level demand numbers. It doesn't matter whether this is used in a "push" system to generate forecasts and inventory levels, or whether this is used in a "pull" system to directly drive rapid replenishment.

It may seem unnecessary to devote an entire chapter to counting demand. However, there are many types of transactions, and each must be evaluated to decide whether it should affect the demand count for an item. These examples are based on auto parts items, but distributors in other industries will surely find similar situations in their products, too.

Time Periods or Time "Fences"

The very first step is to establish the most appropriate time periods for aggregating demand. The best period is a balance between two factors. If the period is too long, the item may change its selling pattern, and past periods may not give the best data to project the future. If the period is too short, the erratic nature of demand will add more statistical noise into the history. This could make it harder to get an accurate forecast.

In general, the period should be as long as possible, to cut down on the statistical noise. It should not be so long that the demand might shift appreciably during one period. It is also important to roughly match the total time span for replenishment. If you order weekly, and lead-time is one to two weeks, then a monthly or four week (thirteen periods per year) cycle is probably best for all items that are reasonably stable.

If the item's demand is changing rapidly, and if the replenishment cycle is short, then weekly history buckets will help show this, and help any forecasting system react more quickly.

If the item's demand is reasonably stable over a longer time span, and the item is not seasonal, then two month (six periods per year) or three month (four periods per year) will help smooth the statistical noise out of the demand history. If the item's demand is seasonal, monthly or four-week cycles might be most appropriate. Some dairy and tobacco distributors use daily demand history periods and "day of the week" seasonal profiles.

Remember that you can accurately update the item forecast only at the end of each period. Another consideration is how frequently you want to update all the forecasts, with the workload of doing this and reviewing items with unusual behavior. It might be productive to forecast many very slow movers quarterly, rather than monthly.

You might want to vary the history keeping periods and forecasting intervals by item. However, the job of understanding this might outweigh the forecasting advantages. For the remainder of this book, monthly history is used in all the examples. This was appropriate for the items in our auto parts inventories. We used it for all our items for 25 years.

Demand is What the Customer Wants

The first step is to make sure you are capturing demand, not shipments or sales data for every item. There is a very simple formula for this:

$$Demand = Sales + LostSales$$

You may assume that capturing sales data is straightforward and accurate for the first part of this equation. However, the real world is not that simple. Not all sales should count, and there are other factors to consider, too. Here are some things to consider in translating the "sales" part of that equation into demand accounting:

- **New Merchandise Returns:** You need to decide whether to count returned items as a negative demand, or whether to disregard them and use gross sales. In almost all cases, we deducted new merchandise returns from the demand count. Here are some auto parts examples.

    o Frequently, the end user does not have enough information to order exactly the right item. In auto parts, mid-year changes are a big cause of this. It is not always possible to determine in advance whether a car has the "early" or "late" part. In this case the customer typically orders all the possible items, matches them against the part from the car, keeps the right one, and returns the rest. Clearly, there is a net zero demand for these returned items, so these returns should be deducted from the demand count.

    o Many repair shops will order all the parts they might need for a job, often before the car arrives at the shop. Once they complete their diagnostic procedures, they know which parts are really needed for the repair. The others are sent back as returns. In this situation, the decision whether or not to deduct the return is not quite so clear. Certainly there is no real net sale for the unused parts. Yet, you still might want to count the demand, to make sure you have all the items available for the next similar job, when all the items might be used.

Here is an example. Suppose a vehicle has a leaking water pump. When you replace a water pump on most engines, you must remove the fan or drive belts and the radiator hoses. So, a shop might order all these items, in case they discover that the belts or hoses have deteriorated, and should be replaced. In many cases, with the owner's permission, it could be prudent to replace them at this time, if it appears they might fail soon. Since they must be removed and re-installed, there is no incremental labor cost to replace them at this time, and it saves the owner another trip to the shop. So, even if these items are not needed on one job, you may still want to make sure you have all these parts for the next job.

Here is another example. Some late model vehicles have four oxygen sensors, two "upstream" and two "downstream" of the catalytic converter. The shop can't diagnose the downstream sensors until the upstream ones are functioning properly, so the shop is likely to order all four at once. If an upstream sensor is the problem, the downstream ones will be returned. They are almost always ordered, but seldom installed. Yet, a shop will want all four, to have all the parts to complete the repair promptly and efficiently.

Most auto parts distributors will only count demand for the parts that are installed, and net out the returned items. However, it should be a decision to count this way, not just a result of your credit entry software.

It is not always easy to determine whether to count an inquiry, or even a purchased and returned item as demand. Ideally, the customer would provide additional input so legitimate inquiries could be logged as demand.

o   Other new merchandise returns can come from a customer's inventory stock adjustment. This is discussed below in the "pipeline" comments.

- **Warranty Returns:** Customers return some items for warranty credit. It is my personal opinion that the warranty return itself should not be deducted from demand. If the item is replaced, there is a sale transaction. The replacement part is needed to satisfy the customer, and should be in inventory. This sale should not be offset by the warranty return. It seems contrary to common sense that some extra inventory is needed to satisfy warranty replacements, but that is a legitimate part of customer service. If you deduct the return from demand, you would show no net demand, and you might not have the part next time it is needed.

- **Transfers for Special Orders:** If an item is not available locally, it is frequently shipped from another location within the company. In most systems, the shipping location gets credit for the sale, but it is not clear which location should count the demand. This depends on how the company wants to fill future similar orders.
  - o If the company intended to serve the customer from the original location, and it should have had the item at that location to fill the customer's need, then the location that took the order should count the demand, even though it had no sale. Counting the demand at the location where the part was needed will, over time, get the inventory in the right place.
  - o On the other hand, it might be a strategy of the company to concentrate their inventory for some product categories in master locations. These might be hub stores or master distribution centers. In any case, the company intends to fill orders for some items from these master locations, not the branches. In this case, the master location, not the branch, should get the demand. That will maintain the inventory in the master location. If the demand is posted to the branch, it will, over time, increase the inventory at that branch, and that would be contrary to the company's strategy.

- **Transfers for Branch Replenishment:** This is similar to the situation just above. There are a number of reasons why a company might have a master location for one product line, and use that location to replenish all other locations. The vendor's terms, freight allowances or freight minimums might make this the best strategy. In the case of very broad lines with thousands of very slow moving parts, this might be the only way a company can justify one big inventory. As above, the master location should count replenishment shipments to the branches as demand. It is a valid purpose for this inventory. If the master location doesn't count these transactions as demand, it won't maintain the needed level of inventory. At the branches, you might want to count the demand only on items authorized for stock at the branch. If you count everything, eventually you'll have a full inventory at each branch.

- **Get the Waves out of the Pipeline:** Adjusting inventories is an ongoing process for auto parts distributors and stores. Items are routinely added to store inventories as they become more popular, and removed from store shelves as they decline in popularity. None of these sale or return transactions should count in demand. If the company owns both the distribution center and the store locations, these are clearly just inventory transfers, and should not be counted as distribution center demand. Even if the DC shipment was made to or received from an independently owned customer's store, and counts as a sale or credit, it still should not count as demand. The part was just moved from one shelf to another as part of a pipeline adjustment, even if it changed ownership in the process.

- **Backorder Fulfillment:** A distribution center will process replenishment orders for their customer's stores. Items that are not in stock, and not shipped, might, in some instances, be recorded as a backorder. In these cases, the customer has given permission for the distribution center to ship the item as soon as it is available. The net result of all this should be to count one demand. If the distribution center posts a demand for the original "lost sale" when the item was not shipped, then it should not count another demand when the item is finally shipped. If, for some reason, the distribution center does not count the original lost sale as a demand, then it certainly should count the demand when the part is shipped. You need to make sure your system records demand consistently, and posts just one demand for these events.

- **End User Demand:** Ideally, you should use the real end user consumption as the true demand. A single company that owns its distribution centers and all its stores can approximate this by using the store demand to forecast the distribution center needs. You still need all the above considerations about what to really count as a demand at the store level. This eliminates the pipeline activity. In many systems it is very difficult to determine which distribution center sales and returns are pipeline movement, and which are events that should be posted to demand. Counting the end user demand bypasses this difficulty, and gives the truest picture.

- **The Remanufacturer's Story:** Many categories of auto parts are available in the aftermarket as remanufactured units. It is possible to re-use the castings and remanufacture items like water pumps, air conditioning compressors, power steering pumps, rack and pinion steering units, front wheel drive axles, starters, alternators, and many other categories. These items are much less expensive than new replacement parts, and adequate for many customers. When a remanufactured part is sold, the customer is expected to return the old part, called a "core". Often a deposit is charged when the part is sold, and refunded when the old core is returned. These cores are then sent back to the remanufacturer, and become the raw material for the next remanufactured unit.

  Manufacturers have the most difficult time forecasting demand, because they are farthest away from the end user's actual demand. The manufacturer's view can be greatly distorted by time lags in replenishing the pipeline, and by all the pipeline transactions of inventory adjustment. Our best remanufacturer kept very careful track of cores that were returned, and used that information to forecast their demand, rather than orders or shipments. They said they knew the pipeline activity distorted their view of the end user demand data.

  However, they were pretty sure that every core that was returned represented a part that was installed on a vehicle sometime within the past few days. So, they used their core returns as a proxy for the real end user demand.

- **Supply Chain Collaboration:** Ideally, all the stores and distribution centers would share their demand data with each other and with suppliers, to get a consensus forecast of end user demand. Unfortunately, most of the automotive computer systems have been incompatible, so very little of this has actually been done in the automotive aftermarket as of this writing. Now, with the Internet, and with industry activity to adopt standards for XML and EDI transactions, this is much more feasible. It would give the best picture of end user demand to everyone in the channel.

Lost Sales

At last we come to the second part of that original equation. It seems simple to say that lost sales should be counted as part of demand, but here again, there are lots of areas that should be examined.

- **Repeated Orders:** Many auto parts stores replenish their inventories daily. If they do not allow the distribution center to hold backorders, then the store will cancel its original order for an item not shipped, and reorder it on the next replenishment order. These stores will order the item every day until the distribution center eventually gets it in stock and ships it. If the distribution center counts these lost sales as demand, they will post every repeated order as another demand. It might take a couple of weeks for the distribution center to get back to an in-stock position. The distribution center could count a lot of false lost sales during this period, even though the real demand is only the original one ordered by the store. If any of your customers are on "ship or cancel", rather than "hold backorders", you need some algorithm to filter out these repeated orders, and only count the initial lost sale as a demand. An ideal system would track this customer by customer.

- **The Hudson Water Pump Syndrome:** There aren't many Hudson cars still in operation. Collectors have a few. Those owners look anywhere and everywhere to find parts for their vehicles. When a Hudson owner needs a water pump, he is likely to inquire about it at every auto parts store in his town. All of those stores are likely to see if any of the distribution centers have it in stock. Every store will log a lost sale for this item. The distribution center may log as many as ten lost sales for this item in one day, if ten different stores all tried to order it from the DC. These are difficult transactions to identify. They look like real orders from different stores that happen to be for the same item. It is almost impossible to tell that it was just one end user generating all this activity. Most systems would faithfully count all these transactions as lost sales and demand. We'll return to this situation in the section on forecasting. If it can't be identified here, then it needs to be filtered out in the forecasting process, or pretty soon everyone would stock a Hudson water pump (or two).

- **Bad vs. Good Lost Sales—The Bentley Story:** It would seem
  that all lost sales should be equal. However, in auto parts there
  can be bad lost sales and good lost sales. Here is an example.
  One of my wife's acquaintances owns and drives a 1936 Bentley.
  When he learned that she owned an auto parts warehouse, he
  immediately asked if he could buy some parts. He wanted a set
  of spark plugs and a fan belt for his Bentley. It took a long time
  for our customer service department to find the oldest catalogs,
  but they did, and were able to identify the needed items. I was
  shocked when we had both in stock. Not only that, we had 30 of
  the spark plugs, enough for 5 sets for this 6-cylinder car. He
  was ecstatic that we had the parts in stock, and he happily
  purchased them. I went crazy until he left, and until I could find
  out why we still had those items in stock. They should have
  been returned to the manufacturer thirty or forty years ago. It
  took a lot of investigation to discover that these items also fit
  other, current model vehicles, too. They were in our inventory
  because they were good sellers for these other applications. It
  was the only acceptable answer.

It would be very bad for an auto parts distribution center to be
out of stock on spark plugs for a 1998 Toyota Camry. That
would cause a bad lost sale. However, the distribution center
should be out of stock on items for a 1936 Bentley (unless they
happened to fit something else, too). Those would be good lost
sales.

You need to sort out your own product lines, to determine what
you really want to stock, and treat any lost sales on those items
as bad lost sales, that should be fixed.

You should be happy to have lost sales on items you have
decided not to stock. You should still track these lost sales to
determine whether to stock the item or not, but you should not
count them against the overall performance of the inventory you
have chosen to carry.

Life Cycle of an Automotive Replacement Part

The graph of sales for an automotive replacement part over its
entire life cycle resembles a turtle. It is shown in Figure 1.

The scale for both the height and width of this chart depends on
the individual item's application and characteristics.

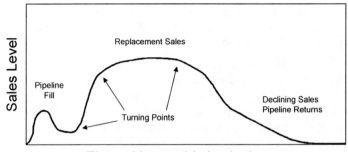

Ch 4 Fig 1. The Life Cycle of an Auto Part—the "Turtle Chart"

When a part first becomes available, there could be some immediate pipeline sales over a fairly short period of time, as distributors fill their shelves. This is the head of the turtle.

The length of the neck of the turtle depends on the item's characteristics. An item will show few sales until replacements begin. End user consumption of an item like an oil filter will begin almost immediately, as owners perform regular oil changes. For an item like a brake pad, sales may not begin to turn up for about 3 years. Most original equipment brakes will last at least 30,000 miles, and the average vehicle is driven about 11,000 miles per year.

Once replacement demand begins for auto parts items, sales increase and then hold steady for some time, based on the number of vehicles that use that part, and the number of times the part is likely to be replaced on each vehicle over its life. The height and width of the body of the turtle depend on the item's application. If there are lots of vehicles, and the item requires frequent replacement, the body of the chart will be both tall and wide. Many items that just fit a few models and years will never be big sellers, and will exhibit a flatter and shorter chart.

Eventually, the some vehicles that use this part are scrapped, and the demand will decline. Also, there will be pipeline returns as the item is removed from store stocks.

The scale of this chart can vary widely. If the part fits a lot of vehicles, it will be tall. If the part only fits a few vehicles, it might be very flat. A part like a muffler will have a long neck on the turtle, as the original equipment mufflers are likely to last eight to ten years, and replacement sales will begin then, and continue as long as the vehicles are on the road. That same muffler might have a total life span of decades. A part like a custom pickup truck accessory might show a very short neck, as owners will begin purchasing it immediately to dress up new vehicles. These items might have a very short total life span, as few people would buy a custom accessory for an older vehicle.

It can be difficult to detect the turning points. However, if your forecasting system can detect those points, you will have a much more efficient inventory. You will know when to begin stocking the item in all stores, just as the real sales begin. You will also know when to begin removing it from inventory, before it dies completely.

Other Considerations

Jon Schreibfeder gives an excellent list of additional "unusual" transactions that should not be counted in demand in Guess Right.[11]

The Value of a Data Warehouse

Only in the past few years could smaller companies afford the computer systems to build a data warehouse of all their transactions. However, this can be an extremely valuable tool to help identify all of the above situations, and develop an accurate counting of demand consistent with the inventory policies for your business.

It permits the analysis to determine pipeline transactions, the "Hudson Water Pump" type of false demands, and can let a company aggregate end user sales at stores that stock each category of parts.

Aggregated transactions at a data warehouse, and decision rules to deal with some of the situations described above will produce the best, most accurate counts of demand.

Chapter Summary

Count as Demand
- Transactions that reflect what the customer wants to buy.
- Returns (as negative demand), except in rare cases.
- Transfers and Drop Shipments. Count the demand at the location where you want to maintain the inventory for inventory transfers or drop shipments direct to a customer, regardless of the location that took the order and did the final invoice.

---

[11] Jon Schreibfeder. Guess Right. NAW DREF. 2003.

- Lost sales (but be careful what you count as a lost sale—see the examples of transactions that should not be counted as lost sales).
- End user demand is better than store, distribution center or factory shipments (if you can capture it with a data warehouse or some other aggregation method).

Don't Count as Demand

- Items ordered for inspection (to choose the right one) and returned. (Or, count the sale as a positive demand and the return as a negative demand to net it out).
- Items going into or coming out of customer inventories (pipeline transactions).
- Warranty returns (in most cases) should not count as a negative demand.
- Transfers and Drop Shipments. Don't count the demand at locations where you do not want to maintain inventory, regardless of the location that took the order and did the final invoice.
- Filling a backorder (as long as you counted the lost sale as a demand in the first place).
- Lost sales that are repeated reorders from the same customer for the same item, as long as you believe the customer only wanted the item one time.
- Lost sales that are repeated orders from the same end user, even if they are placed at different branch locations (see the discussion on backorders).
- Repeated orders from a single customer's effort to find an item (see the Hudson example).
- Orders for items you do not want to replenish (see the Bentley example). Only track these to decide whether or not to stock the item.

If you are not achieving your service level goals, review what you count as demand.

Accurate demand history is the important next foundation step toward good inventory management.

Pete Kornafel

Chapter 5. Inventory Classification

Most manufacturers and most wholesalers do some form of inventory classification to indicate the relative popularity and sales potential of items in their product lines. Many wholesalers also use this classification data in their purchasing process, and base their inventory levels by item class.

For example, Gordon Graham[12] advocated 12 classes, ranked by annual dollar sales, and suggested a number of months supply of inventory for an item based on its class.

Class	% of all items	Cum % of items	Months Supply to Buy	Turns to Expect
1	7.5%	7.5%	1	12.0
2	7.5%	15%	2	6.0
3	10%	25%	3	4.0
4	10%	35%	4	3.0
5	8%	43%	5	2.4
6	8%	51%	6	2.0
7	8%	59%	7	1.7
8	8%	67%	8	1.5
9	8%	75%	9	1.3
10	8%	83%	10	1.2
11	8%	91%	11	1.1
12	9%	100%	12	1.0

Ch 5 Fig 1. Gordon Graham Inventory Classification and Purchasing Guideline

I agree with many of the principles and concepts presented by Gordon Graham. However, even though this is a tidy and appealing chart, this method of classifying inventory does not work well in the auto parts channel, for several reasons:

1. Each automotive product line includes items with a wide range of unit prices. It does not make sense to lump together a $10 item that sells 300 units per year in a distribution center with a $200 item that sells 15 times per year, just because they both generate $3,000 in annual sales. Most stores would want to carry this $10 item, but few stores would want to carry the slow moving

---

[12] Gordon Graham. Distribution Inventory Management for the 1990's. Inventory Management Press, Richardson, Texas. 1987 Pg. 153-154

$200 part. Yet, this method would put these two items in the same inventory class.

For store inventory purposes, the classes should be based on a ranking by unit demand or by return on investment, not by dollar sales.

2. Even at the distribution centers, most people in the automotive industry, including the author, feel it is much more important to rank items by unit movement or return on investment rather than dollar sales, especially if this ranking is used in any of the purchasing formulas. Here again, an automotive aftermarket DC buyer would probably not want to carry the same number of months supply of inventory for the above two items.

3. Most auto parts product lines have a relatively small number of very fast movers, and a very large number of slow moving items. Fewer than 500 items would be in the first class, and more than 50,000 items would be in the bottom class, using the above class break points.

4. Auto parts have a wide spectrum of gross margin percentages. The investment can vary widely, too. For example, remanufactured items carry core deposits, and the inventory investment is higher for these items.

So, virtually all auto parts manufacturers and distributors use unit rankings for inventory classification. Each auto parts manufacturer classifies each of product line into ABC or 123 type codes, but seldom publishes the category break points. This makes it difficult for a distributor or store to understand how to apply their classification codes to store inventory recommendations or DC purchasing.

It is important to understand the main "mission" for inventory classification in auto parts. The primary use is to help determine items to stock at auto parts stores. Stores must select the 15-20,000 items to stock from a universe of about 500,000 items. Since a single distribution center supplies many stores, the decision to stock an item at most or all stores is a much bigger investment decision than stocking it at the distribution center. It is a larger financial risk, and deserves even more analysis and scrutiny than the detailed management of items within the distribution center inventory.

For this reason, a classification scheme has been developed by automotive distributors to do the best job of helping stores select which items to stock. This method is applied consistently across all product lines to give an indication of how any item will perform in a store inventory.

Automotive Classification Schemes

Here is a scheme to classify auto parts by their unit sales potential at the store level. This is the scale used in our company and many other aftermarket firms. The class codes are based on the annual unit sales per average store, for stores that stock that product category. Here is the scale used by the author and many other auto parts distributors.

Class Code	Annual Unit Sales per Stocking Store
Code 1	>4
Code 2	>3
Code 3	>2
Code 4	>1
Code 5	>.5
Code 6	>.25
Code 7	>.1
Code 8	<.1
Code 9	Recall
Code 0	Obsolete

Ch 5 Fig 2. Auto Aftermarket Classification Codes

So, a Class 1 item sells more than 4 units per year per store that stocks that product category. A Class 2 item sells between 3 and 4 units per year per store, and so forth.

Prior to data warehouses, the general method is to establish the number of stores that stock a particular category of products, and use that number to scale the serving distribution center's unit demand. For example, if a distribution center supplies 75 stores for a category like fan belts, then the definition of a Class 1 fan belt is one that sells more than 300 units per year at that distribution center or in those stores. A Class 4 item in this category sells between 75 and 150 units per year, to match the range from 1 to 2 units per store per year.

If aggregated "like" store demand history is available, this is cleaner and better data than distribution center demand.

It is acknowledged that the class codes will be more accurate if they are based on a large universe of demand observations.

However, there is a significant difference in the mix of vehicles across markets in the U.S. The Western states have a large mix of pickup trucks, and the West Coast states have the highest mix of Japanese cars. A typical auto parts distribution center serves 50-150 stores in a region that is generally within 150 miles of the DC.

Because the variation in vehicle mix is significant, most companies provide regional classifications, based on the movement in each regional distribution center. Based on experience, this is more accurate and appropriate than classification based on larger regions, even though that would aggregate more total demand.

It would be even better to aggregate data from stores in similar markets. The rural stores in Colorado had a distinctly different market and vehicle mix than the metropolitan Denver area stores. Even within Denver, neighborhoods varied widely. Without a data warehouse, we just did not have a way to compile data from "like" stores. It would have given us better classification data if we could have achieved that.

Note the important distinction that the number of stocking stores is used to scale the demand. There are many specialized categories of auto parts, and not every store stocks every category. For example, our distribution center in Denver served 75 auto parts stores. All of these stores stocked the category of fan belts. The distribution center demand was scaled by 75 to determine the class codes for belts. However, only 25 stores stocked the category of hydraulic hose and fittings. This is a specialized product category used only by fleets and agricultural customers. Only stores with a significant base of these customers stocked this category. The distribution center hydraulic hose items were scaled by 25 to establish the class codes in this category. If store sales are available, aggregate only the stores stocking each category.

The overall result is that the automotive class codes help stores predict their likelihood of a store selling specific items. In auto parts, this is a far more important use of the codes than to distinguish levels of inventory popularity within the distribution center itself.

There will be much more detail about how these class codes can be used to manage store inventories in a later chapter.

Figure 3 is a summary picture of a typical distribution center's inventory, using this scheme to establish class codes. This is a medium size distribution center in an Atlantic Coast state, supplying about 60 stores, in 2003.

This chart illustrates the small number of good sellers, and the huge number of very slow moving items in the automotive aftermarket.

Category of Items	# of Stock Items	$ of DC Inventory (at DC Cost)	% of DC Inventory	$ of DC Annual Sales (at DC Cost)	% of Total DC Sales	Cum % of Total DC Sales	DC Turns
Code 1	2,563	453,375	10.8%	7,432,849	32.2%	32.2%	16.39
Code 2	934	95,830	2.3%	1,394,152	6.0%	38.3%	14.55
Code 3	1,792	169,755	4.0%	1,960,317	8.5%	46.8%	11.55
Code 4	4,510	377,221	9.0%	3,406,238	14.8%	61.6%	9.03
Code 5	8,584	490,027	11.6%	3,318,843	14.4%	76.0%	6.77
Code 6	9,320	491,980	11.7%	2,156,068	9.4%	85.3%	4.38
Code 7	12,173	554,288	13.2%	1,476,890	6.4%	91.7%	2.66
Code 8	44,007	1,516,125	36.0%	1,783,028	7.7%	99.5%	1.18
9, 0, none	121	58,522	1.4%	120,002	0.5%	100.0%	2.05
Non Stock	159,750						
Total	243,754	4,207,123		23,048,387	100.0%		5.48

Ch 5 Fig 3. Typical Distribution Center Inventory Data by Class Code

There are only 2,563 best sellers in Code 1, of a total inventory of almost 84,000 stocking SKUs at this distribution center. These are good items. They require only 10% of the total inventory investment, but generate almost 1/3 of the total distribution center's sales. This DC turns its inventory of Code 1 items more than 16 times per year.

At the other end of the scale are more than 44,000 Code 8 items. Remember that a Code 8 items sells less than .1 units per year per store, so in this distribution center, each of these 44,000 items sell 6 units per year or less, based on the total of 60 stores.

These Code 8 items represent over 1/3 of the total inventory investment, but generate less than 8% of the distribution center's sales, and give just over 1 annual inventory turn.

What is even more trouble is that the inventory master file for this DC includes another 150,000 items that the DC has chosen not to stock. This DC tracks lost sales, and these items have even lower sales potential than the Code 8 items.

Your first reaction is probably to ask why this DC should stock these slow moving Code 8 items. Please hold that question until the next chapter on selecting items to be stocked.

Coverage by Class Code

If you establish class codes based on the item sales per average store, it is an important note that the coverage of overall demand will vary from product category to category. Here are some examples of the coverage obtained on several product categories:

	Code 1-3		Code 1-4		Code 1-5		Code 1-6		Code 1-7	
	Cum Items	Cum % Coverage	Cum Items	Cum % Coverage	Cum Items	Cum % Coverage	Cum Items	Cum % Coverage	Cum Items	Cum % Coverage
Brake Calipers	14	17.4%	73	45.7%	176	69.4%	297	80.5%	571	91.8%
Chasis Parts	89	50.4%	188	67.2%	346	79.7%	546	87.0%	936	93.6%
Filters	449	88.2%	716	93.7%	995	96.8%	1,317	98.3%	1,819	99.4%
Power Brake Boosters	0	0.0%	3	12.6%	7	25.4%	12	33.9%	40	56.6%
Spark Plugs	61	92.5%	84	96.4%	98	97.3%	123	98.6%	163	99.6%

Ch 5 Fig 4. Coverage by Class Code for Several Categories

Look at the cumulative coverage of items in class codes 1 through 3 (meaning items that sell at least 2 units per year per store). There are only 14 brake calipers that sell that well, and they account for only 17.4% of caliper demand. In filters, 449 items sell well enough to be classified Code 3 or better, and they are 88.2% of total demand, but it takes 1,819 different filters to give 99.4% coverage.

Power Brake boosters are seldom replaced, and no items sell well enough to be classified in code 3. Only 3 items sell well enough to be classified in Code 4. Only 40 items are classed 7 or better. There are another 500+ items that are classed Code 8. The best of these sells less than .1 unit per store per year, but in the aggregate they account for 44% of the total unit demand for this line.

There are 61 spark plug sets that well enough to be in codes 1-3, and they account for 92.5% of all demand, and 163 spark plug items give 99.6% coverage.

So, if a store stocks a uniform depth on all lines, say Code 1 through Code 5, it will have a varying degree of coverage by category, but will stock individual items that sell at least 0.5 units per year per store, regardless of category.

Automotive Oddities

The auto parts channel has several other oddities, and these make classification more difficult.

The first is "units per car or job". Many parts have more than one unit per vehicle, or per repair job. For example, spark plugs are typically replaced in sets, so a single sale is likely to be 4, 6 or 8 units. Should a spark plug that fits 4 cylinder cars be given a lower class code than a plug that fits 8 cylinder cars, if the same number of vehicles are repaired for each item, but that results in only half the unit sales for the 4 cylinder plug versus the 8 cylinder plug? Spark plug wires are sold as complete sets, and one set includes all the wires for a vehicle. Even if the same numbers of vehicles are repaired, there will be 1/4 or 1/8 as many wire sets sold as spark plug units. Should all these items be classified based on the number of units sold or the number of jobs performed?

The answer is that wherever possible, the unit demand should be scaled by the units per repair job. This will give a more accurate picture of the number of repair events, and help the DC and store stock enough units to satisfy each repair.

Another complication is with quality grades of some products. Some categories like disc brake pads come in good—better—best quality grades. There can be three items that fit the same vehicle, but with different qualities and price points. Typically, the largest sales are in the mainstream, better grade. However, there can be significant sales in the high and low end products, too. It is tempting to aggregate these items, to produce a classification based on the incidence of repairs to a specific vehicle, regardless of the quality of part used.

However, it is my opinion that these items should, in general, not be aggregated. The classification for each item should stand on its own. If aggregated, the result would be to apply the same class code to the three like items, and base the code on the total sales of all three items. This is not representative of what happens in the real world. Customers are more likely to spend the money for the best products for newer, more expensive vehicles. They are also more likely to purchase the value grade for older, less expensive vehicles. So, the mix of quality grades varies by item. It is more realistic to classify each item on its own demand history. If a store wants to stock more coverage of all quality grades, to give their customers more choice, that can be achieved by stocking a deeper level in the specialized grades.

There is an exception to this (as there usually is with all "rules"). If the item or category comes in several quality grades, but individual stores are likely to stock only one grade, then that is a different situation. For example, stores in a low-income neighborhood might stock only the value grade, and stores in a high-income neighborhood might stock only the better or best grades. In this case, you should aggregate the movement and apply it to like items in each grade for the purpose of selecting items for store inventories. This will give a balanced inventory within one grade in each store. The store might have to convince the customer to take the readily available item, but it will have full coverage in the selected quality grade.

Pete Kornafel

The Risk of the "Self Fulfilling Prophecy" in Classification

There is one further, significant issue with this classification formula. If a store has an item in stock when it is needed, the store is likely to make the sale. If a store does not have the item in stock, they can offer to source the item from a distribution center, another store in the area, or the factory. However, many wholesale customers will not wait, so the store does not turn all these orders into sales.

A very rough rule of thumb is that a store can convert only about 1/3 of these potential orders into actual, special order sales. The store should log inquiries as lost sales in all cases where the odds are that the store would have made the sale if it had the item in stock. If the store logs these lost sales, then the true demand will be accurately recorded. However, most stores do not do this.

As a result, the stores and distribution center see actual sales for these special orders, and it is only a fraction of their true potential. This classification system can lead to a self-fulfilling prophecy if lost sales are not logged, and if the classification is based on sales, rather than true demand. This is how it would work:

When an item grows in actual sales to a level that justifies stocking it in most stores, then the inventory manager will add it to each store's inventory. In the following period, that item is likely to sell several times better, just because it is in stock at the stores, and the stores convert almost every inquiry to a sale. The inventory manager congratulates himself on his wisdom for adding this item to the store mix. He was right. The item jumped up in sales, and deserved to be put into the store stock.

When an item that is stocked in the stores declines in popularity, it will reach a point where the decision is made to remove it from each store's inventory. In the following period, that item is likely to have an even steeper decline in sales, because the stores cannot convert every demand into a sale, and the only actual sales are to those willing to wait for special orders. The inventory manager congratulates himself on his wisdom here, too. The item shows a big decline in sales, and he was wise to remove it from the store stock.

So, if a company does not capture lost sales at the store level, it runs the risk of biasing the true classifications on these borderline items. Since each better class code indicates a doubling in sales potential, and since this phenomenon can alter actual sales by a factor of three or more, these items can be misclassified by one to two codes.

There will be a further discussion of this in the chapter on Store Inventory Selection.

Classification Calendar

We reclassified our inventory annually. Auto parts have long enough lives that most items stayed in the same code for several years, or only moved up or down by one code from year to year. Popular new items could jump several codes in a single year. We attempted to give new items an initial classification that showed where they would be when their sales reached their potential, but this was a challenge.

Our other reason for classifying inventory only once a year was that we used this classification to select items to move in and move out of store inventories, and we just didn't want to move all this merchandise around more than once a year in each line. Many systems offer the capability of almost continuous forecasting and classification updates. That's fine only if you're willing to move items in and out of stores each time a classification changes up or down past the store's cut line.

We had a calendar for the month each product line should be classified. There were three considerations in selecting the month for a particular product line.

First, if the product line had some general seasonality (air conditioning system parts sell much better in the summer), then we wanted to classify that line in front of the peak season, so all our DCs and stores would have updated inventories going into the season.

Second, if our vendor had a regular time to announce new items, or publish a new catalog, or overhaul their own coverage, then we wanted to reclassify that line quickly after this new information was available to us.

Third, and our least favorite reason, was if the vendor imposed a deadline date for returning items on stock adjustments. If there was a deadline, and it would be our last chance to return some items for credit before the vendor declared them obsolete, then we wanted to reclassify our inventory and recall those items from all our stores and customers in time to make the deadline.

Chapter Summary

The main mission of classification in the automotive aftermarket is to assist in the selection of items for store inventories.

This is a usually a much larger investment decision than tweaking the distribution center inventories.

So, a classification scheme based on unit sales potential per average store worked best for our company in the automotive aftermarket.

Rank items by units or by return on investment, not dollar sales.

If you adjust store inventories based on classification changes, then only classify as frequently as you are willing to handle the pipeline inventory adjustments.

A scheme like this would probably also be the best way to classify other hard goods lines where the big investment decision revolves around selecting inventory to be deployed in the field.

Chapter 6. Selecting Items for Store and DC Inventories

Pre-Computer Systems

Before all the computer inventory management systems, there were a number of manual systems for selecting items. New numbers were announced once a year, in conjunction with each year's new vehicles, and the total population of automotive aftermarket parts was small enough that it was easier to select which new numbers to stock.

It was harder to decide when to discontinue an item. The most general method was the "dust" method. If the package had been in inventory long enough to accumulate a layer of dust, it was a solid clue that it had not sold, and should be discontinued or returned to the vendor.

My parents bought our auto parts business when I was seven, and I was introduced to inventory management at an early age. One of the product lines we stocked was a line of exhaust system parts— mufflers and tailpipes. The dust method worked OK for the muffler boxes, but the tailpipes were stocked in hanging racks, and it was harder to tell how long they had been in inventory. One of my first jobs was to accompany my father when we called on our customer's stores. I carried a can of spray paint. I would walk down the aisle and spray a paint stripe on each tailpipe in a customer's hanging rack. I did that each year, in a different color. The inventory management rule was like baseball— "three stripes and you're out." It clearly identified items that had not sold in three years.

Today, it is possible to use the computer systems in each store and distribution center to help select items to stock and items to discontinue. There is a big benefit in blending data from all sources for these decisions.

Whose data to use? Issues with Individual Store Data

A single store should not base all of its stocking decisions only on its own history. If that is obvious to you, skip to the next heading. If that is not obvious, then here is the reason you also need data from other sources to choose the best items to stock in any store.

Assume that items can be accurately classified into the Class Codes defined in the Classification chapter. I know this is not possible in the real world, but it simplifies an illustration. If items in each Code really do have these ranges of probable sales per average store, that can be converted into the statistical probability that an individual item will sell in one year in a store. Here is a chart of those probabilities:

Class Code	Unit Sales per Store	Average Demand Per Year	Probability of Annual Unit Sales in an Average Store			
			No Sale	Any Sale	One Sale	Two or More
Code 1	>4	5.50	0.38%	99.62%	2.18%	97.44%
Code 2	>3	3.50	2.96%	97.04%	10.48%	86.56%
Code 3	>2	2.50	8.12%	91.88%	20.48%	71.40%
Code 4	>1	1.50	22.23%	77.77%	33.51%	44.26%
Code 5	>.5	0.75	47.19%	52.81%	35.48%	17.33%
Code 6	>.25	0.38	68.72%	31.28%	25.80%	5.48%
Code 7	>.1	0.18	83.94%	16.06%	14.69%	1.37%
Code 8	<.1	0.05	95.12%	4.88%	4.76%	0.12%

Ch 6 Fig 1. Probability of Sales at an Average Store by Class Code.

So, an average store has about a 47% chance of not selling a specific Code 5 item in a year's time. It has about a 35% probability it will sell a Code 5 item exactly once in a year, and about a 17% chance it will sell that item twice or more in a year.

These probabilities illustrate the wide spectrum of demand for individual items. If you combine these computed probabilities with the number of items in each classification code from Figure 3 in the Classification Chapter, you can estimate the number of items in each class code that will sell in an average store.

Class Code	Annual Unit Sales per Average Store	Number of Items	Probability of No Sale in a Year	Estimated Number of Items Not Sold	Probability of One Sale Per Year In Average Store	Estimated Number of Items Sold Once Per Year	Probability of Two or More Sales Per Year in Average Store	Estimated Number of Items Sold Twice or More Per Year
1	>4	2,563	0.38%	10	2.18%	56	97.44%	2,497
2	>3	934	2.96%	28	10.48%	98	86.56%	808
3	>2	1,792	8.12%	146	20.48%	367	71.40%	1,279
4	>1	4,510	22.23%	1,003	33.51%	1,511	44.26%	1,996
5	>.5	8,584	47.19%	4,051	35.48%	3,046	17.33%	1,488
6	>.25	9,320	68.72%	6,405	25.80%	2,405	5.48%	511
7	>.1	12,173	83.94%	10,218	14.69%	1,788	1.37%	167
8	<.1	44,007	95.12%	41,859	4.76%	2,095	0.12%	53

Ch 6 Fig 2. Estimated Number of Items Sold By Code In an Average Store.

This chart illustrates two very important points.

First, it shows you should not use just the store's data to determine which items to stock. The sales of individual items at any single store are small enough that the statistical "noise" will overwhelm the individual store sales data, particularly for slow moving parts.

For example, on the statistics alone, there are about 150 Code 3 items (8% of all the Code 3s), that are likely not to sell at all in a year in an average store, even if these items have a "real" sales potential of between 1 and 2 units sold per store per year. At the same time, there are about 2,400 Code 6 items (25% of all Code 6s), and 2,000 Code 8 items (5% of all Code 8s) that will sell one time in a year. These items have very low overall sales potential, but each store sells some small fraction of all these items. However, the "real" sales potential of a Code 3 item is 8 times as great as a Code 6 item and 20 times as great as a Code 8 item.

If the store's inventory rule is to remove all items that have not sold in a year, they will remove these Code 3 items from stock. If the store's rule is to add all items that have sold at least once, they will add these 2,400 Code 6s and 2,000 Code 8s. Both would be bad inventory decisions.

The second point is just as important. There is one key area where an individual store's demand history should be used to select items to be stocked at that store. This is where the store has a rare customer for very specialized items, and should stock items just for that one customer.

Here is an automotive example. One of our stores was close to a shop that restored and specialized in Corvairs. That's a real niche business, but this shop had a widespread reputation for this specialty. This shop restored about six Corvairs each year, and repaired many others. This shop bought as many parts as it could from our local store. So, we sold ten to thirty units per year on some items that only fit Corvairs. All these sales went to this one store, for this one repair shop customer. These were judged to be very popular parts at that store, and it stocked many of them to give good service to the restorer. However, they did not sell anywhere else in our system. No other store should stock them, even though they had enough overall demand to be classified in categories that looked appealing to larger stores.

A Data Warehouse would be very helpful in detecting these situations. Another big help is "The Rule of 2".

Pete Kornafel

The Rule of 2

Based on the statistics alone, it is extremely unlikely that an average store will sell a very slow moving item twice or more in one year. Just based on the odds, an average store will sell about 50 Code 8 items twice or more in one year, but this is from a universe of over 44,000 Code 8 items. Note that this refers to two separate events. One sale of two shock absorbers for one car is one event. Use units per vehicle or job to scale demand.

So, if an individual store does sell a Code 8 item two or more times in one year, then it is likely that store happens to be the one that actually has the rare customer for a very slow moving part. The Rule of 2 is that an auto parts store should stock every item that it sells two or more times per year, regardless of the overall popularity of that item. Each store may stock roughly 50 Code 8 items that happened to sell twice in that store based on the statistical probabilities, but it will also stock all the Code 8 items that sold twice or more in that store because one of its regular customers has the ongoing need for a very slow moving Code 8 part. The store's local demand data should overrule other data in this case, and the store should stock the item based on its sales in that store alone, even though it is a slow moving part overall.

Stock Depth Profiles, or Base Inventory Profiles

The store's data is also most appropriate to determine the overall level of inventory that store can support.
With classification data that projects unit sales per store, it is possible to set a "stock depth" as the "normal" inventory level. Here are some examples.

- Because the popularity codes have the same scale for all products, a store could use the same stock depth for all lines. A single store will understand that they are likely to sell about 1-2 units per year of any Class 4 item, across all categories of parts, if it is an average size store within the group of stores classified together.
- The store could select an appropriate stock level, and apply it to all lines. If a store decides to stock all items in Class codes 1 through 5, for example, that means it will stock every item that sells at least 1/2 unit per year per stocking store at the distribution center, across all product categories. Because the codes are based on unit demand, this would maximize the unit service level to their customers.

- There are many specialized categories of auto parts, and not every store stocks every category. Return to the example of hydraulic hose. This is a specialized product category used only by fleets and agricultural customers. Only about 1/3 of our stores stocked these items. Denver metro stores without significant fleet accounts would not stock this category at all. A store considering whether to add the category of hydraulic hose would know that items in any specific class code sold at the appropriate rate in stores that already stocked the line. Once they decided to add the category, the same stock depth would work for them.

- An average size store might adopt a general rule to stock all items classified Code 5 or better, plus items below that which sold twice or more in the past year, and less any items in Code 5 or better where the store knows they do not have customers for that item or category, or the item has not sold for 2 years (the Rule of 2 again).

- Also, the stores understand that these codes are based on the average store size, and this size is published. Items in any class code are likely to sell at about twice these rates in a store that does twice the average overall sales. A larger store in a larger market area might stock through Code 6 items, with the same exceptions.

- Finally, remember that stocking all lines at a uniform depth with this classification system gives uniform item movement potential. It maximizes unit service level, but does not give uniform coverage by category, or maximize the store's dollar sales or gross margin, as you will see later in this chapter.

A store that wants to specialize in one or more categories to cater to their particular mix of customers can stock one or two levels deeper in those areas.

We established that we wanted to stock an item at a specific store, and then we also used that store's information to set the stock level at the store. We had a "pull" system, where we replenished every store every day, so the stock quantity for the vast majority of items was one (or the quantity required per vehicle or per job). We used the store data to set all quantities higher than one (or one car's worth).

So, the primary uses of individual store data are to help set an appropriate overall level of inventory, to find special cases of slow moving items that should be stocked just at that store, and to set the item stock quantities where the movement justified stocking more than one (or one car's worth).

Distribution Center or Aggregated Store Data

Our second source of data to help select items for store inventories came from our distribution center classification process.

The laws of statistics show that data from a larger sample will give a more accurate overall prediction, as long as the data comes from comparable sources.

Here's a trivial example. You can't predict the odds of "heads" or "tails" from a single coin toss. You'll get "heads" or "tails", and think that is the only possibility. However, if you toss a coin 10,000 times, you'll feel pretty confident that the odds of getting "heads" on any toss are 50/50. Now mix in a die (1/2 of a pair of dice) that has "heads" on one face, and "tails" on the other five faces. Toss it 10,000 times, too. If you just examine the die, you'll conclude the chance of getting "heads" is one in six. If you merge the results from the coin and from the die, you'll conclude the odds of "heads" on the next toss is one chance in three. That is an average, but not correct for either one. You shouldn't mix coins and dice, or apples and oranges, or stores that don't have the same kind of customers when you aggregate data.

But, if you could aggregate stores that have the same kind of customers, you'll get much better predictions of the "real" demand for any specific item. The general principle is to aggregate as many "like" stores as possible.

In our company, we did not have a good way to aggregate store data. Absent that, we judged that stores served by a single DC, and that actually stocked a category of parts would give the largest consistent sample of demand for items in that category. We did not want to mix in stores that did not stock that category. So, we counted the number of stores that stocked each category, and scaled our distribution center demand by that number to get to a predicted sale per average store for items in that category. A full data warehouse would have been a very valuable tool. But, we didn't have that, and while we knew our system was not perfect, it was the best we could do.

We used the distribution center's data in this fashion to set the overall class codes for all items in our database. We used this classification data to drive most of the decisions to add or remove items from store inventories. It would have been better to group "like stores" and classify them together, but we did not have an easy way to do this.

Vendor Data

Our third source of data was our vendors. The good vendors gave us a lot of information about new items when they announced them. We worked with the vendor's information to make stocking decisions for stores and distribution centers. After all, it was all we had to go on for information on new numbers.

Because of the long life cycle for many auto parts, and the long "neck" on the "turtle" shaped life cycle chart, few new auto parts numbers would show immediate large demand. It is easier to identify the few items that will become popular quickly than to distinguish among the thousands of slow moving items that are introduced each year.

For example, a new oil filter for a new engine that is going to be used on several hundred thousand vehicles will become a popular item very quickly, and should be added to all store inventories as soon as it is available. Or, an item might be introduced which superseded a previous, established item, and demand for the prior item could be used to set an initial forecast for the new item. Other items are introduced which are likely to be slow movers for some time. For example, a new master cylinder for one model and year of a low volume vehicle might not sell at all (other than as a collision repair part) for several years. It clearly should not be added to any store inventories when it is first introduced, and might not even be needed at the distribution centers for several years.

So, our practice was to rely on the vendors and only put items into stock in the stores where we anticipated a lot of immediate usage. Otherwise, we loaded the item to our master data files, and waited for the first "lost sales" before stocking it.

We had some eligibility to return items to most of our vendors as stock adjustments. However, the vendors made the decision when to declare an item obsolete, and ineligible for return. So, we used their data completely to drive all "final recalls", to make sure all these items were returned to the vendor before their deadline. In a few cases where we had ongoing demand, we asked for and received extensions for specific items, but these could still be a problem when we eventually wanted to return them.

So, we primarily used our vendors for information on new items, and on items going obsolete.

Category Management

Category management has been used in food and other channels for years. Here is a brief and probably oversimplified introduction.

The goal is for all stores to submit item level point of sale data to an industry sponsored central agent. The central agent compiles all the data, and supplies it to vendors and distributors. The vendors typically pay for the data, and this funds the project.

The data gives a global perspective of market size and share by brand and by item. It also gives total composite sales for comparable items. With this data, Procter and Gamble knows the detergent market size for every community, and Tide's share, both by geographical areas and by package sizes. Kroger knows their market sizes and shares on Tide, and other items, too.

This data has been widely used in food distribution and retailing to help select items to be stocked in supermarkets, and to influence and measure marketing programs, pricing strategies, promotions, etc. Each category has a "category captain"—usually the lead vendor, who is responsible for analyzing the data and suggesting store items and planograms for each category. The data is used to try to maximize the profit for each store. For example, it is used in grocery stores to determine which items to stock at eye level, and which to stock on the top and bottom shelves, based on the sales potential and gross margin for each item in the category.

Since 2000 there has been an initiative, sponsored by AAIA, the Automotive Aftermarket Industry Association, and spearheaded by Sandy Brawley at Clorox. Sandy knows the benefit of this approach in other channels. Clorox also owns Armorall and STP, two key chemical brands in the automotive aftermarket. Some of the major aftermarket retailers are participating in this project. So far, the approach has only been used on chemicals, accessories, and other "retail" items.

There has been some discussion about extending this technique to long application product lines. At the time of the writing of this book, a study group is working on the category of brake parts, to see if the technique can be used. There are many issues with using these techniques for application parts.

First, it is difficult to directly compare items in many categories. Each supplier has different product design standards, and the items are not one-to-one interchangeable. This means you can get an overview of market sizes and shares, but the item level data may not be very accurate.

Second, in many markets, there are fewer local distributors than in other channels. The process only works if everyone contributes their confidential data, and can analyze the composite results without being able to diagnose any specific competitor's data. In the extreme, with only two participants, one company could subtract their own data from the composite and learn exactly what the other participant is doing. This has happened in other channels. In 2001, Wal-Mart stopped providing their data to the industry wide category management group for groceries and general merchandise. They apparently felt they had more to lose than gain. K-Mart became less of a factor in many local markets, and it became easier for Target to back their own data out of the composite totals and infer what Wal-Mart was doing. In many markets there are only two or three full line automotive distributors, so this is a real concern for automotive companies, too.

The jury is still out on whether this will be a big help in the automotive channel. As of now, it does not play a big role in determining auto parts inventories on the application lines with thousands of items.

Vehicle Registration Data

The automotive aftermarket has a potential advantage, in that a single company, R.L. Polk, collects and maintains a data base of all 200+ million vehicles registered anywhere in the United States. The Polk data includes the VIN (vehicle identification number) and the zip code where the registered owner lives.

There is an industry standard for Vehicle Identification Numbers. They encode the make, model, year, engine, drive train, body style, and a serial number unique to that vehicle. The manufacturers publish the codes so you can get all that detail about the vehicle from the VIN. So, if you buy the Polk data, you could know precisely how many Red 1998 Mitsubishi Eclipse Spyder GT Convertibles with the 2.0 Liter turbocharged engine are registered in zip code 80227. (I could find out if mine is the only one, or how many others there are.)

You can uniquely determine many parts that fit this vehicle based on the information in the VIN. You can aggregate this across all the models and years that a single item fits, and develop a data base with the population and age of specific parts in any defined market area. You can establish the registered vehicle population, and in theory, infer the replacement parts market down to the Zip code level with the Polk data. This should give a great indication of all the prospective customers in any particular market that might need that part.

51

Pete Kornafel

Unfortunately, it's not that easy. We don't have a good handle on wear-out and replacement rates for many items. It doesn't matter how many vehicles in your market have that part, unless it needs to be replaced, and it's tough to predict the failure rates. Not all cars live or get repaired where they are registered. Many people have their cars repaired close to where they work, not close to where they live. Many college towns and towns with armed services facilities have lots of cars that aren't registered locally. Finally, you're never sure what your market share might be for a specific item.

So, even though this data seems very appealing, several distributors, including our company, have failed to develop local forecasts for individual items from this data alone.

However, it is can be helpful in deciding what items to stock (and which ones NOT to stock) in individual stores. There are only about 20 of us with Mitsubishi Turbo convertibles in Lakewood, Colorado. My local auto parts store should not stock items that are specific only to 1998 Mitsubishi Turbo Convertibles.

Implementation at the Store Level

Here is a sample of a cumulative investment table, showing the number of items, the inventory investment for one vehicle quantity of each item, and the percent of coverage obtained from those items in each classification code for each category of items. Here is an example:

CONFIDENTIAL * CONFIDENTIAL

Cumulative Investment by Movement Code by Subline		Denver - 2/28/02			At Jobber Acquisition Cost W/Cores				
		MVTCD							
SLNAME	Data	3	4 TOP	4 BOT	5 TOP	5 BOT	6 TOP	6 BOT	7 TOP	7 BOT
CARQUEST WIPER PRODU	CUM PARTS	65	100	107	132	135	162	161	174	187
	CUM INVEST	543	909	968	1217	1233	1403	1506	1651	1803
	CUM SALES	94.7	97.3	98	98.9	99.1	99.5	99.6	99.8	99.9

Ch 6 Fig 3. Cumulative Investment Table For One Product Line

The column for Movement Code 3 (MVTCD 3) shows that in CARQUEST Wiper Products there are 65 SKUs that sell well enough to be classified as Code 1 through 3. These 65 items have a cost of $543 for a pair of each item (two wiper blades per car). The 65 items give 94.7% unit demand coverage of the wiper blade product line. Then look at the data for the bottom half of Code 5. This requires 135 SKUs, an investment of $1,233, and gives coverage of 99.1%.

52

Would you stock through Code 3 or Code 5? That is the question for an inventory manager. Does the incremental investment of $690 in the next 70 SKUs give a reasonable return? It only improves the store's coverage by 4.5% in this category. While these items sell well enough in units to make this classification code, the tiny bit of additional coverage might not pay a reasonable return on the incremental investment to stock this line at this depth.

So, this table can be used to select a stock depth on each category of parts. If you pick a uniform depth on all categories, you will maximize the unit service level because you are picking all the items that sell at a specific unit level per year in an average store.

What do you want to Maximize?

All of the above shows ranking by item unit movement potential. The real mission of all classification systems is to help achieve the "most efficient" inventory. If most items have roughly the same return on investment potential, this unit movement ranking will work fine.

However, there is a wide range of gross margin percentages across our auto parts categories. There is a wide range of investment requirements, too. For example, many remanufactured items include a deposit on the "core", and have a corresponding lower return on inventory investment.

GMROI

The Gross Margin Return on Investment (GMROI) can be a very valuable way to determine what inventory should be stocked. Here is a formula:

$$GrossMarginReturnOnInvestment = \frac{AnnualGrossMarginDollars}{InventoryInvestment}$$

Here is an example for a product that has a 25% gross margin, $100 annual sales, and a $10 inventory requirement:

$$GrossMarginReturnOnInvestment = \frac{\$100\ Sales * 25\%\ Gross\ Margin}{\$10\ InventoryInvestment} = \frac{\$25}{\$10} = 250\%\ GMROI$$

A $10 inventory investment in this item will generate $25 in annual gross margin. You might want to rank items by this ratio of their forecast gross margin to their inventory investment requirement. This generates an inventory model with the most "bang for the buck"—with the most forecast gross margin dollars for any given size inventory.

The above example on Wiper Blades helps illustrate this point. An average size CARQUEST store in the Denver market sells about $10,000 in Wiper Blades annually, and generates about $3,500 in gross margin. If the store only stocked the top 65 items, they would capture 94.7% of that, or $3,315 in margin with an on-hand investment of $543. That would give a ratio of gross margin to inventory or GMROI of 610%. The store would generate a $6.10 in gross margin for each $1 invested in this inventory.

If the store adds coverage through Code 5 Bottom, or 135 SKUs and $1,233 inventory investment, it would improve the coverage to 99.1%. In this case, the store would capture $3,468 in margin, but that only gives a GMROI of 281% on the $1,233 invested in inventory.

The marginal investment of $690 ($1,233—543) only yields an incremental gross margin of $153 ($3,468—3,315). That incremental investment has a GMROI of 22%. There is likely to be a better place to invest an incremental $690 that would generate more gross margin than this incremental investment in wiper blades.

Here is a larger case study. The chart below has the cumulative investment information for 8 auto parts product categories. It shows the dollar gross margin in the entire category, and then the cumulative part count, percentage coverage, and inventory investment for all the items in each classification code.

CONFIDENTIAL * CONFIDENTIAL

Cumulative Investment by Movement Code by Subline   Denver - 2/28/02   At Jobber Acquisition Cost W/Cores

MFG	Margin $	SLNAME	Data	MVTCD	4 TOP	4 BOT	5 TOP	5 BOT	6 TOP	6 BOT	7 TOP	7 BOT	TOTAL
ACL	$5,300	NEW CLUTCH KITS	CUM PARTS		11	17	32	47	70	93	123	168	
			CUM INVEST		66	904	1576	3020	4566	7057	9574	12927	17732
			CUM SALES		6.1	25.3	33.1	49.7	60.2	72.2	78.8	88	91.7
BAT	$4,385	NEW BATTERIES	CUM PARTS		36	39	45	52	58	59	61	59	65
			CUM INVEST		1334	1474	1902	2101	2430	2549	2727	2928	2936
			CUM SALES		92.3	93.5	97.5	98.4	99	96.5	99.7	99.9	96.9
CFI	$1,600	RED AIR FILTERS	CUM PARTS		49	55	81	89	100	108	111	112	112
			CUM INVEST		208	254	342	309	409	437	440	451	451
			CUM SALES		84.1	87.2	95.2	97.2	98.9	99.7	99.9	100	100
EC	$570	COMPUTERS	CUM PARTS		0	1	1	8	8	10	10	17	32
			CUM INVEST		0	96	66	301	391	850	850	1101	2106
			CUM SALES		0	8	8	23.6	23.8	43.2	43.2	51.4	83.5
FRI	$79	GOLD PADS QD ORGANIC	CUM PARTS		5	3	5	8	8	10	10	12	12
			CUM INVEST		33	84	84	232	232	278	278	330	330
			CUM SALES		33.3	65	65	90.1	90.1	94.8	94.8	98.1	98.1
FRI	$1,733	GOLD PAD GMD SEMI-MET	CUM PARTS		19	16	21	25	32	34	39	42	48
			CUM INVEST		343	543	891	819	1038	1118	1272	1386	1589
			CUM SALES		60.8	75.1	83.9	88.6	94	96	96.7	97.5	98.4
NWF	$6,963	NEW WATER PUMPS	CUM PARTS		27	40	57	81	101	127	153	182	209
			CUM INVEST		770	1131	1993	2313	2947	4006	4853	6178	7123
			CUM SALES		54.4	63.9	72.6	81.1	86.2	90.9	93.8	90	97.3
PQR	$818	PROVEN VALU ROTORS	CUM PARTS		52	110	126	154	164	174	175	179	179
			CUM INVEST		2656	3774	4427	5205	5768	6058	6091	6247	6247
			CUM SALES		90.2	94.6	96.8	98.5	99.3	99.9	99.9	100	100

Ch 6 Fig 4. Cumulative Investment Table for Eight Product Categories

Suppose you can only afford to invest $11,000 in inventory in these 8 categories. That would just cover stocking each category through the Code 4 Bottom level. Here is a chart showing the investment and forecast gross margin in that model inventory:

Product Category	Uniform Unit Coverage Through Code 4 Bottom		
	Cumulative Investment	Gross Margin Potential	Cumulative GMROI
ACL New Clutches	1,578	1,754	111.2%
BAT Batteries	1,902	4,275	224.8%
CFI Red Fuel Filters	342	1,523	445.3%
EC Computers	66	46	69.7%
FRI Gold Organic Disc Pads	84	47	56.0%
FRI Gold Semi-Met Disc Pads	691	1,452	210.1%
NWP New Water Pumps	1,593	5,055	317.3%
PDR Drums and Rotors	4,427	792	17.9%
	10,683	14,944	
Overall GMROI			139.9%

Ch 6 Fig 5. Model Inventory with Uniform Coverage of Unit Demand

If you stocked each category through that level, you would generate about $15,000 in annual gross margin. Clutches, for example, would generate $1,754 in gross margin ($5,300 for the line times the 33.1% coverage through Code 4 Bottom), and require $1,578 investment. Here is a complete table for clutches, with the cumulative and incremental investment, coverage, margin, and GMROI for each step of inventory depth.

Product Line	Code 3 Top	Code 4 Top	Code 4 Bottom	Code 5 Top	Code 5 Bottom	Code 6 Top	Code 6 Bottom
ACL - New Clutches							
Cumulative Investment	85	994	1,578	3,020	4,555	7,057	9,674
Cumulative Coverage %	6%	25.3%	33.1%	49.7%	60.2%	72.2%	78.8%
Cumulative Margin $	323	1,341	1,754	2,634	3,191	3,827	4,176
GMROI on Cumulative	380.4%	134.9%	111.2%	87.2%	70.0%	54.2%	43.2%
Incremental Investment	85	909	584	1,442	1,535	2,502	2,617
Incremental Coverage %	0.061	19.2%	7.8%	16.6%	10.5%	12.0%	6.6%
Incremental Margin $	323.3	1,018	413	880	557	636	350
GMROI on Increment	380.4%	111.9%	70.8%	61.0%	36.3%	25.4%	13.4%

Ch 6 Fig 6. Cumulative and Incremental Data for New Clutches

Look at the Code 5 Bottom column. It requires $4,555 inventory to cover to that depth, and that gives 60% coverage of the whole category. It would generate $3,191 of gross margin, and give a GMROI of 70%. The increment is the additional coverage to go from Code 5 Top through Code 5 Bottom. The increment is $1,535 added inventory (from $3,020 to $4,555), and gives an additional 10% coverage (from 49.7% to 60.2%). It adds $557 in gross margin (from 2,634 to 3,191), and the GMROI on the incremental inventory is 36.3% ($557/$1,535).

The question is whether there is an $11,000 inventory investment that could generate more gross margin dollars than an inventory based on uniform depth of unit movement. The answer is that there is. Here is a chart comparing a uniform depth through Code 4 Bottom with an inventory optimized by GMROI. Rank each category by the GMROI, and build it up to the $11,000 total to derive the optimum mix of inventory by gross margin potential.

Product Category	Uniform Unit Coverage Through Code 4 Bottom			Balanced by GMROI on Incremental Investment			
	Cumulative Investment	Gross Margin Potential	Cumulative GMROI	Optimum Depth	Cumulative Investment	Gross Margin Potential	GMROI on Last Increment
ACL New Clutches	1,578	1,754	111.2%	5 Bottom	4,555	3,191	70.1%
BAT Batteries	1,902	4,275	224.8%	4 Bottom	1,902	4,100	215.6%
CFI Red Fuel Filters	342	1,523	445.3%	6 Top	437	1,595	365.0%
EC Computers	66	46	69.7%	None	-	-	
FRI Gold Organic Disc Pads	84	47	56.0%	4 Top	84	47	56.0%
FRI Gold Semi-Met Disc Pads	691	1,452	210.1%	5 Bottom	1,038	1,629	156.9%
NWP New Water Pumps	1,593	5,055	317.3%	5 Bottom	2,947	6,002	203.7%
PDR Drums and Rotors	4,427	792	17.9%	None			
	10,683	14,944			10,963	16,564	
Overall GMROI			139.9%				151.1%

Ch 6 Fig 7. Optimum Inventory Balanced by Incremental GMROI

The optimum selection should generate $16,564 in gross margin. Would you do this? You could generate an additional $1,600 in gross margin with virtually no change in inventory investment. This could improve your profit significantly.

Would your customers figure it out? Perhaps. In this example, with the optimum solution you would not stock the Computers or the Drums and Rotors at all. That might not be acceptable to customers, so you might have to temper the pure rankings. However, this is clearly a better way to rank the inventory as a starting place.

Here is an overall chart comparing the dollar gross margin generated at each overall inventory level if you stock by uniform class codes, and if you re-balanced that same inventory by the incremental GMROI to maximize the gross margin coverage.

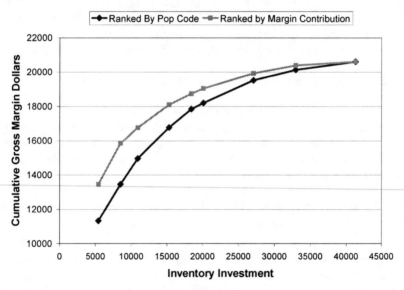

Ch 6 Fig 8. Chart of Gross Margin vs. Inventory Investment for Eight Categories

In every case except where you stock full depth in every category, the GMROI ranking will generate more gross margin for a comparable inventory investment than one based on unit movement. In all cases, these models should be tempered by the need to meet customer expectations. If your customer needs or expects to find certain items or categories in stock for immediate availability, then you have to stock them. If that is the case, then try to improve the GMROI on those items. If you need or want to stock a specific line in depth, you might have to find ways to increase the margin or reduce the investment.

Selecting Items to Stock at Distribution Centers

We used the Rule of 2 at our distribution centers, too. Here again, one lost sale might be just statistical noise, but the second lost sale was a pretty good indicator that some actual demand was beginning for an item. So, if we had two demands for an item at the DC, not in the same day (the Hudson water pump syndrome), then we would add or keep an item in stock at our DC.

Unfortunately, one of our customers figured out our system. Any time he thought we should stock an item, he would order it twice, and that would trigger our system to begin stocking the item. It took a while for us to figure out he was just registering his "vote", and it took even longer to get him to stop doing it. It requires some monitoring to make sure you're counting legitimate demand data.

Why Stock All those Slow Moving Parts at the DC?

If you look at the Code 8 line of Chapter 5 Figure 3., you'll see over 44,000 Code 8 items that are stocked at this DC. A code 8 item sells less than .1 units per year per average store, and this DC supplies about 60 stores, so the best of these items sells 6 times per year or less. I'm sure you have wondered why an automotive distributor would stock all these slow movers. After all, they account for only about 7% of the total demand, and the inventory of this set of items turns only about one time.

The answer is that even with very low sales, these items contribute importantly to the overall customer service provided by this DC. The goal is still to get any vehicle, with any problem, fixed and returned to the customer in one day. These items are needed (even if in small quantities) to complete repairs on a vehicle.

Individual stores are unlikely to stock any of these items, so the DC has the inventory closest to the customer.

Many auto repairs require replacement of more than one part. If any one of the needed items is not readily available, the repair cannot be completed. So, if this DC stocked none of these Code 8 items, as many as 10% of all repair jobs could not be completed in one day. Most vehicle owners would judge that as poor customer service. Even if the vehicle owners did not object, the auto repair facilities would. A repair shop would have a vehicle disassembled, waiting for the proper part. That vehicle is likely to tie up one of their service bays, and they would not be able to work on any other vehicle in that bay until the first job is completed. Repair shop owners are very sensitive to the productivity of their technicians and the full use of their service bays. So, both the vehicle owners and repair shop customers demand a very high service level, even on unusual and slow moving parts.

Also, a slow moving item can generate some contribution to the profit of the DC as long as the DC stocks only one unit, and sells it more than twice a year. An automotive DC typically has about a 25% gross margin. When a slow moving item is ordered, it will either be sold by the DC or recorded as a lost sale. There is almost no incremental variable operating cost at the DC to supply an additional item on an order. The warehouse pickers are already circulating in the warehouse, and the variable cost to pick an incremental item is very small. Most automotive DCs deliver goods to their stores daily on their own trucks. The truck is going to run the full delivery route, so there is almost no variable cost in delivering an incremental part along with all the other freight. Most DCs receive shipments from vendors weekly. A shipment consists of all the items to be replenished in a product line. Here again, there is almost no variable cost in stocking one more incremental part to replenish the inventory after a sale. Most manufacturers of auto parts provide some inventory stock adjustment allowance, so an item can be returned for cost if it does not meet a minimum sales level, and there isn't much obsolescence risk, even on these slow moving parts.

So, almost all of the gross margin on an incremental sale can flow through to operating profit. The only significant cost is the investment and carrying cost for the inventory. A DC can more than cover that carrying cost if it can stock one unit, and sell it twice or more per year.

When you combine the positive customer service with a minimal financial risk and even a potential small contribution to profit, it makes sense to stock these slow moving parts.

The key, however, is the word "moving". If an item does not sell in a reasonable period of time, it should be returned to the vendor and not replenished. For our auto parts, with very slow changes in overall demand levels, we required at least two years of zero demand to determine that a part was unlikely to sell in the future.

Pete Kornafel

Silver[13] gives a complex formula for computing whether to stock an item or not based on the inventory carrying and handling costs if the item is stocked versus the transaction costs for special orders if it is not stocked. This does not take customer service requirements into account, but it could be used as a decision rule.

Retail Auto Parts Chain Stores

Many significant sellers of auto parts have large store inventories, but do not attempt to stock the slow moving items in their distribution centers. Their store inventory is their only way they can service customers on a "same day" basis, so they concentrate their investment at that level. These chains typically stock this same mix at their distribution centers, just for store replenishment, and typically replenish their stores weekly. These chains cannot give same day service on items that are not in store stocks. Most of the retail auto parts chains follow this model. They typically stock about 20,000 items in their stores and distribution centers, and typically replenish their stores weekly.

These chains generally offer a special order service, with fulfillment by the manufacturer. They give overnight, UPS, FedEx or Parcel Post delivery, but usually pass through the shipping charges to the consumer.

A retail consumer is apparently not as fussy as a shop owner with a bay tied up. The retail chains have judged that overnight service including the freight charge is adequate for their customers.

Even those companies, however, must still choose items to stock in their stores. Since they do not see a full spectrum of demand, they must rely on their suppliers and on their own special order sales to guide which items to add to their store mix.

Self-fulfilling Prophecy

Don't forget the lesson from the chapter on Classification about this. Unless lost sales are captured meticulously at the stores and incorporated into the overall demand data, the true demand for items that are only stocked at the DC level and classified on DC actual sales could be understated by a factor of two or three times.

---

[13] Pg. 377. Edward Silver, David Pyke, Rein Peterson, Inventory Management And Production Planning and Scheduling, Third Edition, 1998, John Wiley and Sons.

This is because the store can only convert about 1/3 of inquires for these items into actual "special order" sales.

If you do not have all the lost sales data, then a compromise is to make sure that you do not draw a "bright line" at the classification break points to determine which items to stock in the stores.

The actual DC sales for all items not stocked in the stores could be scaled up by some factor to represent how the item would do if it were on the store shelves. The result of this is that an item classed one or even two levels below the store stock depth but not already in the store could be added to the store inventory. Its "true" demand, when parts are available from store inventories should justify that.

Chapter Summary

It is important to define which items to stock (and which not to stock) for every store and distribution center. This should be done regularly.

In our company, we did a complete reclassification once a year for each product category. If we did it more frequently than that, we would have the handling cost for many more "pipeline" sale and return transactions between our DC and its store customers. Also, most of our vendors updated their lists of items going obsolete and being recalled once a year, so that helped set the time when a stock adjustment was necessary.

For most auto parts items, with long life cycles, once a year was often enough to update the store and DC inventories. We did add new items to the DC, and new, immediately popular items to the stores, on an ongoing basis throughout the year.

Once the decisions are made about which items to stock, then, all the purchasing techniques can be used to replenish those items.

Here is a summary of the rules we used at stores and at DCs:

Pete Kornafel

Summary of Sources of Information to Use for Store Inventories
Use individual store data

- To set the stock depth profile by category of parts and the overall inventory size.
- Stock all items at that level or better in each category.
- Plus, local items (based on 2 or more sales per year).
- Minus, items that do not sell in this store (for 2 years), even if they are within the overall class depth that the store stocks.
- To set the quantity to stock on popular items.

Use the DC or aggregated "like" store data

- To determine the overall class code for all items.
- To give an early indication of actual movement on new numbers
- To give an early indication of items declining in popularity

Use the Manufacturer data

- For availability of new numbers and new applications.
- For notice on recall and obsolete items to return.
- For consolidations, and supersessions.

Summary of Sources of Information to Use for DC Inventories

Use the DC or aggregated "like" store data

- To determine the overall class code for all items.
- To decide when to start stocking a new number (at least 2 lost sales).
- To decide when to stop stocking a slow mover (less than 2 sales per year over a 2 year period).
- To set the order point on all items stocked.

Use the Manufacturer Data

- For availability of new numbers and new applications.
- For a "double check" on the DC classification, to make sure no important items are missed.
- For notice on recall and obsolete items to return.
- For consolidations, and supersessions.

Chapter 7. The Benefit of Short Lead Time

Frequency beats Forecasting

If your supply chain can replenish forward inventories almost immediately, you might not need strong forecasting techniques for those inventories, even if items exhibit erratic demand. You could just replenish items immediately when they are sold. Fairly simple techniques could tell you how many units to stock on each item. The only risk of lost sales would be for single orders or single day demands greater than the stock level in that forward inventory.

Frequent replenishments are the best antidote to uncertain forecasts.

Our company replenished all our stores every day from our distribution centers. An individual store didn't have to forecast most items—they just replaced what they sold daily. The only forecasts were to determine stock quantities for items that needed more than one unit for one day's demand. The opportunity for lost sales was minimized with daily replenishment. Some auto parts distributors get parts from their distribution centers to nearby stores as frequently as every two hours.

But, You Still Have to Forecast in Many Cases

The situation at our distribution center was different. Item demands were higher, since a DC served about 75 stores. We reviewed most major product lines weekly, and most lines had lead times of one to two weeks. With some safety stock, we needed to forecast about one month's usage on most items to set an accurate stock level.

So, frequency beats forecasting, but if you can't replenish inventories almost instantly, you need forecasts to set stock levels. If we missed a forecast at the DC, we could be out of stock for a week or more. A week's lost sales at the DC could be many times larger than those in a single day at a single store. A good forecast was key to good order fill at our distribution centers. We spent a lot of time on DC item forecasts. If you need to forecast usage for periods of a week or more, you might as well use the best forecasting techniques possible.

Short Lead Times help on Slow Moving Items

Glenn Staats developed probabilities of multiple sales over various lead-time cycles. This shows the benefit of short lead times on slow moving parts[14]:

Annual Demand	10 Day Cycle Sold = 2	Sold > 2	20 Day Cycle Sold = 2	Sold > 2	40 Day Cycle Sold = 2	Sold > 2
1	0.048%	0.0004%	0.051%	0.0005%	0.203%	0.0040%
2	0.189%	0.0030%	0.199%	0.0040%	0.760%	0.0330%
3	0.415%	0.0110%	0.748%	0.0310%	2.680%	0.2430%
4	0.718%	0.0260%	1.580%	0.1000%	5.320%	0.7490%
5	1.090%	0.0510%	2.650%	0.2280%	8.320%	1.6220%
10	3.810%	0.3730%	11.460%	2.7600%	23.890%	14.7900%
24	14.780%	4.0070%	27.110%	21.2000%	20.990%	63.0500%
60	30.200%	32.2000%	13.690%	79.3900%	0.648%	99.2050%
Data reprinted with Permission from Cooperative Computing, Inc.						

Ch 7 Fig 1. Probability of Demands in Various Periods.

This chart shows the probability for strictly independent events. It can be a rough gauge for stock levels on slower moving items, based on the service level goal. For example, look at an item that, on the average, sells 4 times per year. The odds that it will have 2 demands in any 10-day period are less than 1%, but they climb to 5% for a 40-day period. If you want to achieve a 95% service level, you need to stock two of this item if the total review and lead-time is about 40 days.

For an item that sells 10 times per year, or almost one per month, the probability is almost 4% that there could be 2 demands in any 10 day period, and almost 3% that there could be three or more demands in any 20 day period, so you would need to stock 2 if the cycle time is 10 days, and 3 if the cycle time is 20 days and your goal is 96-97% service.

This illustrates an important point that is essential to good service. The need for good forecasting, to accurately show the overall average demand, and the need for safety stock, to cover erratic demand, both grow very rapidly as the time span you must cover increases.

If you are fortunate enough to have cycle times (review time plus lead time) of just a few days, then you might not need all the detailed techniques of the next few chapters on forecasting and setting lead time.

---

[14] Data with permission from Glenn Staats and Cooperative Computing, Inc.

However, if the cycle time is anything longer than just a few days, your service level and inventory performance will benefit from good forecasting techniques.

"Pull" Systems beat "Push" Systems

Pull systems use actual end user demand to "pull" inventory through the distribution channel. Pull systems are likely to give the best service level and minimum inventory investment. They usually require frequent replenishment, and they can only be used if the "upstream" points in the distribution channel can support them.

Push systems use manufacturing requirements or a central inventory controller to set the overall schedule and drive replenishment shipments into the distribution channel at levels and frequencies based on the needs of the "upstream" member of the channel (farther away from the end user). In some categories the manufacturing process has to be controlled or scheduled to such an extent that the manufacturer has to drive the process, and push inventory into the channel. The most extreme example was our vendor for replacement wheels. The plant was mostly geared to supply the vehicle manufacturer assembly lines, and they only made aftermarket inventory when they had some slack time in their production schedules. They didn't want to keep any inventory, so they solicited orders and then scheduled and made a batch of an item. The only way we could give good service was to purchase about a 6- month supply of each item whenever they offered it. This was a tough line to get any kind of return on investment, and we eventually discontinued the line completely.

Chapter Summary

Demand patterns are almost always erratic, so there is always some uncertainty about the accuracy of a forecast based on them. If you can recover quickly, the risk to your service level is minimized. Frequent replenishment minimizes the risk of lost sales, even with uncertain forecasts.

If the replenishment cycle is more than a few days, then you might as well develop a good forecasting system, and have as much accuracy in your forecasts as possible.

In general, the longer the replenishment time, the more important it becomes to have accurate forecasts.

Pete Kornafel

Chapter 8. Item Level Forecasting—Part 1. Regular Items

Why Forecast at All?

An item level forecast, however derived, is needed to establish an estimate of the demand for the item in the near future. This can be translated into a usage requirement over the time span needed to replenish the item.

Even in "pull" systems with very frequent replenishment and very short lead times, it is still necessary to establish a stock level, or an order point and a replenishment order quantity. The answer might be as simple as "stock one unit, and replenish it with one more unit every time it is sold". It still takes some diagnosis to make sure that is the right answer for the item (to decide when it is necessary to stock 2 or 3, for example).

Forecasting becomes more critical as the time span increases. If the item can only be replenished once a week, and if the lead-time from ordering is also a week, then a good forecast is needed to project the requirements for the next two weeks.

If the item is imported, and the lead-time is 60-90 days, then a great forecast is needed to project requirements much farther into the future.

If the item is seasonal, it is critical to purchase for the increased projected demand at the right time, just in front of the season. It is equally critical to purchase less near the end of the season.

"Just-in-time" systems and Vendor Managed Inventory push the responsibility to the supplier. Even in these systems the supplier still needs to carry inventory and needs good forecasts.

For all these reasons, good item level forecasts are the next building block of a good purchasing system.

Not all Items are Equal, and Items Change over Time

Any distribution inventory includes a mix of items with very diverse demand patterns. Some items show solid, steady demand. Some are erratic. Some items are seasonal. Others are "lumpy", with infrequent but large demands. Others are just plain slow movers. Successful promotions introduce major changes in an item's demand history.

No one forecasting model works in all these situations. An individual item might exhibit several of these demand patterns over its life cycle. So, a good forecasting system needs several models, and needs to apply the most appropriate one to each item at a specific time.

This same technique is the heart of Bernard T. Smith's book on Focus Forecasting.[15] He only reveals a few of his 14 different forecasting models in this book. I guess you have to buy his software package to learn all of them. In any case, I agree with his premise, that you should have several forecasting methods. Each time you forecast an item, find the model that fits best, and use it.

Smith states that based on his experience, his model beats exponential smoothing. I confess I do not have actual experience using his system. If he is benchmarking his variety of methods against a system that only uses exponential smoothing, I bet he is right.

The system we used in our auto parts business used exponential smoothing for one class of items, but other systems for items with irregular patterns. It worked fine for us.

"Regular" Item Forecasting

This is the simplest case, so it is the best place to start. A "regular" item has the following attributes:

- An overall level of demand that is high enough that a good forecast is important (and can be a reliable prediction for the near future). In our auto parts business, we used about 25 units per year as the lower limit of regular items.
- An overall level of demand that is fairly stable around an average, even if there are erratic, large swings from period to period. The average can change over time. The system proposed below can "keep up" with change on the order of 10% per period compounded, and will flag items changing more rapidly than that.
- An item that does not have upcoming special situations. There are no promotions, special purchasing opportunities, or significant seasonality in the time horizon of the next couple of orders.

---

[15] Bernard T. Smith. Focus Forecasting. Bookcrafters. Copyright 1997.

Many early inventory management systems used pure averages, or weighted averages, to develop an item level forecast.

In general, the principle is that the past history will predict the near future for an item, and that the most recent past history should influence the forecast more than older history data. Remember that this does not work for "fashion" items with rapidly changing demand.

The forecast is updated at the end of each history-keeping period. A very easy way to achieve this is to use a forecasting technique called "Exponential Smoothing".

In Exponential Smoothing, each new demand history value is used at the end of the period to update the forecast. It is weighted into the old forecast by a "Smoothing Constant", and the symbol α (alpha) is used to denote this.

This technique is the one used in the IBM INVEN packages for regular items. It is reprinted here with permission from IBM.

The formula is:

$$NewForecast = OldForecast * (1-\alpha) + Most\ Re centDemand * \alpha$$

For example, suppose the old forecast was 10 units per month, the actual demand for the most recent month was 13, and alpha, the smoothing constant, is .3. Then, the new forecast is:

$$NewForecast = 10 * (1-.3) + 13 * .3 = 7 + 3.9 = 10.9 UnitsPerMonth$$

The most recent demand represents 30% of the new forecast, and all the prior history represents the other 70%.

A key in this process is to establish the smoothing constant. A small α like .1 will give more weight to the past history, and the forecast will change less rapidly over time. A larger α like .3 will give more weight to the most recent period, and the forecast will change more rapidly.

There are different types of items, and cases where you would like both of those levels of responsiveness.

You'd like a small α for an item that might be somewhat erratic from period to period, but has a very slow change in the overall average. That way, the forecast wouldn't overreact to the statistical variations from period to period. However, it would gradually track a gentle overall change in the demand level, matching the actual rate of change. This would be best to predict the future for items with very slow overall changes, as it would "dampen out" the period-to-period volatility.

You'd like a big α for items that show changes to their overall average demand quickly (over a few periods). You want these forecasts to "keep up" with the rapid demand changes. A small α will cause the forecast to lag the actual changes, and this could hurt the performance of this item.

It can be difficult to distinguish between period-to-period volatility and actual changes in the level of demand. So, the next step is to develop a measurement of the changes from period to period. This will help determine whether they are just statistical erratic behavior, or a basic change in the demand level.

The traditional way to measure variation in demand has been to calculate the Mean Absolute Deviation in demand, or MAD. This is a simple example for one item, just using averages.

	Period 1	Period 2	Period 3	Period 4	Sum/Avg
Actual Demand	8	14	12	6	40
Forecast	10	10	10	10	40
Forecast Error	-2	4	2	-4	0
Absolute Value (MAD)	2	4	2	4	12
MAD as % of Forecast	20%	40%	20%	40%	30%

Ch 8 Fig 1. Example of Mean Absolute Deviation as a % of the Forecast

Over the four periods, the sum of the demands was 40. The item actually averaged 10 units per period, even though 10 was never the actual demand for any one period. The sum of the absolute value of the errors (disregarding the sign) totals 12 units, or 30% of the item's total demand of 40 units. So, the Mean Absolute Deviation in demand for this item is 30% of the forecast.

We retained the MAD as a percentage of the forecast, and used exponential smoothing to update the MAD% at the end of each period. The formula looks a lot like the one used to update the forecast itself:

$$NewMAD\% = OldMAD\% * (1-\alpha) + AbsoluteForecastError\% * \alpha$$

Suppose the old forecast is 10, the most recent demand is 14, The MAD is 3 units, the initial MAD% is .3 (30% of the forecast), and α is .2. Then,

$$NewMAD\% = 3 * (1-.2) + 4 * .2 = .24 + .08 = .32$$

The MAD% is important, as it measures how erratic the actual demands are. MAD%s of 50% of the forecast or more are not unusual for automotive replacement parts. The MAD% is also a key

70

measure to establish safety stock, as you'll see in a couple of chapters.

However, since the MAD% uses the absolute value of the errors, it measures how erratic the demands are, but, by itself, it doesn't help determine whether the overall average is stable or changing.

Signed Error and "Tracking Signal"

For that, we need another measure, the "Signed Error". In our first example, the sum of the forecast errors was zero, showing that the overall average was stable at 10 units per month. Here is a second example, where the level of demand changes:

	Initial	Period 1	Period 2	Period 3	Period 4	Period 5	Period 6	Period 7	Period 8
Actual Demand		8	10	6	8	13	15	13	15
Sum over 4 periods					32				56
Exp Forecast (α = .2)	8.0	8.0	8.4	7.9	7.9	8.9	10.2	10.7	11.6
Actual Forecast Error		-	2.0	(2.4)	0.1	5.1	6.1	2.8	4.3
MAD% (α = .2 start at .3)	0.30	0.24	0.24	0.25	0.20	0.29	0.37	0.35	0.36
Signed Error (α = .2)	(0.05)	(0.04)	0.02	(0.04)	(0.03)	0.10	0.22	0.23	0.26
Tracking Signal (SE/MAD%)	0.17	0.17	0.07	0.17	0.16	0.35	0.59	0.66	0.73
Forecast (Var α = TS)	8.0	8.0	8.3	8.2	8.1	8.9	11.0	12.2	14.0

Ch 8 Fig 2. Using Signed Error to get a Variable Alpha for Forecast.

In this example, the average demand jumps from 8 per period in the first 4 periods to 14 per period in the second 4. An exponentially smoothed forecast, using .2 for α hovers around 8 for the first four periods, and then starts to climb as the average changes, but is still under 12 by period 8. It is pretty good that it has moved almost half way from the old average to the new average in 4 periods, but this company is likely to lose sales on this item during that time, and perhaps for several more periods until the forecast catches up to the new overall level.

So, a second measurement is needed. The Signed Error is an exponentially smoothed percentage of the forecast, but includes the sign of the forecast error. If the demand is generally level, the signed error will be stay close to zero as plus and minus deviations net out. If the demand level changes, the forecast will be consistently under (or over) the actual, then the Signed Error will build up. In our example above, it stays below 10% of the forecast in the first four periods, but builds up quickly when the forecast error is in the same direction for several periods.

The best measure of a change in the overall level of demand is the "Tracking Signal". It is the absolute value of the signed error divided by the MAD%.

This shows how well the actual demands track the forecast. If demand stays about level, the signed error will stay close to zero, and the tracking signal will be small, even if the item is somewhat erratic. If the level of demand changes, the signed error and the tracking signal will begin to build up.

The magic in the INVEN forecasting system is to use the tracking signal as the α in the exponential smoothing of the forecast. When the tracking signal stays small, the forecast will be even more stable than with any normal fixed value for α. If the Tracking Signal grows, then the most recent demand will influence the new forecast much more, and the overall forecast will "catch up" to the new demand level more quickly. An item with erratic demand around a stable average will have a small tracking signal, so the forecast will not try to track the erratic movements. On the other hand, if the item has begun to change level, then even a few small changes all on one side of the forecast will build up a large Tracking Signal. This will make that forecast react much more quickly to a change in the overall level.

This can be seen by comparing the two forecasts, one using a fixed .2 for α, and the second one using the Tracking Signal as the α value. In Figure 2 above, the forecast using the tracking signal has caught up to the new average demand rate of 14 per period in only 4 periods.

Here is a graph of the item with fixed and variable smoothing constants.

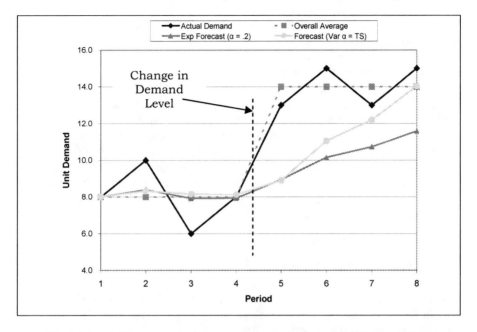

Ch 8 Fig 3. Responsiveness of Several Forecasting Models

As you can see, the forecast using the Tracking Signal as the smoothing constant catches up to the overall change in demand much more quickly.

This is the forecasting algorithm used for regular items in the IBM INVEN/3 package. It is a great way to have stable forecasts for items that have a generally unchanging average, but a quick reaction time when needed.

Note for New Items

It takes about six periods of good demand data for this forecast model to "settle in" to a reasonable value for the forecast, MAD, and tracking signal. For new items, an initial forecast is required. For this model, if you also have an initial value for the MAD, it will help the forecast get up to speed more quickly. Silver (Pg. 126) suggests a formula for estimating an initial standard deviation. This works back to setting an initial MAD% at about 50% of the forecast for new numbers with annual demand forecasts under about 100 units per year, and roughly 30% of the forecast for new numbers with annual forecasts of 300 units per year or more. While these are not as precise as his formula, they would give the process a much faster start than an initial MAD value of zero.

Reporting Forecast Accuracy

At the end of each period, you need a Forecast Accuracy report, to show the aggregate demand forecasts and actual demands for the period. This could be segmented into whatever categories make sense for your company. If you have multiple people doing forecast adjustments, you might want a report by person. You might want it by product category. You might want it by the forecasting model used, to see if the "regular" items are forecast more accurately than slow, seasonal, or promotional items.

This is really just a scorecard…

Item Level Forecast Monitoring

At the end of each period, your software should update the forecasts for all items based on the actual demands, and whatever forecasting algorithms and parameters you use.

If your algorithms are great, and if your items all behave themselves, then this forecasting process will update all the items, and they'll be purchased with the new forecasts in the coming period.

Life is seldom that simple. Items seldom behave themselves.

There are a number of measurements you can use to flag items that have unusual behavior for review by an inventory manager. These items can be ranked and grouped into an exception list, and presented for review with their pertinent information.

The inventory manager should review these items and make any desired changes to the forecast prior to the next replenishment of the items. The Inventory Manager might fix errors in demand data, or know if an item has changed its overall demand level. If the inventory manager judges that the demand history is incorrect, it should be corrected.

Here are several criteria for flagging an item for review:

- **Service Levels.** If the actual service level is far below the goal for an item, an inventory manager should review it. The item could be on backorder from the vendor. The lead-time could be wrong. The item's general level of demand could have changed. The demand data could be wrong. In any case, the inventory management system should achieve close to the target service level. Unless the cause is discovered and fixed, the item may continue to give poor performance.

- **Demand Validation and Filtering.** It is possible to set a window of "reasonable" demand numbers, as the forecast plus or minus some number of MAD% times the old forecast. If item demands were truly "independent" events, then the results would follow the "normal" distribution. The probability that the demand would be within the range of plus or minus 2 MAD% times the forecast is about 95%. The probability it would be within the range of 3 MAD% times the forecast is over 99.5%. That is to say, the odds that an actual demand would be outside the range of 3 MADS from the forecast is about 1 chance in over 200. So, if a demand is observed that is outside a range such as that, then it could be: 1) an error, 2) a real change in the level of demand, or 3) an extremely unlikely event.

Here is a brief example. An item has a forecast of 100, and a MAD% of .2, or 20 units. There is a 99+% chance that the next demand will fall between 40 and 160 units (forecast plus or minus 3 MADs). If the next period's demand is outside this range, an inventory manager should review the item. The manager might discover an error, or decide that the item has changed its overall demand level, and manually reset the forecast.

We used a validation limit of 3 MADs, and that seemed to work well for our auto parts inventory. This is a limit that should be set based on actual experience. It is recommended that the limit be set fairly small at first (2 MADs) and then opened up gradually until the inventory manager feels it is flagging an appropriate number of items.

Further, a demand outside this range is so unlikely that it should not be used to automatically update the forecast. It would be safer to use the reasonable upper or lower demand limit in developing the next forecast, and flag the item for review. Suppose the next demand was 200 in the above example. It would be safer to use the upper limit of 160 to update the forecast and also have a person review the item. You run the risk of trimming off some valid demand data in rare cases, but you will trim off unusual demand data caused by errors. A typical case in our auto parts inventory was when a customer ordered 100 of a hose item, thinking he ordered 100 feet, but we counted it as 100 rolls of hose. It was almost always an error, and almost never a valid order for 100 rolls.

We used this "filter" for many years, but a better system would be to define specific types of transactions that should not count in demand, and use a data warehouse to back out those individual transactions. Return to the example of a customer who does not let you hold backorders, and reorders an item every day. You should have some rule to exclude these repeated reorders and lost sales from the item's demand. Our rule was to only count the first lost sale to a specific customer and ignore repeated orders for the same quantity of the same item during the following week. If you have a full data warehouse, you can extract the transactions you want to count as demand, filter out ones that should not count as demand, and use it to develop the actual demand value. If you can do all that, then you should use that number to update the forecast. I know that our method of limiting the demand count cut off some valid "outlier" data in some cases.

If the limits are too close together, this system will flag more items for review, and not react as quickly to major changes. If the limits are too far apart, the system might make bigger changes than the inventory manager is willing to allow without some review. It requires some adjusting for each kind of product.

- **Tracking Signal warnings**. The tracking signal value will grow if the actual demands are consistently over or consistently under the forecast for several periods. This may be a strong sign that the item's overall level of demand has changed. An inventory manager should review items with large tracking signals. We used a limit of about .50-.60, and reviewed items with larger values. If you look at the sample part in Figure 2, the tracking signal reaches .59 in period 6, after three straight periods where the actual demand exceeded the forecast. The system was increasing the forecast, but it continued to lag behind the actual demands each period. It is appropriate to flag this item for review at this time. An inventory manager would update the forecast manually if they know that the basic level of demand has shifted.

- **Bookmarks**: There could be items which an inventory manager would want to review every period. There should be way to bookmark an item so it will show in each exception report until the bookmark is removed.

- **New Items:** An inventory manager may want to review "new" items every period. The manager should be able to set the number of periods that define a "New" item. This number of periods depends on the kind of item, and how quickly it reaches a steady level of demand. Think about the "turtle chart"... You'd like to classify the item as "New" until you're past the "head" and "neck", and into the "body", where a "normal" level of demand is reached. We did not have a way to do this in system. We had many new numbers, and it took a long time for some of them to start to sell. We relied on the other monitors to catch them at that time, if they took off faster than the system could track.

- **Change Forecasting Category:** An item might have demand pattern changes that would take it out of the "regular" category. Another forecasting technique might fit the demand history better. This should be done automatically. It should be at the inventory manager's discretion whether these changes are all reported for review.

Manually Changed Forecasts

If an inventory manager decides to change a forecast, it is also a vote that all the prior history is no longer appropriate for that item. Whatever the inventory manager decides should not be undone by the forecasting programs.

So, the forecast updates should "start over" at that point. It is appropriate to retain the MAD% value, but the Signed Error should be set to zero, to signify that the inventory manager has given his best estimate of the future demand level. The system should still use some amount (perhaps .2) as the α to calculate a new forecast for the first period after a forecast has been manually set. Then, the regular tracking signal algorithm could resume.

Adjust the History and Forecasts When Needed

There are some changes that clearly void the prior demand history's value in predicting future demands. The addition or loss of a major customer, or the shift of customers between distribution centers, or the opening or closing of stores all can cause a significant shift in the overall demand level for almost all items in the inventory. It is appropriate in these situations to scale all the item forecasts and all the item demand history to reflect a best estimate of the impact of these changes. The sales history data may be needed for audits and other reports, but the item level demand history should only be used for inventory management forecasts, so it can be changed in most companies. For example, one of our competitors suddenly closed their branch distribution center in Denver, and we picked up ten of their stores overnight as new customers. Those 10 stores were forecast to add about 8% to the volume of our DC. We scaled all the forecasts up by that amount to increase our DC inventory levels immediately. We also scaled all the demand history by that same amount. This was needed since the seasonal item model (in Chapter 10) looks back at the history. We felt those stores would buy the same mix of items as our regular customers, and it was important to preserve the historical seasonal patterns, but at this higher overall demand level.

Chapter Summary

Forecasting is needed in many situations. Many items fit a "regular" demand pattern, with enough movement to require forecasting, and no seasonality or other dynamic conditions. The above model is very stable for items with slowly changing demand, but also reacts quickly when there is a significant change in demand.

For our auto parts inventory, this system maintained forecasts without intervention on about 98% of our "regular" items. There are criteria to determine and flag exceptions for review.

Not all items fit this "regular" pattern. The next chapter will deal with items that have other patterns of demand.

Thanks again to IBM for permission to reproduce this forecasting technique.

Chapter 9. Item Level Forecasting—Part 2. Unusual Items

The regular item forecasting model does not work well for items that exhibit other types of demand patterns. These include:

- **"Lumpy" items:** These exhibit infrequent sales of one or multiple units per event, and are likely to have many periods with no demand at all. They have low enough annual total sales that these "lumpy" events stick out in the demand history, and can be several times the pure average demand per period. The forecasting method for regular items will not give a good service level on items with this type of demand pattern, as it will not predict or handle the multiple unit sale events.

- **Slow Movers:** Items with annualized sales below an established limit (we used 25 units per year) also require slightly different forecasting techniques. They also require special treatment when establishing service level goals and safety stocks.

- **Trend Items:** Some systems can infer or accept a demand trend, as a percentage increase or decrease in forecast demand per period. We did not use this in our company, as we felt few items exhibit a steady trend over many periods. Unchecked, it could lead to severe overstock or lost sales. However, there is a discussion below of situations where this might be appropriate.

This chapter will cover these three types. Subsequent chapters will also cover:

- **Seasonal Items:** Items with a repeating seasonal pattern can be identified. The pattern can be converted to a seasonal profile, and it can be used both for forecasting and for computing usage requirements.

- **Promotions:** Items with promotions require special treatment, both for the promotion, and for the periods following a promotion.

"Lumpy" items

In our auto parts inventory, we had thousands of fairly slow moving parts where the sales, when they did occur, could be for more than one unit. A good automotive example is the category of internal engine replacement parts. A vehicle has one piston per cylinder.

Standard size pistons were usually purchased one at a time, to repair a vehicle with one damaged part. However, if the engine had significant wear, the engine block could be bored to an oversize, and oversize pistons are sold in sets of 4, 6, or 8 units, depending on the number of cylinders in the engine. Engine valves were purchased singly, to replace damaged valves, but were also occasionally purchased in full sets. Some engines have two intake and two exhaust valves per cylinder, so a single sale event might be for 1 unit or up to 16 units. If the total annual sales are low enough, each of these events can stick out like a "lump" in the demand history.

A regular item with annual sales of about twenty-five units, weekly replenishment and a one to two week lead time would probably have a stock level of two or three units, depending on your service level target. If this item is truly a regular item, you might lose a sale for one unit in an unusually large period. If it is a lumpy item, it might have annual sales of about 25 units, but in 3 or 4 events of 6-8 units each. If you don't have a full quantity for the largest expected unit sale in stock, you could lose the sale for the full set quantity.

So, the issue with "lumpy" items is to establish the number of units necessary to cover the largest expected single sale event, and the likely frequency between events. Then it is possible to decide whether it is profitable to stock enough to cover one or more likely sale events during the required replenishment time.

The quantity sold on each order would be easy to determine with a data warehouse, where you can see the exact quantity ordered on each transaction.

It is more difficult to determine when only a total demand number is retained for each period. In that case, you can't distinguish between eight independent sales for one unit each, or one sale for a set of eight units. Also, these items can have many periods with zero demand. Regular forecasting will develop a low overall average, and fail to adequately cover the events with multiple unit sales.

Alan Miller of Mercia Software[16] advocates removing the zero periods, and developing a forecast just based on the periods with positive demand. This gives an estimate of the size of an average sale event. Mercia also uses the history without zeros to compute the demand deviation and set a safety stock.

Once you've determined an average or biggest quantity you need to cover for a sale event, then you can decide if it is profitable to carry

---

[16] Alan Miller, Managing Slow Moving and Difficult Products Throughout the Supply Chain. White Paper. Mercia Software, 1999.

that much inventory. See the chapter on Safety Stock and Service Levels for more information on this.

If you decide it is profitable, you can establish a stocking minimum as the average or biggest quantity required per sale (or for two sales if the probability of two sales during the lead time is high enough). Then, continuously replenish the inventory up to this minimum level. You should always have enough in stock to fill an order for a full set quantity.

Mercia develops a probability of two or more sales events occurring during the forecast horizon. The probability that two sales will occur during the required time span can be measured against the service level goal to determine whether to stock one or two sets, and to set an order point. There is also a reference to this type of forecasting model in Silver.

If you cannot strip out the zeros, and use the regular forecasting method for all history periods, it will generate a very large MAD% (probably greater than 50-60% of the forecast). That can be one indicator that the item should be treated as lumpy.

You should routinely check the forecasting method at the end of each period. If the item continues to qualify as a lumpy item, then it is necessary to re-compute whether to keep the minimum stocking quantity.

Slow Movers:

Slow movers exhibit annual sales below a defined limit (we used 25 units per year for our auto parts inventory).

At that level of sales, the normal forecasting method will compute fractional unit forecasts and fractional unit usage per period. For slow movers, the decision on how to round these fractional quantities has a big impact on the inventory.

So, the special requirement here is to have more direct control over the stock levels. You may not want the system to round up the stock level to two units by itself. There is really very little difference between an order-up-to-level of 1.39 units (which would round down to 1) and 1.54 units (which would round up to 2).

In these cases, the forecasting technique can recommend a fractional unit stock level, but you really want to set the actual stock level based on an estimate of the relative profitability of stocking 1, 2, or 3 units, etc. There is a full discussion of this in the chapter on Safety Stocks and Service Levels. In general, if the item's stock level is under about 5 units, it is better to use the technique in that chapter to set the level each period or each time the item is purchased.

Here again, the item should be reviewed at the end of each period to see if it continues to qualify for this special category of forecasting.

Trend Items:

If an item exhibits a fairly steady growth or decline in demand from period to period, it is possible to apply a trend factor, as a percentage per period, to scale up or scale down the forecast usage.

$$ForecastForPeriod = OldForecast * TrendFactor$$

$$NewForecast = ForecastForPeriod * (1 - \alpha) + ActualDemand * \alpha$$

We did not use this in our auto parts inventory, for several reasons.

- Few of our items changed demand levels quickly enough to establish a uniform trend.
- No trend lasts forever. It is just as important to decide when to remove a trend factor as it is to decide to set one initially. Unchecked, when the item stops moving with the trend, you could wind up with a lot of overstock or a serious service level problem.
- This only makes a material difference in the computed usage when it is necessary to forecast over a very long lead-time, or if there is a large and steady growth or decline from period to period. If the trend in demand is not more than 10% per period, and if you do not have to forecast over a time span of more than about 3 periods, you probably do not need trend forecasting. In our auto parts inventory, there were few items with lead times of several months, and even fewer of them had any steady trend.

Silver[17] suggests using downward trend forecasts at the end of the life cycle of an item, to help reduce the order point and inventory.

So, there might be situations where you need it, but use it carefully.

Chapter Summary

"Lumpy" items have infrequent sales of more than one unit. Some auto parts are items sold in pairs or "sets" for one repair job. It is

---

[17] Pg. 130, Edward Silver, David Pyke, Rein Peterson, Inventory Management And Production Planning and Scheduling, Third Edition, 1998, John Wiley and Sons.

necessary to determine the likely number of units per sale event, and the likely frequency of events to determine whether to stock inventory for one or more sale events.

Slow movers have annual sales below a benchmark level (25 units per year for our auto parts inventory). For these items, you need to translate forecasts into integer stock levels, not just "rounded" fractions.

Trend items show a definite up or down trend in demand over several periods. If you conclude that trend is likely to continue, then it can be applied to the forecast to estimate future usage. This should be done with caution, as no trend continues indefinitely. You must have a mechanism to spot the end of the trend.

Pete Kornafel

Chapter 10. Item Level Forecasting—Part 3. Seasonal Items

A seasonal item is one with a demand pattern that consistently repeats on an annual, monthly, or weekly cycle. Demand patterns can be affected by the calendar (holidays, or "back to school" time, etc.), or by weather patterns (summer items, winter items, etc.).

This chapter describes a technique for identifying items with repeated seasonal patterns, a way to build a "profile" of the pattern, and a way to use the profile to forecast usage.

It is very important to separate seasonal from non-seasonal items. A regular forecasting model will give the wrong answer for seasonal items at the most critical times.

Just before the beginning of the item's seasonal peak, a regular forecast will look at recent low demand, and project that into the near future without recognizing the coming peak. When the item begins to sell at the season high level, you are likely to have a service level problem.

Just before the end of the item's season, a regular forecast will look at recent high demand, and project it into the near future, too. When the item's sales start to slow, overstock inventory could build up rapidly.

What is needed is a seasonal profile and a way to use it to look ahead, not back, when computing future requirements. A regular forecast can be scaled by the index for the upcoming period(s) to estimate the future demand.

Here is an actual item from our inventory as an example[18]:

				Demand History for a GM Car and Truck Distributor Cap									
Year	Jan	Feb	Mar	Apr	May	Jun	Jul	Aug	Sep	Oct	Nov	Dec	Total
1	97	71	109	149	89	67	120	126	140	166	152	95	1,382
2	111	92	113	138	107	84	120	121	134	168	90	89	1,369
3	89	105	112	105	124	107	133	132	120	142	109	105	1,386
4	97	90	137	111	103	139	125	131	150	165	115	99	1,466
Profile	0.8	0.8	1.1	1.0	0.9	1.0	1.1	1.1	1.2	1.3	0.9	0.8	12.0

Ch 10 Fig 1. Sample Seasonal Item.

---

[18] Data from Hatch Grinding Co., Denver, CO.

A seasonal pattern is not immediately evident by a simple inspection of this actual item's yearly demand history. However, the technique used below classified this item as a mildly seasonal item, and computed the profile shown. If you look closely, the demand in the peak months of August through October has repeatedly been about 50% greater than the low months of December through February.

Stock levels for this item should be raised in February, to get ready for a mild increase in March through July. They should be raised again in August, to get ready for better selling months. In mid October, they should be cut to get ready for winter.

The overall average demand is about 120 units per month over the full four years of history. The process is to look ahead, and scale that by the upcoming month's index to project demand. So, the forecast for October would be 156 (120 x 1.3) and the forecast for December would be 96 (120 x .8). With the required quantity computed by looking ahead, not back, you will buy appropriately for each season.

We expected some auto parts to be seasonal. Air conditioning system repair parts sell best in the summer. Starting fluid, de-icer, and similar items sell only in the winter. Those are all obvious candidates. However, we also found several thousand items like the distributor cap above, which had very predictable mild seasonal patterns. Our conclusion for the distributor cap and related items is that people in Colorado tend to have more tune-ups in the spring and fall.

It is important that this be done at the item level. While the overall category of spark plugs exhibits the same characteristics in our market as the distributor cap example, there are exceptions. The spark plugs that fit lawn mowers peak in the spring. The spark plugs that fit marine applications peak through the summer. The spark plugs that fit chain saws peak in the fall.

Batteries fail most often in winter in Colorado, so we expect to sell more in the winter months than in the summer. However, we did not know until we used this model that the high capacity, high price batteries peak in October, and the low price models peak in February. We concluded that people who were serious about maintaining their vehicles had them inspected in the fall, to be ready for winter. Those customers were more likely to buy a premium battery. Other vehicle owners made it to the coldest part of the winter, and then had a morning where they couldn't get their vehicle started. Those owners tended to buy cheaper batteries, just to get through the rest of the winter. In our New Mexico market, batteries failed more frequently in the hottest summer months. Different profiles were needed for each location.

Seasonal items occur in lots of other industries, too. One of the most unusual examples is toothpaste. A distributor once told me toothpaste was seasonal. It seems hard to believe. He explained that while the overall consumption of toothpaste is very level throughout the year, people tend to buy smaller tubes in the summer for travel, and larger tubes the rest of the year for home use. So each package size had a mild seasonal pattern, even though the total usage was constant.

All these examples are based on 12 monthly periods per year. However, this same technique, with appropriate control factors, would work for 13 four-week periods or even weekly periods.

In an extreme case, one cigarette distributor uses daily seasonal profiles. This distributor services stores and vending machines in several different states, and has to affix the proper tax stamps for each state. They deliver on a weekly schedule, so their demand for cigarettes with specific tax stamps depends on the direction of their truck routes each day. Their goal is to operate with four days inventory, so they used a weekly seasonal profiles with an index for each day of the week to accurately forecast daily demand for each route truck going to each different state.

There are a number of forecasting programs available today that can identify and forecast seasonal items. The discussion below is one way to achieve this. Software that identifies and forecasts seasonal items is available from JDA, Evant, Oracle, SAS, and others.

In our total auto parts inventory, about 8,000 items qualified as seasonal using the criteria below. Those items accounted for about 35% of the total dollar value of our inventory. We used this model for 15 years. We consistently had our most accurate forecasts on seasonal items.

Determining Seasonal Candidate Items:

The first process is to analyze each item's demand history to determine if it is a seasonal candidate. All the control values were determined empirically. They worked fine for auto parts, but might need some adjusting for other products. These are the values and limits we used in our auto parts forecasting, and we let this software run "unattended" to find candidate items and set seasonal profiles for them (with some exceptions noted below).

Pete Kornafel

Here is the math model we used:

1) Only consider items with annual demand large enough to show a seasonal pattern. In our auto parts business, we only considered items with annual demand of at least 36 units. Below this, even if the item is truly seasonal, it is unlikely that a seasonal pattern can be validly separated from the statistical "noise" in the actual demand history.

2) Build arrays backward from the most recent complete month to up to three years of monthly demand history. This can be done in any month. If you were forecasting in August, then the three arrays would be this July back to last August, and so on for prior years. Build only complete year arrays. You must have a minimum of two full years of history. Three full years is better. These arrays are called H1, H2, H3 in the formulas below, where H1 is the most recent complete 12 months.

3) Compute the annual total demand for each year of history:

S1 = sum of H1, S2 = sum of H2, etc.

4) Compute the ratio of S3/S1. If it is out of bounds disqualify the third year of history. In our auto parts inventory, we felt that if the demand has more than doubled or decreased to less than half of what it was, then the third year of history should not be used to establish a seasonal profile. In this case, only the most recent two years history will be used.

5) Compute the ratio of S2/S1. If this ratio is out of bounds, disqualify the item as a seasonal candidate. For our auto parts, we used limits of about 35% up or down. This says that we want two or three years of established history without large total demand changes to apply a seasonal profile. Items that show big growth or decline are disqualified because the growth or decline is likely to mask a seasonal demand pattern.

6) Now, determine if there is a repeated "matching" pattern in the two or three years of validated history. If the third year qualified, take the sum of the squares of the differences between $H1_n$ and $H3_n$ where each is scaled by that year's total demand. The smaller this value, the more the history patterns match. If this sum is greater than the LIMIT, there is no good match. Disqualify the third year of history. The formula is:

$$MatchYearOneToYearThree = \sum_{N=1}^{12}\left\{\left(H1_N * \frac{12}{S1}\right) - \left(H3_N * \frac{12}{S3}\right)\right\}^2 \le LIMIT_{13}$$

Using the squares of the differences to evaluate the degree of "matching" is a normal statistical analysis method for determining the degree of correlation between two sets of data. Each company will need to review their own data and set an appropriate limit.

7) Perform the same calculation for the sum of the squares of the differences between each element of H1 and H2. If this value is greater than a second LIMIT, disqualify the item as seasonal, since the patterns do not match closely enough. If the value is less than the limit, the history patterns repeat closely enough from year to year that seasonal forecasting should be an accurate model. This formula is:

$$MatchYearOneToYearTwo = \sum_{N=1}^{12} \left\{ \left(H1_N * \frac{12}{S1} \right) - \left(H2_N * \frac{12}{S2} \right) \right\}^2 \leq LIMIT_{12}$$

8) The final test is to determine if there is a significant seasonal peak or valley in demand. To do this, compile the two or three years of history into a single composite year. We used a weighted average of each element in the H arrays, weighting H1 by 2/3 and H2 by 1/3 if there are only two valid years, or H1 by .5, H2 by .3 and H3 by .2 if there are three valid years of history. Then take the ratio of the sum of the three largest contiguous months to the sum of the three smallest contiguous months. In our auto parts inventory, we used a ratio of greater than 1.50 to show enough of a seasonal peak or valley in demand to require seasonal forecasting. Each user should set their own factors to set an appropriate weighting to the prior year(s) of demand history.

9) If the item passes all these tests, it has the following characteristics:
   - It has enough demand in units per year to reveal a seasonal pattern.
   - It has at least two full years of demand history.
   - It does not have significant year to year changes in total demand
   - It has a close match of the month-to-month pattern when the most recent year is compared to the previous year and possibly the year before that.
   - It has a significant peak or valley in the demand pattern.

10) If an item passed all these tests, we qualified it as a seasonal item. A profile can be computed as shown below.

Pete Kornafel

With all these empirically set factors, it must look like this is not a very scientific model. That is true. I confess I'm an engineer, not a scientist. The model was developed with a great deal of love, care, simulations, and beer. It survived the real test - it worked in the field. It may not be elegant math, but it works.

Compute the Seasonal Profile:

Once an item was validated, we established a seasonal profile for the item. Take the composite year of history, and scale it so that it is a series of 12 monthly indices that sum to 12. These 12 indices are the profile. Here are the steps to do that.

1) Establish a "normal" monthly demand forecast in units. We started with the average of H1, and then used exponential smoothing to maintain this average each month.
2) Use the numbers for each period's demand from the "composite year" array in step 8 above, and scale them so that they add to 12.0 (for 12 periods per year). This, rounded to one decimal place, set each month's index.
3) Assign a name or serial number to that profile, and store it for use with this item, and possibly other items.

For our sample item, the result is the profile shown as the last line in Ch.10 Fig 1. This sample item has an average demand of about 120 units per month, but we expect January and February to be .8 or 80% of that value, and we expect October to be 1.3 or 130% of that overall average.

Using the Profile to Forecast Future Demand:

First establish the forecast horizon as the number of days supply needed for review time, lead-time and safety stock. Then use the forecast and the profile index for the coming periods to look ahead and compute estimated future usage.

Here is an example with our item in Fig. 1 with an average of 120 units/month. This shows the forecast for September 10 and November 10, when you have to forecast for 45 days future usage in each case. You can use the monthly index values to "look ahead" and calculate the usage at the forecast rate times the monthly demand index, for the number of days to look ahead.

	September	October	November	December	Forecast Usage
Monthly Seasonal Index	1.2	1.3	0.9	0.8	
Seasonal Unit Forecast	144	156	108	96	
45 Days Usage from 9/10					
Days in each Month	20	25			
Usage in Those Days	96	130			226
45 Days Usage from 11/10					
Days in each Month			20	25	
Usage in Those Days			72	80	152

Ch 10 Fig 3. Computing Usage with Seasonal Forecasts

A level forecast for 1-½ months would be 180 units. During the peak, the seasonal index adjusts this to 226 units. After the peak, a 45-day forecast is 152 units. Even with mild seasonality, the peak forecast usage is about 50% more than the off-season.

This forward looking forecast can be used to establish replenishment orders throughout the year.

The model looks ahead and uses the seasonal index for each month to compute a forecast unit usage over a future time period. This will increase the order point going in to a seasonal peak, and reduce it near the end of the season.

About Profiles:

We maintained the profiles in a separate file, and only the profile number (the record number in that file) was assigned to the item. An inventory manager could view the profile library, and manually assign an existing profile to any item. We moved the existing seasonal profile to a new item if it superseded a seasonal item. We assigned an existing profile to a new item that was expected to be seasonal.

We had a way to test profiles against items. The software simulated the forecasting process starting with two-year-old history, and moving forward, using regular item forecasting and seasonal forecasting with the assigned profile. It computed the MAD% each way. If the MAD% was lower with the seasonal model, it meant that the profile fit the history better than a flat forecast.

Exceptions:

It should be noted that this forecasting model finds seasonal items, but only if they have a pattern that repeats from year to year. It may

NOT find items with very sharp spikes that depend on weather. For example, if air conditioning parts peak with a very large one month spike in June one year and July the next year, the history might fail the "repeat pattern" test, even though the item is seasonal. We identified items with a large ratio of the biggest quarter to smallest quarter, even if they failed the repeated pattern matching, and examined them to find this kind of situation. We manually assigned profiles to these items.

It should be noted that this method may also conclude that items are seasonal if there are repeated promotions with similar results from year to year, and if you do not "normalize" the demand history to exclude the promotion sales.

For example, some of our air conditioning parts showed a peak in March and April, because of an annual pre-season sale to help our customers stock up for the peak season. If we did not "normalize" this demand, the forecasting software would conclude there was a consistent peak in the spring, and set a profile. Once a profile was established, we would buy for this anticipated peak in an upcoming year, as though it was a normal seasonal peak. That was fine only if we were consistent in running these promotions every year. The seasonal model would stock up whether we were going to run the promotion or not.

If we did not run a promotion every year, or did not have consistent results from year to year, then the item would probably fail the validity tests, and not be classified as seasonal.

We used this model at our distribution centers, but we did not use it or need it for our stores. We had few items with the necessary level of demand in individual stores. Also, the short replenishment cycle at the stores made this unnecessary.

Off Season note:

While our system did not do this, I wished we could change the way forecasts were updated based on the season. Bernard T. Smith cites the example of fly swatters. His fly swatter philosophy says that winter fly swatter demand has nothing to do with summer fly swatter demand.[19] I agree with this. Deviations in actual demand during the "off" season when the total demand is small impacted our forecast, and that would be reflected in the peak month usage computations. An extreme example is an air conditioning system compressor. We sold about 10 units per month in the summer, and

---

[19] Bernard T. Smith. Focus Forecasting, Bookcrafters, Copyright 1997.

less than 1 unit per month through the winter. If the demand in January or February happened to be 2 instead of 1, that factored into our overall forecast, and predicted a bigger than usual summer peak. That was probably not a valid prediction. This was an error in our system. We could have done it better.

Examples:

Here are several items from one of the CARQUEST DCs that show clear seasonal patterns in the two years of available demand history:

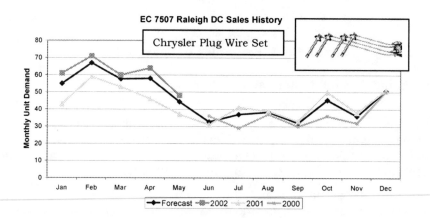

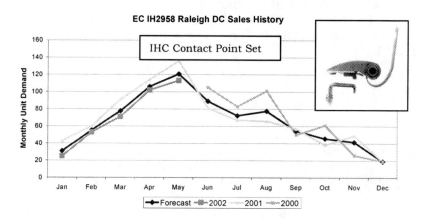

Pete Kornafel

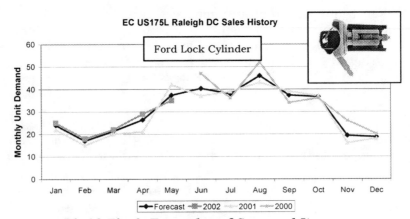

Ch 10 Fig 4. Examples of Seasonal Items

Updating Demand History and the Forecast

It is important to record each period's actual demand in the item's demand history array. This will give an accurate record for that item. It is what you need to validate the current seasonal profile, or compute a new one, or determine if a trend factor should be applied

However, the actual demand should be scaled by that period's seasonal index before it is smoothed into the overall item forecast. That forecast is intended to represent the ongoing overall average demand for that item. The forecast will be scaled again by the upcoming period's seasonal index to compute expected future demand.

Here is the formula for obtaining a new overall forecast for a seasonal item:

$$NewForecast = OldForecast * (1-\alpha) + \frac{ActualDemand}{SeasonalIndex} * \alpha$$

Take our sample item from Ch 10 Fig 1. Suppose the actual demand for January of the 5th year is 110 units. The expected demand is the forecast times that month's index. This would be 120*.8=96 units. The actual demand of 110 is about 15% above the forecast, and it should raise the overall average somewhat. If the α (Tracking Signal) is .3, then here is the new forecast:

$$NewForecast = 120 * (1-.3) + \frac{110}{.8} * .3 = 125.25$$

94

This same process should be used to scale the actual demand by the current period's seasonal index before it is used to compute new MAD%, Signed Error, and Tracking Signal values.

Application:

We ran this program twice a year to assign seasonal items and establish profiles for all items that passed these tests.

This forecasting process also produced a list of previous seasonal items that did not meet the criteria this time. We reviewed these items, and in some cases, reassigned a profile.

Grouping Items

Once you have established profiles for each item, it is possible to compare them and develop some "typical" profiles that would handle many items each. This offers a couple of possible advantages. First, if you have a profile that fits a logical category of items (high quality batteries, for example), it is likely to be better than individual item forecasts. The larger sample of data is likely to eliminate a little statistical "noise" that might appear in individual profiles built from just one item's history. Second, it provides a smaller library of known good profiles that could be assigned to new items in that category. Since this model requires two years of history to develop an individual item profile, it is necessary to assign an existing profile to a new item that you feel is highly likely to be seasonal.

We had some software to compare seasonal item profiles, and then run simulations against established items to determine the "fit". The measure of fit was the MAD generated when the simulation was run against the item's past history. If the MAD was close to the same value when the item was forecast with two slightly different seasonal profiles, either one was judged to be acceptable for that item. A tally was kept for each profile showing how many items it fit within acceptable limits. The most "popular" profiles were categorized as group profiles, and used for all items they fit.

We did not have the computer horsepower to run this very often. We did not develop a good way to classify the profiles (summer peak, fall peak, double peak, etc.) The "brute force" computation was to take each item and simulate it with all of the 8,000 profiles to see how many gave a good fit. It took several days to run on our early IBM AS/400. I have not tried this on newer faster computers, but it would be one more enhancement to the overall seasonal forecasting model.

Pete Kornafel

Chapter Summary

You can match 2 or 3 years of history to detect repeated patterns
and significant seasonal peaks, and qualify items as seasonal.
You can use the history to build a profile of monthly seasonal index
values.

You can use the index values to "look ahead" and adjust the
forecast.

For more than 15 years we found this was the most accurate
forecasting model we used. Our monthly review compared forecasts
to actual demand, and seasonal forecasting was always the most
accurate of all the models.

This is a complicated process. You could contact JDA or other
vendors of supply chain software and use their current seasonal
forecasting software.

Chapter 11. Item Level Forecasting—Part 4. Promotion Items

One type of promotion is a special offer from a vendor for a limited time. In most cases, the vendor hopes or requires that the distributors and stores pass some or all of the terms through to their customers.

A second type of promotion is generated within a distribution company, in the hope that extending an additional discount or terms for a limited time will raise overall profits.

Promotions require special attention throughout their life. Before the promotion, it is necessary to forecast sales and source the products. During the promotion, it is necessary to monitor sales and place reorders if they are allowed. At the end of the promotion, there might be an opportunity to make an additional purchase on the special terms for your own inventory. After the promotion, it is still necessary to monitor sales and reorders in case the impact of the promotion was to advance sales into earlier periods and depress sales for some time after the promotion ends.

Forecasting for Promotions

In our auto parts company, we had a difficult time forecasting sales during promotions. Occasionally, a promotion was announced with enough lead-time that we could "book orders" from our customers, and make an accurate order. More often, we had to forecast performance and place orders for the promotion before we could notify our customers.

Here are some "do not" rules for promotion forecasting.

- Do not let your Sales department forecast promotions. You pay them to sell, and they're confident they can sell anything. They are likely to buy way too much on promotion.
- Do not let the Financial department forecast promotions. They feel promotions are more likely to screw up the inventory than sell more products, so they won't buy enough.
- Do not let your Purchasing department forecast promotions, especially if you measure them by inventory turns. They may ignore promotions as an added risk to their performance measurements.

97

- Do not assume an item or category will go back to normal sales immediately after a promotion ends. In some promotions, it is likely that people will buy earlier than usual to get the special terms. Some promotions are designed to be "loaders" and put inventory into the distribution channel. In either case, sales could be significantly below normal for several periods following the promotion.

In our company, we finally found a person in our Marketing department who had a good sense of what our customers would do for each promotion, and no stake in the outcome other than a review of her accuracy of forecasting. We let her do all our promotion forecasting for several years.

The forecast should include all the periods when the promotion is running, and periods after the promotion until sales are forecast to return to their normal level.

Buying for Promotions:

The safest situations are those where the distributor can place multiple re-orders during the promotion, and where the lead time is short enough that it is unlikely the distributor will run out of stock, even if the promotion exceeds the forecast.

The most difficult situations are those where the distributor can only place one order, in advance of the promotion. In this case, the distributor has only one chance to buy against the entire forecast. The risk of either stock outs or overstock is greatly increased.

Measuring the Financial Impact of a Promotion:

It is possible to chart the profit outcomes based on the terms of the promotion and various sales levels. This can be very helpful in testing the validity of a promotion, and in benchmarking the results.

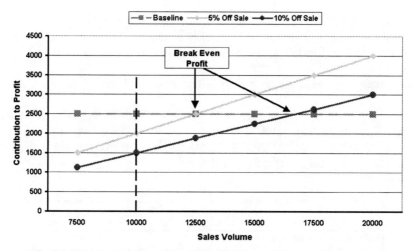

**Ch 11 Fig 1. Promotion Break Even Chart—Sales and
Contribution to Profit**

Here is an example of an internal promotion for headlamp bulbs.
We considered extending an extra discount of 5% or 10% for a 30-
day period. Our normal sales were $10,000 per month for these
items, and they contributed 25% to profit (gross margin minus
variable costs for filling orders and delivery). If we gave a 5%
discount and did not increase unit sales, then we would give up
$500, and achieve a $2,000 contribution to profit. We had to
increase sales 25% to $12,500 to break even on a 5% discount. We
had to increase sales 67% to $16,700 to break even on a 10% extra
discount.

It is important to consider the total sales change, including periods
after the promotion. If you sell more during the promotion, but sell
less immediately afterward, then both should be considered in
evaluating the total sales with a promotion versus normal sales.

This kind of chart is very helpful to assess a promotion. In this case,
it is necessary to sell 67% more product to break even after a 10%
extra discount. That helps everyone understand and sign up to do
what is necessary for a successful promotion.

Forward Buying at the End of a Promotion:

When the supplier runs a promotion, a distributor can purchase
goods at the special terms and pass those terms through to its
customers during the promotion. It may also be possible for the
distributor to place one final order to secure the extra deal for its

own inventory. This final order should be analyzed as a Forward Buying situation, and not as part of the promotion. See the chapter on Forward Buying for more detail on this opportunity.

Recording Demand During and After Promotions:

If the promotion is unlikely to be repeated, then the actual sales during the promotion should not be used to update the forecast. Rather, the actual sales should be scaled by the promotion index, or normalized, to update the forecast.
Here is an example:

	Periods				
	1	2	3	4	5
Before the Promotion					
Normal Forecast	100	100	100	100	100
Promotion Index	1.50	1.50	0.75	1.00	
Promotion Forecast	150	150	75	100	100
During the Promotion					
Actual Observed Demand	170	140	65	105	100
Normalized Demand	113	93	87	105	

Ch 11 Fig 2. Promotion Forecast and Normalized Demand

This example shows an item with a regular forecast of 100 units per period. The promotion forecasts a 50% increase in sales for two periods, followed by one period where sales are likely to be 25% below normal.

The second block shows the actual demands recorded for these periods. In this case, the item sold better than forecast in the first period of the promotion, but less than forecast in the second period of the promotion and the first period following the promotion.

You may want to save both the actual and normalized demand values in your demand history files. The normalized values (actual divided by the promotion index) should be used to update the forecast, MAD%, tracking signal, etc.

By doing this, the ongoing forecast will continue to be updated with variations from the planned levels to the actual demands.

Possible View as Seasonality:

If you run the same promotion at the same time each year, get similar results, and record the actual sales, then the seasonal item forecasting model might interpret these as seasonal sales.

For example, in our auto parts company we promoted air conditioning parts every spring, to make sure our stores and their shop customers updated their inventories before the summer peak season. We solicited large "stock-up" orders, and gave extended terms to permit our customers to prepare their own inventory for the season. After several years, the actual demand figures showed a peak in March as well as in June-August.

If you don't back out the promotion index values, your seasonal forecasting model might assign profiles to these items that include this pre-season peak. If you don't run the promotion in a subsequent year, your system will still buy for those extra sales, but you aren't likely to realize them.

"Backward Promotion Forecasting":

There is also an opportunity for some good market research by doing "Backward Promotion Forecasting".

This is what you should do in cases where one of your competitors is running a promotion and your company is not matching it.

The process of backward promotion forecasting is to closely monitor your own sales on the affected items during the competitor's promotion.

If your own sales go down while the competitor is running a promotion, then it is likely that they are stealing some of your sales.

If your own sales are unchanged, then that other company is not your competitor on those items. You won't know where they are selling their product, but you can conclude they're not taking any of your business, and so they are not really your competitors.

If your sales happen to go up, then it is possible that the other company's efforts have influenced the market so much that everyone, including your own company, benefited with extra sales. Then you could conclude their efforts temporarily increased the entire market size.

Regardless of the outcome, there is some valuable market intelligence information from analyzing your own sales when others are running promotions.

Chapter Summary

You need to forecast promotional demand, and purchase adequate inventory to cover the forecast.

If the promotion is likely to pull demand ahead from future periods, you need to forecast demand after the promotion—until the demand returns to normal levels.

You should not include promotional inventory if you measure buyers on turnover.

You can develop a simple break-even chart to show the profit impact of reduced margins, and the additional sales required to increase profits from a promotion.

It is best if a vendor will allow you to place multiple orders during the promotion, and perhaps one last order as a "Forward Buy" (see Chapter 21).

You should look at your own demand when others are running a promotion, to determine if they are taking your customers, or raising the overall level for everyone, or show no impact on your own sales.

Chapter 12. Forecasting Summary

The preceding chapters present several different forecasting methods. Each is appropriate for items with specific types of behavior.

Part of the routine process is to verify that each item is in the right category, or switch it to a different forecasting model if its characteristics have changed.

Here is a summary table of the various types:

Item Class	Characteristics	Most Appropriate Forecasting Model	Update and Review
Regular Item	Reasonably stable level (with period to period fluctuations) and demand greater than about 25 units per year.	Exponential Smoothing with Alpha based on Tracking Signal.	Update Forecast, MAD, and Tracking Signal Each Month. Flag items with unusual demand or tracking signal values for review.
Slow Mover	Basically level demand less than about 25 units per year	Exponential Smoothing with Alpha based on Tracking Signal. Set stock level, service level and safety stock based on integer stock level computations.	Update Forecast, MAD, and Tracking Signal Each Month. Flag items with unusual demand or tracking signal values for review
Lumpy Item	Occasional demand in multiple units, and periods with zero demand	Forecast units per sale and time period between sale events. Evaluate Profitability of stocking one or more "sets".	Ideally, update the forecast after each event.
Trend Item	Consistent growth or decline rate of change in overall level, with period to period fluctuations	Apply a Trend Rate to Forecast, and then use Exponential Smoothing with Alpha based on Tracking Signal.	Update Forecast, MAD, and Tracking Signal Each Month. Flag items with unusual demand or tracking signal values for review. Tracking signal errors may indicate trend level has shifted.
Seasonal Item	Repeated seasonal pattern over at least 2 years, with some period to period fluctuations.	Compute Seasonal Profile. Apply each period's index to overall forecast level. Then use Exponential Smoothing based on seasonal forecast and actual demand with Alpha based on Tracking Signal.	Update Forecast, MAD, and Tracking Signal Each Month. Flag items with unusual demand or tracking signal values for review. Do not update forecast in periods with very small index values and actual demands. Recompute profiles once or twice a year.
Promotional Item	Any other kind of item plus a promotion	Establish Promotional Profile for promotion and periods afterward until demand is forecast to return to normal. Use each period's index normalize demand values. Then use Exponential Smoothing based on promotional forecast and actual demand with Alpha based on Tracking Signal.	Use the "normalized" demand history to update Forecast, MAD, and Tracking Signal. Flag items with unusual demand or tracking signal values for review. Save both normalized and actual demand values for reference.
Item with Manually Set Data	Any item where the Inventory Manager has overridden the forecast	Use the manually selected or most appropriate forecasting model or values for forecast or stock level.	"Bookmark" the history and disqualify periods prior to the manually set forecast.

Ch 12 Fig 1. Forecast Model Summary Table

Pete Kornafel

How to Decide Which Forecast Model to Use:

At the end of each period your system should test each item to determine the best forecasting model to use. Once that is done your system can update the forecast and other values appropriately.

Another way to determine the best forecasting model for an item is to use the recent demand history for an item, and forecast it with each model. The model that gives the lowest MAD% fits the demand history best. Again, this presumes that the near future can be estimated by the recent past history.

If an inventory manager updates a forecast, or reassigns an item to a different model, then they are declaring that the history prior to that is invalid, and should not be used. These tests should only be applied to periods after that "bookmark".

Adjust the History When Needed

See the note in Chapter 8, and don't be afraid to scale all of the history when a major change occurs. This can be the gain or loss of a major customer, or a reassignment of stores to a different distribution center.

Since you are using the history only to generate forecasts, you want to use the portion of the history that applies to future sales potential. If you add or lose a major customer for a category of items, scale your history up or down on those items, and re-do the forecasts.

Chapter Summary

Items with different patterns of demand require different forecasting techniques.

Forecasts should be compared to actual demands at the end of each period, to:

- Verify that the right forecasting technique is being used for each item.
- Update the forecasts within defined limits.
- Flag items outside the defined limits for review by an inventory manager.

Chapter 13. Item Level Order Quantity

For almost 100 years an Economic Order Quantity (EOQ) formula has been used to balance the ordering and carrying costs of individual items, and to establish an optimum order quantity. In manufacturing, this is called the "Lot Size Formula", where it balances the setup costs with carrying costs to establish batch sizes for individual items in a job shop environment.

The key to this formula is understanding the variables so you can provide the proper input. You have to establish your process, and it will help determine what data to use in the formula. The most appropriate data may vary widely in different situations. Carrying costs may change with interest rates, and handling costs may vary from location to location.

The classic situation is that you have only one item on an order, and you have full flexibility to determine how much you want to order, and when you can place orders.

The classic formula is:

$$EOQUnits = \sqrt{\frac{2 * AnnualUsageInUnits * OrderCostInDollars}{AnnualCarryingCostPerUnit}}$$

Here is an example:
Item Annual Usage = 1,200 Units
Item Cost = $25
Inventory Carrying Cost = 25% of value of inventory per year
Annual Carrying Cost per Unit = $6.25 ($25 x .25)
Order Cost = $5.50

$$EOQUnits = \sqrt{\frac{2 * 1200 * 5.50}{6.25}} = 46Units \approx 26OrdersPerYear \approx OrderEvery14Days$$

In this classic case, the inventory carrying cost includes the physical costs to store the goods, the opportunity cost of the funds invested, and any risk costs for obsolescence, etc.

The ordering costs include all the variable costs of computing, reviewing, approving, and placing a purchase order, receiving the goods, stocking them, and processing the packing lists and invoices clear through payment.

For this sample item, the formula works out to 26 orders per year, or an order about every 14 days. The total cost curve is pretty flat for moderate changes in the ordering and carrying costs, so it is reasonable to round the answer a bit if it permits a convenient quantity or frequency of orders. For example, if this item came in an overpack of 50 units, it would be much more convenient to place 24 orders for 50 units each over the course of a year.

An EOQ Formula that Includes Size

Chuck LaMacchia, in an excellent article[20], points out that the classic EOQ formula only includes a single value for the inventory carrying cost. Yet, the definition of carrying cost includes economic factors and space based factors.

Economic factors include the cost of capital, obsolescence risk and price deflation risk. The cost of capital clearly depends on the item's prices. Other factors are space-based costs, including warehouse space rental, utilities, warehouse property taxes, and warehouse maintenance. Items require these space costs based on their size. This article breaks down carrying cost into the two components. It develops an EOQ formula that includes both types of cost and uses both the price and the cubic size of the item. In the example, total carrying costs are 28% of the value of the inventory, but this is made up of 13% of the item cost and $3.75 per cubic foot of the item's size. Here is the formula and an example:

$$EOQspace = \sqrt{\frac{2 * AnnualUsageInUnits * OrderCostInDollars}{UnitCost * ValueBasedCarryCost\% + UnitCost * CarryCostPerCube}}$$

Sample Items:

Characteristic	Office Chair	Toner Cartridge
Annual Usage In Units	1,200	1,200
Order Cost in Dollars	$20	$20
Unit Cost	$50	$50
Cubic Feet—Each Unit	12	0.25
Combined Carry Cost Rate	28%	28%
Value Based Carry Cost %	13%	13%
Carry Cost Per Cubic Foot	$3.75	$3.75

---

[20] Chuck LaMacchia, Sizing it Up, APICS, January, 2003

The Classic EOQ formula gives the following result for both items:

$$EOQUnits = \sqrt{\frac{2*1200*20}{50*.28}} = 59 Units$$

The Space EOQ gives a different result for both of these items:

$EOQChair = \sqrt{\dfrac{2*1200*20}{(50*.13)+(12*3.75)}} = 31$	$EOQToner = \sqrt{\dfrac{2*1200*20}{(50*.13)+(.25*3.75)}} = 80$

This revised formula gives a better answer where space is a constraint, and should generally help minimize overall costs. It will recommend smaller quantities and more frequent replenishment of large cube items that take up a disproportionate amount of warehouse space or volume, and larger quantities on smaller size items.

Non "Classic" Situations—Product Line Orders

The normal distributor has very few items that fit the classic model, and are ordered with only one item per purchase order. Most items are purchased as part of a product line or category, so the "order cost" applies to a group of items. They are likely to be received, stocked, and processed as part of that overall shipment, so it is very difficult to assign a variable cost to any individual item.

In these situations, the EOQ formula should only apply to individual items if there are significant variable costs on that item. In our auto parts inventory, we received shipments of starters and alternators on pallets. Each item had to be individually handled when it was stocked. It really didn't matter how many of an individual item were in the shipment. (There was one exception. If we could buy a full pallet of a single number, there were significant handling savings— see the exception below for item level "deals".) Except for those pallet quantity items, we did not use the EOQ formula on starters and alternators, and ordered as many as we needed of each item on each shipment.

In these cases, the governing costs are those of placing an order for and handling an entire shipment. See the later chapter on Order Frequency. It's the same kind of math, but at an aggregate level.

Exceptions—Item level Deals

If there are discounts, better terms, or handling cost savings that apply to quantities of individual items, they need to be considered when establishing an EOQ for the item. Take the example of the starter above. It has a $25 cost, 1,200 annual unit demand, and is available in full pallets of 100 units. We concluded it was worth about a $5.00 savings in direct labor in our receiving department to stock the entire pallet in a special picking area for palletized items, rather than handle 100 individual units. Here is a table showing the costs as though that $5.00 savings is $.05 per unit.

Quantity Per Order	Item Cost	Annual Item Savings	Average Cycle Stock Units	Carrying Cost of Cycle Stock	Order Cost per Order	Number of Orders per Year	Annual Order Cost	Total of Order and Carry Costs	Total with Savings
25	25.00		13	78.13	10.00	48	480.00	558.13	558.13
50	25.00		25	156.25	10.00	24	240.00	396.25	396.25
62	**25.00**		**31**	**193.75**	**10.00**	**19**	**193.55**	**387.30**	**387.30**
75	25.00		38	234.38	10.00	16	160.00	394.38	394.38
100	**24.95**	**60.00**	**50**	**311.88**	**10.00**	**12**	**120.00**	**431.88**	**371.87**
125	24.95	48.00	63	389.84	10.00	10	96.00	485.84	437.84
150	24.95	40.00	75	467.81	10.00	8	80.00	547.81	507.81

Ch 13 Fig 1. Economic Order Quantities with Item Cost Savings

This shows that even a $.05 per unit cost savings makes enough difference that the best, lowest total cost, strategy is now to buy this item in pallets of 100, about once a month. Except for a tiny difference in the carrying cost, the answer would be the same if the handling cost savings were shown as a reduction in the order cost from $10.00 to $5.00 if the item was purchased in pallets. Note that if the item is purchased 125 or 150 at a time, the savings only apply to the full pallet quantities.

Software that can handle item level discounts, payment terms, or handling cost differences is a big advantage in determining item level order quantities. The software should compute the regular EOQ, and then use that quantity and the input values to compute the total carrying cost for the cycle inventory. The cycle stock is one half of the quantity ordered. The average inventory on hand is the cycle stock plus the safety stock. The safety stock will vary with changes in the quantity ordered. A complete system would evaluate it for each strategy, and use it in the carrying cost to compare various frequencies. As shown in the table above, the EOQ can be converted back into a number of orders per year, and that can be used to calculate the handling cost. Save the total of these two costs for the regular EOQ quantity. Then compute the cycle stock carrying cost, the handling cost, and deduct any handling cost savings, discounts or other values at each quantity break point. If the total here is less than the regular EOQ costs, then it pays to buy in that quantity.

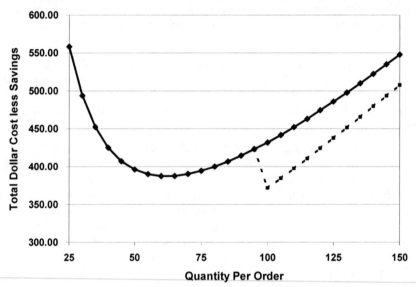

Ch 13 Fig 2. Economic Quantity Cost Chart with Quantity Savings

This is the same data from the table in Figure 1, but as a graph. The costs for handling and carrying are shown as the solid line. This shows that the regular EOQ curve is fairly flat around the regular optimum quantity of 62 units. The savings from buying pallets of 100 units is deducted from these costs, and shown as the dotted line. It shows that the lowest total cost is achieved by buying exactly one pallet of 100 each time you order.

Exceptions—Minimums, Maximums, Schedules

If an item has a vendor required order minimum, or a shelf life maximum, or a vendor imposed order schedule, all of these will take precedence over the EOQ formula. You can run the formula to see how far away the imposed levels are from the optimum quantity, but you will still have to honor these factors over a computed EOQ.

Pete Kornafel

Rounding to Standard Overpacks

Many items are available "each" or in standard overpack quantities at the customer's option, like the automotive starter sample item above. If you determine you have a real variable cost savings from handling the case quantities, then you should include that when deciding whether it makes economic sense to buy it "each" or in cases.

Some replenishment purchasing systems show both the exact quantity needed and the full case quantity. They suggest that if you only need a few units, just buy them, but if you reach some break point (typically 60—70% of a case), then you should round that order up to a case.

I do not agree with those systems. If the item level savings are enough to buy an item in cases or pallets, then you should do that all the time, even when the required quantity is just a few units. Our sample item illustrates this point. It sells 100 units per month, so a pallet of 100 is one month's supply. Suppose you review this line once a week. In the week you get below the order point, you'll probably need about 25 units. If you buy that quantity, then you're likely to keep buying about 25 units each week. You'll never order a pallet, and never achieve those savings. One exception would be on small fill-in orders, where you pay freight or incur discount penalties, and would want to order the exact number of needed units.

Remember that you need to determine the proper variable costs. The variable costs of handling a single item are likely to be different when that item is part of a full product line stock order.

If you trust your estimated costs, then this math will give you the lowest cost strategy for each item.

Computations

It is important to compute the EOQ quantities whenever there is a change in the input values (e.g. if you change the carrying or handling cost rates), or when there is a significant change in the item's forecast. This would change the duration of an EOQ quantity, and affect the number of orders placed per year. An ideal software system would compute them for each suggested order, based on the current input values and any special conditions for each item.

Chapter Summary

When you can accurately assign item level variable costs, it is appropriate to use the EOQ in establishing item level order quantities.

When items are purchased as part of a complete product line and there are no significant variable costs that vary with the quantity of an individual item, the item level EOQ formula is inappropriate. For those products, the best strategy is to order as much as needed of each item on each order. Use the Review Time as the Order Cycle for these items. If you order the product line once a week, on average you'll buy one week's worth of each item each time. This is covered in detail in Chapter 17 on the order frequency for product lines or groups of items.

An optimum software system would have a flag at the item level to show whether a computed EOQ should be used, or the product line's review time, or an imposed minimum or maximum in units or days supply.

A good article on Optimizing Economic Order Quantity (EOQ) with more detail is by Dave Piasecki[21].

---

[21] Piasecki, David, article at
http://www.inventoryops.com/economic_order_quantity.htm

Pete Kornafel

Chapter 14. Lead Time Forecasting

The replenishment lead-time is a key measurement. It is part of the time horizon for computing an item's usage.

Definition:

The lead-time value that should be used in order point formulas should encompass the entire time span from the time your data is used to compute a suggested order until the goods are received, stocked, and posted to the inventory to be available for sale.

In our automotive business, because of the large number of SKUs, we processed suggested orders as an overnight batch process. We therefore had one day of lead-time for our own internal time to prepare an order. We transmitted virtually all orders to our vendors, but that usually took another day to pass from our computer to theirs. They typically took 1-3 days to process the order, and it typically took 5-7 days for the shipment to arrive on our dock. Our internal standard was to receive, check in, stock, and post the shipment within 3 days. The proper lead-time to use in the replenishment formula is this entire time span. Our typical lead-time was 10-14 days for most of our vendors.

Shipment Lead Time Variability:

We tracked the actual lead-time by capturing a transaction record at key times in the purchasing process. We tracked three dates for each purchase order: the date of the original order, the date the shipment hit our dock, and the date it was posted into inventory. This helped us measure the vendors' performance and our own performance in our receiving/stocking department.

We used the start and end date records to create an observation of lead-time for that product category. We maintained a forecast lead-time at the category level by exponentially smoothing each observation of the shipment lead-time into an ongoing forecast, and computed and maintained a MAD deviation in lead-time.

Virtually all of our orders were for groups of items—a product line or category of items. So, this category level lead-time established a minimum lead-time for the whole order.

These techniques were used in E3's Lead Time Forecasting addition to IBM's INVEN packages. Contact JDA for more details.

Pete Kornafel

Item Level Lead Time Forecasting:

If a vendor has perfect service levels, and ships every order with 100% service levels, then every item's lead time will be the same as the shipment lead time.

In our auto parts world, no vendors achieved this. Our inbound order fill from our suppliers was typically 90-95% on the first shipment. Then, most of our vendors would hold a "backorder" and ship the item as soon as it became available. These items clearly had longer lead-time than the category first shipment lead-time.

We tracked the lead-time on each individual item receipt. We logged an item level transaction record at the time we received an item, including the dates and the quantity received. We used an exponential smoothing routine to process these records and maintain an item level lead-time forecast and lead time variability. If the vendor consistently had a longer lead-time for some items, this would increase the forecast usage, and our order point, just for those items.

We scaled the smoothing constant for each transaction by the ratio of the quantity received to the item's forecast. This was to keep the overall impact on the forecasts the same across all items. Each company should select a smoothing constant that gives them appropriate "response time" for their specific supply chain. An item ordered once a month would only have one lead time transaction, typically for an amount close to the forecast, and the actual lead time would be smoothed into the ongoing forecast by the regular smoothing constant amount. An item that was ordered weekly would typically have four transactions in a month. Each would be for about 1/4 of the forecast, and each observation of lead-time would be smoothed into the forecast using a much smaller smoothing constant. This made the overall rate of responsiveness to change about the same for all items, regardless of our ordering frequency.

Where a vendor held back orders and shipped the item when it was available, we used the actual lead-time from original order to eventual receipt. If a vendor shipped part of the quantity ordered on their first shipment, and the rest as a backorder later, that generated two transactions and both were used (scaled by the quantities) to update that item's lead-time forecast.

Some vendors processed our orders as "ship or cancel". When they did not ship an item, they cancelled the order, and we had to reorder it. For these items, we created a lead-time transaction that had the

114

cancelled quantity and a lead-time that included the time from the order to the notice of cancellation, plus one full review cycle time. This item must be reordered on the next replenishment order, and the minimum lead-time it could have would include one extra order cycle, so this should increase our lead-time forecast for that item. Some vendors can give you an ASN (Advance Ship Notice) well before the shipment arrives. This can be an earlier warning they are canceling the order for one or more items, and you can get a head start at reordering them. When this item is reordered and received, that will log a regular lead-time observation and start to bring the item's lead-time forecast back down.

Here is a formula for forecasting item lead-time:

$$NewLeadTime = OldLeadTime * (1 - \beta) + ObservedLeadTime * \beta$$

Where:

$$\beta = \alpha * \frac{QuantityInLeadTimeObservation}{MonthlyUnitForecast}$$

Each user should select an appropriate value for the smoothing constant. A larger value will make the system respond more quickly, but might also give undue weight to temporary changes. We also established an overall maximum lead-time, and would not let the forecasting routines go beyond that. This was just a safeguard so that the forecasting system could not get unstable. In the worst cases, a vendor would not ship an item, hold the backorder for a long time, and then eventually cancel the order. Several of those transactions would produce a huge lead-time forecast for that item. As the forecast lead-time increased, so did our reorder quantities. These situations could produce unreasonably large suggested orders if there is no upper limit on the lead-time forecast.

It is also important to exclude unusual transactions from this forecasting process. Any "emergency orders" with a different shipping method should not be used to forecast routine replenishment lead-time with normal shipping methods. Any "booking" or "preseason" orders should be excluded, as their lead-time will not be reflective of normal replenishment. In situations where a distributor places a blanket order and then releases against that order, the distributor should decide whether to use the full time or the time from each release based on each situation. Part of this decision depends on how much flexibility the distributor has in changing the quantities on each release.

There could be other situations where the lead-time is managed as part of the supply chain process. In these cases the inventory manager should decide on the appropriate data to use in a lead-time forecast.

Auto Parts Item Level Observations:

It should be understood that the total impact of item level lead time forecasting could be to raise your inventory, to achieve higher service levels on items where the vendors cannot ship them reliably. There can't be any reduction, since no item's lead-time can be less than the lead-time for each overall shipment.

We accumulated about one year's lead time observation transactions, and ran a simulation to determine the impact on our inventory before we decided to implement item level lead time forecasting. The simulation showed we would add roughly 5% to our inventory if we used all the item level lead times. We pondered this decision for some time. At that time, this was a $100,000 increase to a $2 million inventory, and a material investment for our company.

We expected to carry safety stock for the erratic demands from our customers. Until we developed the lead-time forecasts, we did not realize we also had to carry some additional safety stock to cover individual items our vendors could not ship consistently. We asked for some extra terms from some vendors to support this extra inventory, with the explanation that this was their fault. We got "deer in the headlights" stares from a few vendors, but the smart ones worked with us.

We eventually decided to proceed. We set initial item lead-time forecasts with the accumulated transactions, and started updating them with live lead-time observation data. Overall, this raised our company service level to our customers by almost one full point. That was based on a full coverage auto parts inventory. It is likely that the same thing would happen in other product categories with broad line coverage and lots of skus.

If you don't have item level lead time forecasts, and have a vendor whose order fill is well below your expectation, your only option is to raise the lead-time and inventory level on the entire line or category. That increases the overall inventory level, and it will help the service level, but it only helps on items that show significant lead-time variability.

We learned that this item level forecasting caused a much smaller increase in our inventory to achieve the same service level improvement.

Why there is Item Variability in Lead Time:

What we discovered was that most of the longer item level lead times were in the "middle" level of items. Very little additional inventory was needed for the most popular and for the slowest moving items.

Our vendors typically shipped fast moving items very reliably, so these items did not require much extra inventory. In many cases, vendors had continuous production lines for these very fast items, and they were almost always available.

The system didn't have much impact on very slow moving items. It was unlikely that a slight increase in the lead time forecast for an occasional backorder would actually increase our order point by one full unit on a very slow moving item.

The middle range showed the most impact. Many of our vendors produced these mid-range items in a job shop / batch environment. If the vendor ran out of one of these items, they typically took some time to react and produce another batch, so the lead-time was likely to be significantly longer than normal. The backorders moved from item to item, so this system tended to raise our lead times a bit on many of these mid-range items. That was OK, as we observed that many of our vendors were consistently inconsistent in lead times for the middle range of parts.

So, most of the incremental investment for item level lead-time and lead-time variability went into the middle range parts. It paid off in better overall service levels to our customers, and they appreciated that very much.

We also observed that our customers noticed this improvement. They expected us to ship the most popular items very well all the time, and they expected to have trouble getting very slow moving items. They expected consistent good service in the middle range. If we could not deliver that then our customers had a perception that our service level was poor on everything.

If you have vendors who manufacture goods this way, but can't get item level lead time forecasts from your computer systems, perhaps you should add a little extra safety stock to the mid range items. Some of these supplier processes might be unique to auto parts, but many apply to a wide range of hard goods.

Lead Time vs. Lead Time Variability

We often asked our vendors to improve their performance. This usually led to a discussion about improving (reducing) their lead-time, and improving their order fill (reducing lead time variability). Of course we wanted both, but that was difficult for most vendors. Our observations were that the best way we could improve our service level on slow and lumpy items was to order frequently. That replenished our small inventories sooner. In effect, we reduced the total cycle time on those items.

On fast moving items, we generally felt that the improving the lead-time variability was more crucial than the shortening the lead time itself.

One of the attractions of some "Vendor Managed Inventory" systems is that they can provide extremely consistent lead times with very little variability.

In our auto parts business, we ordered weekly from most of our large vendors. If they did not ship an item, the earliest we could receive it was one shipment, or one week later. We felt reducing the variability would help our outbound service level more than reducing the actual lead-time by a day or two.

There is a full discussion of lead-time variability and formulas in a paper by Philip Evers.[22] It includes the math to determine the impact of changes in lead-time and lead time variability for various kinds of items. His general conclusion matches our experience. "In the case of slow moving items with lumpy demand, reductions in average lead time tend to have more effect (on reducing safety stock requirements). In the case of fast moving items having stable demand, reductions in the standard deviation of lead time tend to be more effective (in reducing safety stock requirements) up to a point."

Using the Forecast to Discover Lost or Overdue Shipments

The order date plus the lead-time minus in-house processing time gives an expected arrival date for each shipment. Some vendors provide a Purchase Order Acknowledgement or an Advance Shipment Notice (ASN), at the time the shipment leaves their dock. We used this and a variety of online systems provided by the carriers to track shipments in transit, and anticipate their delivery.

---

[22] Philip T. Evers. The Effect of Lead Times on Safety Stocks. APICS Journal, Second Quarter, 1999.

All of that gave us an early warning system to discover shipments that would not arrive when needed. That let us beg the common carriers for expedited handling, if the shipment was in transit, but late. In a few cases we had to reorder the goods when the vendor never filled the purchase order.

Without some system like this, either someone would eventually notice the absence of a shipment, or you would see it when your service level declined sharply on one product line. In either case, it is far too late to react and preserve good customer service.

Using the Forecast Lead Time to Prioritize Put-Away

We flagged each purchase order record at the time the shipment hit our dock. Each morning we generated a report of all the shipments on the warehouse floor. This was ranked by the date we needed to have that shipment stocked and available for sale. That same report also showed the size of the shipment and the anticipated lost sales on items that were expected to arrive in that shipment. These were based on the item level forecasts, and the on hand and on order quantities.

Our receiving department prioritized their work by this report. We could sequence their work to stock shipments in the order we needed them for customer service, not in the order they arrived on the dock.

Be careful, or this could create another self-fulfilling prophecy. If the shipments from one vendor consistently arrive a few days early, this kind of system would keep them at the bottom of the priority list, and sequence other shipments ahead of them. That could lead to a consistent longer time for put-away, since this shipment might sit for several days. This could maintain an artificially long overall lead-time for that line. We had a company wide benchmark that said every shipment had to be processed in three days or less, and that kept us out of this trap.

Acknowledgement

This lead-time forecasting system was developed by E3 Associates and tested and used at Hatch Grinding Company from 1981-1996. Once we had enough observations of lead time to get fairly stable item level forecasts, we used this system without any intervention. A Lead Time Forecasting system is available today from JDA. The only changes we made to lead times were when a vendor changed our logistics—and shipped from a different location or by a different method. Then, we reset all the forecasts and started over on those lines.

Lead Time Seasonality

We did not have the capability to apply seasonal profiles to lead time, but we felt there was significant seasonal variation on some product lines. This usually compounded our problems, as the vendor tended to have longer lead times during the peak season. In our system, this showed as increased lead-time variability, and increased our safety stock somewhat. If we could have applied a seasonal profile, it would have scaled the lead-time itself, and had a more direct effect on our inventory stock level. JDA's Lead Time Forecasting system has the capability to incorporate seasonal profiles for lead-time.

Chapter Summary

Both lead-time and the variability in lead-time can be tracked and forecast.

If you can't improve both, then improvements in overall lead time will help the service level more on slower moving items, and improvements in lead time variability will help the service level more on faster moving items.

It requires some special forecasting techniques to handle items ordered with different frequencies, and to handle back orders and cancelled orders.

A good lead-time forecast can help discover lost or overdue shipments.

A good lead-time forecast can be used to prioritize shipments for put-away.

Each day of inventory removed from the system, and each reduction in lead-time variability flows directly to improve service levels and profits.

Chapter 15. Setting Safety Stock Amounts

This chapter and the next form a unit. This chapter discusses how to set safety stock based on a service level goal. The next chapter discusses how to set that goal.

A strict replenishment formula recommends just enough inventory to exactly cover the forecast demand over the planned lead-time. Any variability in demand or lead-time will lead to stock outs whenever the actual demand or lead-time is larger than forecast. The purpose of safety stock is to cover some level of demand greater than forecast, and some level of lead-time longer than forecast.

The amount of safety stock required is very sensitive to the variability in demand, the planned lead-time, the variability in lead-time, and the service level goal.

If the item has very little fluctuation in demand from the forecast level, then a small safety stock will cover most replenishment cycles without a stock out. Items with very short lead time and review time require little safety stock, too, as the potential for lost sales is limited to a very short time until the item can be replenished. Items with more variability of demand, longer review times and lead times, and some variability of lead time can require significant amounts of safety stock.

The Noise Balancing Method:

One classic way for a buyer to set safety stock amounts is to practice noise balancing. Here is how it works:

- When the service levels are too low, the company sales manager yells at the buyer to put in more inventory.
- When the inventory investment is too high, the company financial officer yells at the buyer to reduce inventory.
- Many buyers set safety stock levels to balance the noise generated by these two sides.

This is a difficult task. Most sales managers are noisier than most financial people. Pure noise balancing can lead to too much inventory. However, many inventory departments report to a financial officer, so the buyer's job may depend on meeting investment or turnover targets, regardless of the service level generated.

Obviously, this is not the best way to maximize the productivity of the inventory and the profits of the company. There is a better way. The optimum process sets safety stock at the item level. No two items are the same. Using the same amount of safety stock for an entire line, or even for a category of items will not yield the best results. Items with higher variability of demand or lead-time will not have enough safety stock, and you may not achieve your service level goal. Items with less variability of demand and lead-time will meet or exceed their service goals, because they will have too much safety stock, but the extra investment is wasted.

The best practice is to compute a safety stock amount each time an item reviewed for a possible order.

The remainder of this chapter gives two different formulas for safety stock based on a target service level and the characteristics of each individual item. One is based on the mathematics of probability, and the other is an empirical formula developed at IBM, used at our company, Hatch Grinding. The next chapter presents a way to determine optimum service level targets to maximize the overall profits of the company.

Classic Safety Stock Formulas:

Observations of truly independent events will form a Normal Distribution around a mean (average) value. They will distribute tightly around the mean if there is very little variability in the process, or widely around the mean if the process has a lot of variability. The Standard Deviation is a measure of this spread.

An example is tossing coins. If you toss a fair coin 20 times, the number of times you get heads should average about 10. However, there is some probability that it could be 8, or 14, or even 20. Everyone intuitively understands the probability of getting 20 straight heads is very small, but it is not zero. There is actually a little less than one chance in a million you could get 20 straight heads. A normal distribution chart is the classic "bell curve", and looks like this:

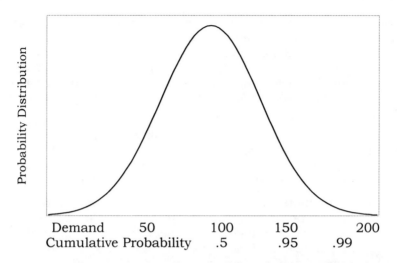

Ch 15 Fig 1. Normal Distribution—Item with Mean of 100, Standard Deviation of 30

This is the chart of expected demand for an item with average demand of 100 units per month and a standard deviation of 30 units. The area under this chart measures the cumulative probability that an observation will be below or above a certain level. For this item, there is a 50/50 chance, or a .5 probability, that the demand will be above or below 100 in any future month. 100 is the average, or mean value. With a standard deviation of 30 units, there is a 95% chance the demand will be 150 or less, and a 5% chance the demand will be greater than 150. If you provide safety stock to cover 150 units of demand in a month, you should not have a stockout in 95% of the order cycles for this item. The probability the demand will be 170 or less is 99%, so you should only have a stockout about once in one hundred order cycles if you stock at this level. For an item ordered weekly, that would be one stockout about every two years.

The normal distribution probabilities can be used with each item's mean, standard deviation, lead-time, and target service level to establish a safety stock. If you have an order level of ½ of a month on the above item, you would expect the demand to be 50 units during that period of time. A safety stock of another 35 units, to cover demand up to 85 units in the ½ month should provide enough inventory that you would expect to complete 99% of the order cycles without a stockout.

Microsoft Excel has several functions that can be used to compute normal distribution values. The NORMDIST function with TRUE argument gives the area under the curve from minus infinity up to the value. The arguments are the value, the mean, the deviation, and TRUE or FALSE. For the sample item, NORMDIST(170, 100, 30, TRUE) = .990185. There is a 99% chance the value will be 170 or less. This predicts the percent of cycles with no stockout. The False argument gives the specific probability of a single value, but only for continuous functions. It isn't meaningful here.

The function NORMSDIST gives the probability for a normal distribution with a mean of zero and a standard deviation of 1. NORMSDIST(2) = .977. This means that a safety stock of 2 standard deviations should prevent stockouts in almost 98% of order cycles.

The NORMINV function can be used to compute an amount of safety stock required for a target service level. It uses the cumulative probability (the target service level), the mean, and the standard deviation. For example, NORMINV(.99,100,30) = 169.79. So, the cumulative probability of all demands up to 169.79 is 99%. Providing safety stock to cover demand up to 170 over this period should cover 99% of cycles with no stockout.

The function NORMSINV gives the probabilities for a normal distribution with a mean of zero and a standard deviation of 1. NORMSINV(.977) = 2. So this can translate a service goal into a number of standard deviations to use for safety stock.

The amount of safety stock grows rapidly as the service level goal approaches 100%. Here is a chart for the above sample item:

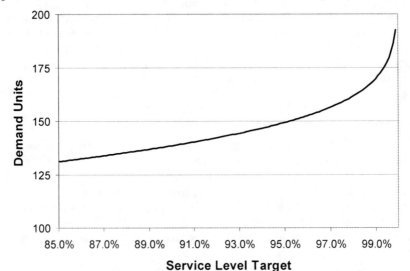

Ch 15 Fig 2. Percent of Order Cycles without Stockouts for Normal Distribution

The simplest way to use the normal distribution in calculating order points is to convert the service level goal into the number of additional standard deviations of inventory that are required over the regular forecast for the period. Here is a table using the Excel NORMSINV function.

Target Percent of Order Cycles with no Stockout	Number of Standard Deviations Required
85.0%	1.04
87.5%	1.15
90.0%	1.28
92.5%	1.44
95.0%	1.64
96.0%	1.75
97.0%	1.88
98.0%	2.05
99.0%	2.33
99.5%	2.58

Ch 15 Fig 3. Standard Deviations vs. Service Levels with Normal Distribution

For example, this shows that if the service level goal is 99%, then you need 2.33 standard deviations of safety stock. For the sample item, with a standard deviation of 30 units, you need 2.33 x 30 = 70 units of safety stock. This should be added to the lead-time and review time supplies to reach an order point. Remember that this targets stockouts, not the actual service level. It says that with that safety stock, you should have 99% of order cycles without a stockout.

This formula can be scaled for the time supply required. If you have to forecast for ½ month instead of one full month, you could use ½ this number of units for safety stock.

Stockouts vs. Order Fill

Appendix 1 gives a chart and table of the Normal Distribution probabilities. Again, these Normal Distribution functions predict the number of stockouts, not order fill. They show the probability that in any one order cycle the demand will exceed the selected level, resulting in a stockout in that cycle. They do not show what the amount of the stockout will be, and therefore they do not predict the actual order fill. Most inventory managers want to control the order fill, not the number of stockouts. There is a good discussion of this in a paper by Coleman.[23]

The Real World of Auto Parts

The classic formula is based on several requirements and assumptions.

- All the events of a demand for this item are independent of each other.
- The mean and standard deviation do not change over time.
- There is no variability in the lead-time (the vendor ships 100% on schedule).
- The formula targets stockouts, not the actual order fill.

None of these conditions were a perfect fit for our "real world" of auto parts.

The demand events for some auto parts are not quite independent of each other. One example is warranty replacements. Warranty is a significant factor for categories of remanufactured auto parts like alternators, starters, and air conditioning compressors. These items have alleged warranty return rates of almost 10%, and many of those returns occur immediately after the part is installed. Not all these parts are defective. Some are used as a "known good part". A technician will install a "known good part" to replace an item that might be malfunctioning. If it fixes the problem, OK. If not, the item is usually removed and returned to our stores. These items are not salable as new, and generally treated as a warranty return. Some items are mis-installed or damaged during installation, and returned as well. In all these cases, the customer expects these items to be credited or replaced at no charge. We replaced these items whether the part was really defective or not. On these items, the probability of another sale shortly after the first one is slightly higher than the ongoing average because of this. Some of these "next events" are dependent on the first ones, not independent.

The mean, or average demand and the variability in the average change over time on all items. The rate of change might not be

---

[23] B. Jay Coleman. Determining the Correct Service Level Target. APICS Journal, First Quarter, 2000.

large, but if the item were growing, the classic formula would not give enough safety stock to achieve the service level target.

All our auto parts had some variability in lead-time. None of our vendors was capable of shipping 100% exactly on schedule. A typical vendor could give us about 90% order fill (measured in dollars) within the normal lead-time. We used the item level lead-time forecasts from the previous chapter, but we also needed an extra amount of safety stock to handle the variability in lead-time.

We really wanted to target the actual order fill, not the percentage of cycles with stockouts, and this required a slightly different formula for computing the safety stock amounts.

Each of these factors required slightly more safety stock than the classic formula to achieve the target service level.

So, an empirical formula was used.

Empirical INVEN/3-38 Formula:

Anders Herlitz developed an empirical method for computing safety stocks while he was at IBM. It was incorporated into IBM/s INVEN/3, INVEN/34, and INVEN/38 programs.[24]

We used this formula for our auto parts distribution center inventories for 20 years.

The formula is complex, involving several steps of computation, and then conversion of the results by looking up the intermediate answers in an empirical table to get the final safety stock factors.

I am not going to reprint the entire formula here, because it is complicated, and only a few readers might be interested in the details.

Here are some observations about the results versus the classic formulas above:

The INVEN empirical formula gives slightly more safety stock than classic normal distribution formulas, even without lead-time variability.

It gives even more safety stock when you include the lead-time variability.

Lead time variability requires some more safety stock. In our auto parts business, when business was good, items were selling above

---

[24] IBM INVEN/3, INVEN/34, INVEN/38 Program Description and Operations Manual. Copyright 1974, IBM Corporation.

forecasts. At that same time, our vendors were more likely to run out of items, so we experienced longer lead times, too. Extra safety stock for the variability in lead times was an important element of delivering the target service level.

Silver (Pg. 283) gives a formula for incorporating the deviations in demand and lead-time into a single standard deviation.

In some cases, the empirical formula gives zero safety stock. In practice, these are unusual conditions. For example, an unusual item with a Review Time of 1 day, a Lead Time of 1 day, an Order Time Factor of 7 Days, a very small demand variability of .5% of the forecast, no lead time variability, and a service level goal of 85% yields a computed safety stock of—1 day. In this case, it makes sense that if you have to buy a week's worth of a very stable item, but can reorder it every day, and get replenishment shipments in one more day, you don't need any safety stock to deliver good service.

Here is a comparison chart for our sample item, showing the safety stock days supply for the Inven formulas with and without lead-time variability, and for the classic normal distribution formula.

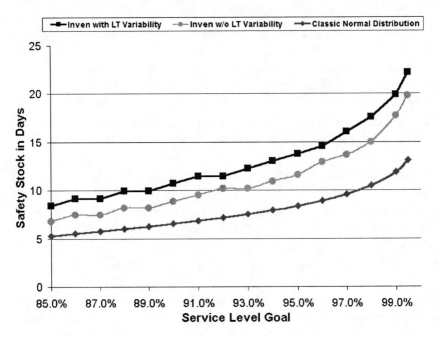

Ch 15 Fig 5. Item Safety Stock with INVEN and Classic Formulas

This shows that the Inven formulas give a few more days of safety stock for all service level goals.

It also shows that the addition of lead-time variability (35% of the sample item's 10 day lead time), adds about 2 more days of safety stock for almost all service level goals.

Small differences in some of the input variables can change the safety stock by a lot. It is one more reason to compute safety stock for each item, and compute it each time you review the item for a possible order.

Measuring Actual Safety Stock

Regardless of the formula you use, there is a fairly simple way to validate your safety stock computations.

The amount on hand just before you receive a shipment is really what you have in safety stock. If you capture that amount for each item as part of receiving a shipment, and use each item's forecast to convert it to days supply, you can get an actual measurement of the safety stock for that item.

Over a number of receipts this would show an average of the actual safety stock. It can be valuable feedback to show whether your system is performing to your goals.

99% is not 100%

This is a story that is almost 30 years old, but I've seen the same thing happen recently at other companies, so it is still appropriate. At our automotive company, the Fram brand of oil, air and fuel filters was one of our largest product lines for many years. We had to purchase this line in exact trailer loads to get the best discount and payment terms. When we ordered the line with our manual system, we would order what we needed in each item, tally that amount, and then add pallets of the best item, PH8A to make the order come up to a full trailer load. It was a safe investment (after all, PH8A was the best item), and we always got the best discount.

Several months after we went on our computer ordering system, we ran out of PH8As. It was the first time in memory that we had been out of that very important item, so it made news all over our company. I collided with our sales manager when we both hit the purchasing agent's office door. We were both yelling at her about the fact that we had just run out of the best selling oil filter. She looked up and said, "Don't panic—I'm just getting the service level

DOWN to 99%. The next shipment arrives tomorrow, and PH8A will be back in stock quickly. We'll make our 99% order fill goal."

I realized that she used the computer to balance the truckload orders (more on that later), and we didn't need those extra PH8As to fill up the truck. I also realized we must have had a huge overstock in that item, as it had taken months to run out. We reduced our inventory a lot, just in that one item. So, I went away happy that our new system was working. Our sales manager never understood. Even though our service levels improved, he never fully trusted the system after this incident. This story is also a good preamble to the next chapter, which discusses how to set service level targets.

Chapter Summary

The classic formulas using the normal distribution are easy to implement, especially with the routines available in Excel and Access.

In practice the classic formula will probably not give enough safety stock to achieve the service goal, because it does not include lead-time variability and other factors. You should add some extra safety stock beyond the classic formula to cover these other factors, and measure the actual order fill and actual safety stock amounts to validate your formula for your particular items and industry.

Our empirical formula's strong point is successful use in our auto parts company, and in many other IBM customers who used the various Inven packages.

The safety stock is very sensitive to the service level goal. The next chapter will give one method for establishing this important input.

Chapter 16. Establishing Service Level Goals

The prior chapter showed that the required amount of safety stock grows almost exponentially as you attempt to achieve higher service levels from inventory. Inventory managers have long realized that there is a point of diminishing return on the investment in safety stocks. The purpose of this chapter is to show a way to analyze this, and establish a service level goal for each item that will maximize the return on investment for the inventory.

The purpose of safety stock is to achieve higher service levels. If there is not enough safety stock, the business will run out of inventory and lose sales in periods with higher than average demand or longer than average lead-time. The inventory manager can estimate these lost sales. A cost can be assigned to these lost sales. The target service level balances that cost against the cost of increased investment in safety stock. The optimum goal minimizes the combination of those costs, and maximizes the profit generated by this item.

Individual items can exhibit great differences in the variability of their demand and lead-time. The optimum profit solution is to establish these service level goals at the item level.

The Cost of a Lost Sale

The first step is to evaluate the cost of a lost sale, or the incremental contribution to profit from an additional sale achieved by reaching a higher service level. To begin, look at two extreme examples.

First, consider a company that makes custom furniture with a lead-time of several weeks or months for delivery. Their customers do not expect immediate delivery, so there is no cost for "lost sales". There is no value for safety stock (or even for basic inventory) in this business. They need samples for display, but maximize profit with no inventory for immediate delivery.

At the other extreme, consider the drug inventory in the surgical department of a hospital. The inability to deliver a needed drug immediately could cost the life of a surgical patient. Clearly, the "cost of a lost sale" is huge in this situation, and this department should have adequate inventory of every drug that might be needed in any situation in the operating rooms.

Most items are somewhere in between these extreme examples.

In our auto parts business, we concluded that when we lost the sale for an item, we lost our entire gross margin on that sale. On the expense side, we incurred almost every operating expense to process the order, whether or not we filled the order for an incremental item. We collected the order. We tried to pick it from inventory. We spent all the internal operating costs whether we had the item or lost the sale. We delivered goods on our own trucks. Each truck ran a full route every day, so there was no incremental expense to deliver one more item. In many cases the customer could not wait for delivery, sourced the item somewhere else, and we lost the revenue and gross margin permanently. Even when the customer would wait, and we filled the order later as a backorder, we eventually captured the gross margin, but incurred extra operating costs in maintaining the back order files. The only variable expense we avoided when we did not fill an order was a commission to our sales force. In cases where several parts were required to repair one vehicle, we could lose the order for all the items if we missed any one of them. Then, the margin lost from one missing item was the margin on the whole order.

Our normal practice was to value the cost of a lost sale at 100% of the gross margin on the item not sold. See more at the end of the chapter about using this parameter to drive the overall inventory performance.

Each user should evaluate their own customer's expectations and behavior, and assign a cost to lost sales for their business or categories of items.

Carrying Cost for Incremental Inventory:

There have been numerous write-ups with methods of establishing a carrying cost for inventory. It is expressed as an annual percentage of the value of the inventory. It includes the physical costs to store and care for the inventory, and the opportunity cost of funds (what you could earn with the money if it wasn't tied up in your inventory). There are a number of references to help determine your inventory carrying cost.[25,26,27] Over time, if you improve the productivity of

---

[25] Inventory Management Part 1. Ohio State University Article by Thomas Goldsby, 2002. Located at http://www.cob.ohio-state.edu/~goldsby_2/classes/780/(780)05_Inventory_I.ppt.

[26] Ownership Cost. Article at http://www.remassoc.com/news/ownership.htm. REM Associates, Management Consultants.

your inventory, you need to raise this level, to reflect that you have the opportunity to earn a higher return by investing money in your inventory. For our auto parts inventory we initially used 20%, but reached a point after several years where we used 40% per year as a carrying cost. That was high enough to keep our inventory lean.

The appropriate cost for a lost sale can be combined with the cost of carrying safety stock. The lowest combined cost is the highest profit service level goal for this specific item.

Why This Should be at the Item Level:

Fast moving items with small variability in demand and lead-time are ideal for an inventory manager. It takes little safety stock to deliver a very high service level. The profit of incremental sales from a high service level will outweigh the incremental carrying cost for the small safety stock needed to achieve that high service level. In our auto parts inventory, using the above measures, we routinely set service level goals of 99.5% order fill on these steady items, and achieved them.

Expensive, slower moving items with very large variability in demand and lead time require a lot of safety stock to reach each increment of higher service. At the same time, if they are slow moving items, the incremental contribution to profit from a higher service level is small. So, on these items, these costs balance at a lower service level target. In our auto parts inventory, for very slow, expensive items like power brake boosters and carburetors, these formulas would assign a service level goal of 90-93%.

By setting item level service goals, you can allocate a limited amount of safety stock investment across all items to achieve maximum profit.

We performed this computation at the end of each period, after the forecasts had been updated. We used that service level goal for the next period, and performed the actual computation of units of safety stock at the time a suggested order was prepared, with current values for lead time, etc.

Let's return to our sample item from the previous chapter. This is the "regular" item with an average demand of 100 units per month, variability in demand of 30%, a review time of 7 days, a lead-time of 10 days, and a lead-time variability of 35% of the lead-time. This

---

[27] The Mysterious Cost of Carrying Inventory.
http://www.effectiveinventory.com/article35.html. Jon Schreibfeder.

item has a selling price of $20 and a gross margin of 20% or $4 per unit. For this example, use 35% as the annual cost of carrying inventory. That's a fairly large value, and it will push the answer toward minimizing the inventory. Use the safety stock amounts from the prior chapter, including safety stock for the lead-time variability. This is the dotted line data from Fig. 5 in the previous chapter. This is converted to the cost of carrying that safety stock by the inventory carrying cost rate.

$$AnnualCostOfLostSales = AnnualUnitDemand * (1 - ServiceLevel) * CostOfLostSalePerUnit$$

$$AnnCostOfSafetyStock = SafetyStockDays * \frac{ForecastUnits / Month}{30} * UnitCost * CarryCostRate$$

Here is a chart of these two, and the combined costs:

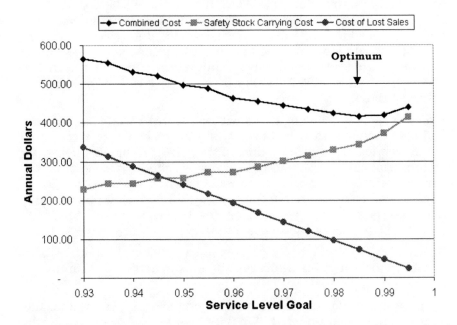

Ch 16 Fig 1. Optimum Service Level for Sample Regular Item

Each loss of one percentage point of service level means you will lose sales on 12 units annually (1% of 1,200 annual forecast), and lose $48 of gross margin. Each additional percentage point of service level requires more safety stock, and this is valued at the carrying cost of inventory. The optimum service level goal for this item is 98.5%.

An Alternate Formula:

A different formula for computing the optimum service level goal is presented in a paper by B. Jay Coleman. [28] This formula defines the service level as the probability of a stockout during each order cycle. This is not the same as trying to achieve a specific order fill goal. The formula, and the math for our sample item is:

$$ServiceLevelGoal = 1 - \frac{CarryingCostPerUnitPerYear * OrderQuantity}{LostSaleCostPerUnit * AverageAnnualDemand}$$

$$ServiceLevelGoal = 1 - \frac{(16*.35)*25}{4*1200} = 1 - .029 = .971$$

This is slightly different than the charted costs, but it also would be applied to a different safety stock formula that uses the normal distribution function.

Slow Moving Items:

Slow Moving items require special consideration to achieve the target service levels. On these items, the goal is to decide exactly how many units to stock. The cost balancing should be computed for integer unit inventories to find the stock level with the highest forecast contribution to profit.

Here is a different example item.

Forecast	2 units / month, with MAD = 50% of forecast
Prices	$50.00 selling price, with 20% gross margin
Times	7 Day Review Time, 10 Day Lead Time with 35% variability in lead time

Inventory Carrying Cost—35% / year

Using the same formulas, but rounding both safety stock units and lost sale units to integer values gives this chart of costs:

---

[28] B. Jay Coleman. Determining the Correct Service Level Target. APICS Journal, First Quarter, 2000.

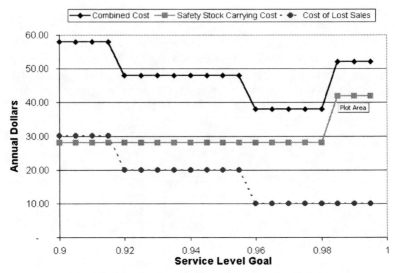

Ch 16 Fig 2. Optimum Service Level for Sample Slow Moving Item

For this slow moving sample item, the safety stock formula shows that 2 units of safety stock (a month's worth) should cover the large variability of demand for all service level goals up to 98%. If the goal were 99%, the safety stock formula would round up to three units of safety stock. The carrying cost of 2 units is $40 cost x 2 units x 35%, or $28. That increases to $42 for three units. To achieve a 96% service level or higher, you could lose only one unit sale per year, or $10 of margin and lost sale cost. If you set the service level goal between 92% and 96% you imply you are willing to lose 2 units per year, and below 92%, you expect to lose 3.

The combined cost is lowest with a service level goal from 96-98%, a safety stock of 2 units, and an estimate that you will lose 1 unit sale per year with this safety stock.

Lumpy Items:

With lumpy items, the further complication is to determine whether it is profitable to carry enough inventory to fill orders for the largest anticipated number of units on each single sale event, and the number of events expected over the forecast horizon.

The analysis can be the same as slow movers, except that the carrying cost and the cost of a lost sale should each be valued at the quantity you expect to sell each time. Here again, the numbers are likely to be small, and the formulas should be computed with integer values to evaluate the expected costs.

Overall Control Values

This system uses two "global" values. One is the inventory carrying cost. It applies to all items. Increasing the value for carrying cost pushes the safety stock cost up, pushes the combined costs to balance at a slightly lower service level on many items, and reduces safety stock inventory somewhat. Decreasing it has the opposite effect.

The second is a multiplier on the cost of a lost sale. We used a percentage of the lost gross margin as another global control value. In "normal times", this was set at 100%, to value a lost sale at 100% of the lost gross margin. However, we could set this to other values. If we wanted to push up the inventory and our service level goals, we valued this at greater than 100%. If we wanted to bring down our inventory and service level goals, we set it at less than 100%. Our business had an overall mild seasonality favoring the summer months. It was not enough to trigger seasonal forecasts, but it could swing 10-15% between winter months and summer months. We typically set the value up to about 120% in March through May. That added a little inventory in extra safety stock where it would generate the most value in incremental margin, and increased our inventory a bit going into the higher selling summer months. We set it back to normal 100% June through October. We set it down to about 80% from late October through November, to reduce our overall inventory slightly going into the slower winter months, and then set it back to 100% from December to February.

Special Items

Here is a short poem by George Herbert (from Jacula Prudentum— early 1600s):

For want of a nail the shoe was lost,
For want of a shoe the horse was lost,
For want of a horse the rider was lost,
For want of a rider the battle was lost,
For want of a battle the kingdom was lost.

We had some "horseshoe nail" items in our inventory. Most of these were small items that related to a big-ticket item. For example, if we couldn't fill an order for a fitting, we might also lose the sale for an air conditioning compressor we had in stock. We did not have the capability to set the value of a lost sale by item, but we wished we could value the lost sale on these kinds of items at 10-20 times the item's lost gross margin, to reflect that we were likely to lose related items, too.

Also, please refer back to the discussion in Chapter 13 about Chuck Lamacchia's article on carrying cost. His concept of splitting the carrying cost into financial and space costs should apply here, too.

What our customers thought:

We did not tell our customers (or our sales people) we were using this system to set item service level goals. We told them we were trying to do the best we could on all items.

We felt our customers would not have understood our real goal. In 20 years, they never figured out that we were really trying to optimize our profit by putting the safety stock inventory in the places where it would generate the most additional gross margin dollars.

Our overall service level was good enough that they were satisfied, and we optimized our profits, too.

Chapter Summary

In our auto parts business, we felt that whenever we lost a sale, our profits went down by the entire gross margin on that sale.

We ran a program that performed calculations against our entire inventory at the end of each month after the forecasts had been updated. It assigned a service level goal for each item based on the minimum combined cost of safety stock investment and potential lost sales. This gave us the greatest overall profit by optimizing each item's safety stock.

The control factors to scale the cost of a lost sale and value inventory carrying costs also gave us an overall way to adjust our safety stock investment.

JDA offers software that can perform this kind of cost analysis to determine optimum service level goals.

Chapter 17. Setting the Best Review Time for Product Line Orders

The next step is to determine the best frequency of orders, or Review Time, for orders that cover a full product line or category of inventory.

The Bermuda Strategy

A lazy buyer would arrive at work on January 2nd, order a full year's worth of everything, and go on vacation to Bermuda for the rest of the year. Don't try it. Your boss will call you and tell you to stay there, as you will not be needed to train your replacement.

Frequency beats Forecasting, again:

Chapter 7 gave reasons why short lead times are beneficial. Those same benefits apply to more frequent ordering, or short Review Time. When you order more frequently, the short review times will improve your service level. There are many reasons for this.

- You have more opportunities to reorder slow moving or erratic items where you might stock only a few units. You will replace that inventory more quickly, and be ready for the next sale, even if it occurs sooner than forecast.
- If your vendor holds backorders and ships them with your next order, these will arrive sooner when you order more frequently.
- If your vendor does not hold backorders, but cancels your order for items they can't ship immediately, you can reorder them sooner.
- In many wholesalers it is easier to check in and stock small shipments. If you process small shipments more quickly than large ones, more frequent ordering will also reduce the internal component of your overall lead-time.

Establishing Categories or Product Lines

In a few cases, a distributor can order items individually. In the majority of cases, the distributor will order all the items in a group or product line on one order. Identify items ordered individually, and assign all other items to some specific group. The item EOQ will set the frequency for items ordered individually. It is necessary to determine an optimum order frequency for each product line or group of items ordered together.

It is also important to note whether order dates and order frequency can be selected by the distributor, or are imposed by the vendor.

Economic Order Quantity applied to Groups or Product Lines

The EOQ concepts work, with some modification, for groups of items ordered together.

We started with a simulation of a year's worth of activity on a product line or category, under various ordering strategies. If you order the line every other week, you would place 26 orders in a year's time. An item with an EOQ less than two weeks would be ordered on every purchase order, or 26 times per year. Even though you might want to buy these items more frequently, you only order them with the group, so you have to order two week's supply each time. Not every slower moving item will be on every order.

You can establish a "purchase order handling cost" (we used $30 in our auto parts business). This is the variable cost incurred each time you issue a purchase order. It includes the costs of ordering, receiving a shipment, handling the paperwork in receiving and in accounts payable, and issuing payment for each purchase order. These are costs incurred regardless of the number of items on a single purchase order. You can also establish a line item variable cost to apply to each line item on a purchase order. Over a year, the handling cost will be the purchase order cost times the number of orders placed plus the line cost times the aggregate number of lines ordered.

As you order a category more frequently, both the "per order" cost and the total number of line items will increase. If you ordered once a year, you would incur one "per order cost" and a line item cost for ordering each item in the category one time. If you order weekly, you would incur 52 "per order" costs. The number of aggregate line items won't be 52 times the number of items in the line, as you will not buy every item every week, but it will approach that for product lines with fast moving items that all have short EOQ times.

You can compute the average cycle stock and aggregate safety stock for all the items in the line for each proposed order frequency. The average cycle inventory is ½ the average order size. Your average total on hand inventory would be that cycle inventory plus the aggregate safety stock. You can apply your carrying cost rate to this amount of inventory. If you order once a year, you would average ½ year's inventory in cycle stock, but little safety stock since you only have one chance a year to stock out of an item. If you order weekly, you would have ½ week's inventory as a cycle stock, plus enough safety stock to achieve your service goal, even with a chance to run out of stock every week.

If the vendor offers any incentives for ordering in a certain size, the value of these incentives should also be applied as an offset to the handling and carrying costs, just as they were on individual item EOQs. Vendors can set all kinds of criteria, usually to reduce their freight or handling costs. They might offer prepaid freight for orders above a minimum size in units, dollars or weight. They might offer discounts or deferred payment for orders that hit other sizes. Some of our auto parts vendors offered discounts for trailer load orders, as a way to pass through lower shipping costs. These can be an amount per order, or a percentage of the cost of the goods.

It is a big simulation, but it is possible to construct a table of the costs for various strategies. Here is an example for a line with annual purchases of $500,000 and 500 items. The vendor offers a 1% discount for orders of $20,000 and up.

Number of Orders Per Year	Review Time Between Orders	Average Order Size	Cycle Inventory	Avg Safety Stock Days	Safety Stock Inventory	Carrying Cost Inventory @ 30%	Order Cost per Year @ $30/order	Number of Lines on a Year's Orders	Line Handling Cost Per Year @ $.50/line	Total Costs	Savings in Discounts or Terms	Total Costs after Savings
1	364	500,000	250,000	0	-	75,000	30	500	250	75,280	5,000	70,280
2	182	250,000	125,000	4	5,495	39,148	60	990	495	39,703	5,000	34,703
4	91	125,000	62,500	6	8,242	21,223	120	1,940	970	22,313	5,000	17,313
6	61	83,333	41,667	8	10,989	15,797	180	2,820	1,410	17,387	5,000	12,387
10	36	50,000	25,000	9	12,363	11,209	300	4,500	2,250	13,759	5,000	8,759
12	30	41,667	20,833	9	12,363	9,959	360	5,220	2,610	12,929	5,000	7,929
17	21	29,412	14,706	10	13,736	8,533	510	6,970	3,485	12,528	5,000	7,528
20	18	25,000	12,500	10	13,736	7,871	600	8,000	4,000	12,471	5,000	7,471
25	15	20,000	10,000	10	13,736	7,121	750	9,500	4,750	12,621	5,000	7,621
37	10	13,514	6,757	11	15,110	6,560	1,110	13,320	6,660	14,330		14,330
52	7	9,615	4,808	11	15,110	5,975	1,560	17,680	8,840	16,375	-	16,375

Ch 17 Fig 1. Table of Product Line Order Sizes, Costs and Savings

This table shows that the overall carrying cost goes down with more frequent orders, as the reduction in cycle stock is more than the increases in safety stock. On the other hand, handling costs increase as you place more orders and have more total line items. The 1% additional discount gives a significant reduction to overall total costs. The absolute lowest cost strategy is 20 orders per year, or an order of about $25,000 every 18 days. It gives the best balance of handling and carrying costs. However, the table also shows it costs only slightly more to place 25 orders per year, with orders of $20,000 about every 15 days. Since frequency beats forecasting, it is likely this will give a slightly better service level, with faster replenishment of the slow moving items in this line. The incremental profit from that slight better service level is likely to more than offset the tiny cost increase. So, the best strategy for this vendor line would be to place an order each time you can make the $20,000 size to achieve the 1% discount. On average, this would be about every 15 days, and you would place about 25 orders per year.

Here is the same data in a graph:

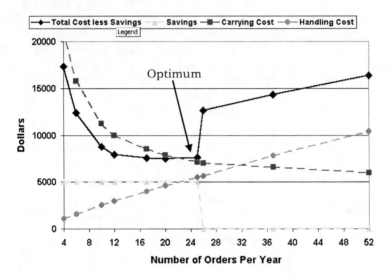

Ch 17 Fig 2. Chart of Product Line Order Frequency, Costs, and Savings.

This shows the importance of achieving the 1% discount. Once that is achieved, the total costs are very flat for strategies from 25 orders per year down to 12 orders per year. Since these costs are close, the best strategy is to order as frequently as possible. The best strategy for this line is to order every time you reach $20,000 in needed items.

Imposed Order Dates, Frequencies, or Sizes

Many vendors impose a schedule, or a required order size on distributors. Some vendors deliver their goods on their own trucks, or use third party logistics companies to arrange shipments to reduce their freight costs. These vendors might impose a day of the week or month for distributors on certain routes. In these cases, the review time is fixed, and the distributor must place each order at that interval of time. This fixed review time interval requirement needs special treatment in the ordering formulas.

Other vendors will require minimum order sizes to prepay freight costs, or require orders in exact truckload or container quantities.

The distributor usually must comply with these requirements or pay a stiff penalty. The cost analysis above can be used to diagnose the required frequency and determine if it is close to the optimum for the distributor.

If the required order interval is close to the best frequency, that is very good. The distributor can comply without increasing internal costs. If not, the distributor will have facts to attempt to negotiate a policy change or waiver.

Value of Deferred Payment Terms

Some vendors offer deferred or installment payments for certain order sizes. One of our vendors offered "30-60-90 day terms" for truckload orders. We would pay the invoice in three equal monthly installments.

You have to analyze terms against the order sizes and frequencies to determine what they are worth to you.

Here are several situations to illustrate this. In one case, you could place orders large enough to qualify for these terms every week or so. You would earn the terms on every order, and carry an accounts payable balance for the later installments. If your company is a net borrower, you could delay borrowing the funds to pay for the later installments and you would save the interest cost on the deferred amounts. Here is a little example of a $12,000 order—with 30 day or with 30-60-90 terms.

	Now	30 days from now	60 days from now	90 days from now
30 day Terms	Order $12,000	Pay $12,000		
30-60-90 day Terms	Order $12,000	Pay 1st $4,000	Pay 2nd $4,000	Pay 3rd $4,000
Deferred			$4,000 for 30 days	$4,000 for 60 days
Interest 6%/yr			$20	$40

Ch 17 Fig 3. Savings on $12,000 order with 30-60-90 day terms

So, you would save a total of $60 in interest by deferring the need to borrow for the delayed installments. This is the same as deferring the entire $12,000 for 30 extra days, and the interest savings is equivalent to a ½% discount on the order at this interest rate. That is only true if your company uses short-term borrowing, and you achieve an interest savings.

If your company is not a borrower, then the value depends on what you can do with the free funds during the dating period. If you can invest these funds, the earnings on that investment are what you gain from the dating. This is called the alternate investment return. If your company does not borrow, and you do not invest the surplus funds, then there is no value or gain from the deferred terms.

All of that works only if you consume the goods very quickly.

Take a situation where you have to order three months supply to get the 30-60-90 day terms. These terms are worth nothing, since you could place an order each month for 1/3 of the total amount, and pay for it with the regular 30-day terms. You would make the payments at exactly the same time.

	Now	30 days from now	60 days from now	90 days from now
30 day Terms	Order $4,000	Pay $4,000 Order next $4,000	Pay $4,000 Order next $4,000	Pay $4,000
30-60-90 day Terms	Order $12,000	Pay 1st $4,000	Pay 2nd $4,000	Pay 3rd $4,000
Gain in Cash		0	0	0

Ch 17 Fig 4. Savings on $12,000, 3 month supply with 30-60-90 day terms

In this case, you would choose to place monthly orders and forego the terms. Remember, frequency beats forecasting. With the first strategy you must forecast every item for 90 days. With the second strategy you get to review the line each time you order, but achieve the same cash flow.

Take an even worse situation where you would have to order six months supply to get the 30-60-90 day terms. In this case you would actually pay sooner for the goods consumed at the end of this cycle if you placed the large order with terms, versus regular small orders with no extended terms.

	Now	30 days later	60 days later	90 days later	120 days later	150 days later	180 days later
30 day Terms	Order $2,000	Pay $2,000 Order $2,000	Pay $2,000 Order $2,000	Pay $2,000 Order $2,000	Pay $2,000 Order $2,000	Pay $2,000 Order $2,000	Pay $2,000
30-60-90 day Terms	Order $12,000	Pay 1st $4,000	Pay 2nd $4,000	Pay 3rd $4,000			
Cash		-2,000	-4,000	-6,000			

Ch 17 Fig 5. Penalty on 6-month supply with 30-60-90 day terms.

In this case, you actually pay earlier when you place the 6-month order with 30-60-90 day terms, and you have to forecast the entire line for the full 6-month time span. This is clearly not a good way to go.

As you can see, you need to understand your company's cash situation, and also the size of the order versus the schedule of payments to place an accurate value on terms.

Consigned Inventory

Consigned inventory is another case of deferred terms. In this case, the appropriate way to compute the proper order frequency is to adjust the carrying cost rate to reflect what you can do with the funds saved by the consignment amount.

Chapter Summary

A simulation of a year's worth of activity on a product line with various possible order frequencies can be used to determine the best order size and frequency based on forecast handling and carrying costs, offset by any vendor discounts or the value of extended terms.

The strategy should be reviewed whenever the vendor changes their "deal", or whenever the product category has a significant change in overall sales. Even if those do not change, it should be reviewed at least once a year.

In our auto parts company, the result of this analysis was that most of the major lines were ordered weekly. One line was ordered twice a week. A few big lines were ordered on a frequency to hit trailer load quantity discounts. The best frequency for small lines was generally set by the vendor's prepaid freight requirement.

Chapter 18. Establishing a Schedule and Budget

The next step in organizing the entire purchasing process is to establish a schedule and budget for all lines.

Once you know how often each line should normally be ordered, you can begin to build a calendar.

Building a Schedule for Ordering

Some vendors will have a required schedule. In our auto parts company, our shock absorber supplier was a "build to order" vendor. They had converted their manufacturing process to produce very small batches in production cells. They could switch each cell quickly to build a different part number, or even a different brand. They built their own brand most of the time, but converted the manufacturing cells to build CARQUEST brand shock absorbers every Thursday. All the CARQUEST distribution centers ordered shocks on Tuesday. On Wednesday, the supplier aggregated all the orders, built a production schedule, and organized the proper quantity of each raw material. They manufactured and packaged the exact quantity of each item on Thursday, staged the product for each CARQUEST distribution center, and shipped all orders on Friday. So, every CARQUEST distribution center had to place a weekly stock order each Tuesday.

Two of our suppliers of remanufactured products delivered the goods on their own trucks. Those orders had to be submitted on the proper day each week so the supplier could process them in time to meet their own truck schedule.

These and a few other lines were ordered on a specific day each week. We had flexibility to set our schedule all other product lines. It was tempting to build the schedule for the convenience of the buyers. We could have easily leveled the daily workload for each buyer. However, it was much more productive to build a schedule to accommodate our receiving and stocking department. Monday was our busiest day. We preferred to have very few shipments arrive on Monday, so we could focus on outbound orders. We wanted a level workload for our receiving crews on the other days of the week. We made many arrangements with our major suppliers and carriers to establish a consistent day to place orders for each line, and a consistent day to expect delivery. That helped control our labor cost in our receiving department. The reduction in lead-time variability also reduced our safety stock requirement.

So, most of the major lines were ordered once a week, on a specific day. One big line was ordered twice a week. A few big lines were ordered every other week or every third week to achieve trailer load discounts and terms.

Scheduling most of the major lines covered enough of our total product to provide a consistent workload in our receiving department.

We did not schedule a specific day of the week to place orders for the smaller lines. Medium and small lines were ordered according to the frequency model for each line.

The result was a calendar with target order dates for all of the big lines. The small lines were ordered whenever the suggested order added up to enough product to make a prepaid shipment or the vendor minimum order amount, or when the order was needed to maintain our service level.

This gave a very good roadmap of work to be done in our purchasing department.

Building a Forecast Budget

This data can also be used to build a weekly or monthly forecast of purchases, and this can be used as a forecast budget for purchasing. The order frequency analysis gives an average order size, and this can be merged with the schedule to produce a forecast of purchases. Here is an abbreviated budget for one month and just a few product lines from our auto parts company.

		Monday		Tuesday		Wednesday		Thursday		Friday		Total
	Filters	27,000	Shocks	10,000	Gaskets	6,000	Brakes	45,000	Ignition	14,000		
Week 1	Rebuilts	18,000	Spark Plugs	3,000	Chemicals	7,000	Engine Parts	8,000	Tools	4,000		
	Bearings	5,000	Wiper Blades	2,500	Oil	20,000	Bearings	5,000	Belts/Hose	25,000	199,500
	Filters	27,000	Shocks	10,000	Gaskets	6,000	Brakes	45,000	Ignition	14,000		
Week 2	Rebuilts	18,000	Spark Plugs	3,000	Chemicals	7,000	Engine Parts	8,000	Tools	4,000		
	Bearings	5,000	Wiper Blades	2,500	Special Tools	1,500	Bearings	5,000	Belts/Hose	25,000	181,000
	Filters	27,000	Shocks	10,000	Gaskets	6,000	Brakes	45,000	Ignition	14,000		
Week 3	Rebuilts	18,000	Spark Plugs	3,000	Chemicals	7,000	Engine Parts	8,000	Tools	4,000		
	Bearings	5,000	Wiper Blades	2,500	Oil	20,000	Bearings	5,000	Belts/Hose	25,000	199,500
	Filters	27,000	Shocks	10,000	Gaskets	6,000	Brakes	45,000	Ignition	14,000		
Week 4	Rebuilts	18,000	Spark Plugs	3,000	Chemicals	7,000	Engine Parts	8,000	Tools	4,000		
	Bearings	5,000	Wiper Blades	2,500	Preseason AC	90,000	Bearings	5,000	Belts/Hose	25,000	269,500
Grand Total												849,500

Ch 18 Fig 1. Monthly Schedule and Forecast Budget

This shows we plan to order Filters every Monday, and expect each order to be about $27,000. We plan to order a truckload of Oil, worth $20,000, every other week on Wednesday. We order Bearings twice a week, and expect each order to be about $5,000. We can only order Special Tools once a month, and make the vendor's minimum order size of $1,500 for prepaid freight. In the fourth week, the buyer expects to place a $90,000 special preseason order for air conditioning parts. Overall, we expect to spend about $850,000 in the next four weeks on these product lines.

We never (thank goodness) used this as a fixed "open to buy" budget. We were always able to order whatever we needed to achieve our service level goals.

However, this forecast budget was a superb tool for both buyers and management.

For buyers, it was very valuable as a benchmark to validate suggested orders. If the total of a suggested filter order was close to the $27,000 average size, it gave the buyer a lot of confidence that all the item quantities were reasonable. This allowed the buyers to approve many suggested orders without having to review every item in detail. They had already spent time reviewing the item forecasts, lead times, order frequency and schedule, so the suggested order should "make sense".

If a suggested order was very different than the forecast budget, then something unusual must have happened. Either we experienced unusually large or small actual sales on a line in the prior week, or someone made a big adjustment to on-hand inventory values, or some error had been made in the data. In any case, it was a strong signal that the buyer should carefully review individual items on that suggested order.

For management, this was an excellent planning tool. It gave a pretty good forecast of future accounts payable and cash requirements, well in advance of receiving and processing invoices. It also let the buyers and management agree in advance on any unusual orders. In the above example, the buyer plans to place a preseason order, required by the vendor, for $90,000 in air conditioning parts. It is good practice for the buyer and management to know in advance that this will be done, and that it is a sensible amount.

Each buyer created this schedule for a month in advance, and had a brief review of it with management. Each buyer kept track of orders actually placed, and accumulated a total against this expected amount. If the actual orders were running significantly larger or smaller than the forecast budget, it let the buyer alert their manager, to make sure this was appropriate based on recent actual sales or other activities.

Chapter Summary

A calendar of planned orders and typical order sizes can be used as a roadmap for buyers, and as a great communication tool with management.

It should not be used as a hard "open to buy" budget.

It can help the buyers schedule orders to optimize productivity in a distributor's receiving department.

Chapter 19. Replenishment of Stores

The previous chapters on determining order frequency, setting a schedule and budget, and replenishment purchasing all apply to distribution centers, or other locations served by ordering products on various cycles from many vendors.

In our auto parts business, we also owned some of our store locations.

The techniques in the previous chapters still apply to the inventory in stores that is purchased on some logical cycle directly from "outside" vendors. We had a few lines like paint that were purchased on a weekly or "make freight" cycle directly from that vendor.

However, the vast majority of inventory in our stores was replenished daily by one of our company distribution centers.

This allowed us to use a much simpler process to replenish the stores.

"Pull" vs. "Push" Systems

Most early inventory management systems were "Push" systems. This is where the manufacturer or central controller makes the decisions, and "pushes" inventory into the distribution channel. There has been a huge amount of development of Distribution Requirements Planning (DRP) and Manufacturing Requirements Planning (MRP) systems to support this. It is the best you can do without aggregated end user data.

Over the past 20 years or so, there has been a major switch toward "Pull" systems, where the end user demand drives the entire system and pulls inventory into the channel. Just-In-Time and Lean Manufacturing systems are an effort to respond quickly to actual end user demands.

Pull systems have the potential to be vastly better than Push systems. If the channel can adequately support a Pull system, it is likely to give much better customer service (from faster reaction to changes in demand), and much less overall inventory and obsolescence (since inventory only goes where it is needed). In our auto parts company we practiced a pull system to replenish our stores from our distribution centers.

"Pull" Daily Store Replenishment System

Here are the steps we took to establish our pull system for our stores.

- A store inventory manager established a stock quantity for each item in each store.
- An "ok to order" flag was set for each item. Only items with this flag "on" were replenished. If we knew an item was slowing down, we had the capability to set this flag to "off". In that case, when the item was sold it would not be replenished. This was one way to sell down our inventory of items that began to decline toward obsolescence.
- For most items, our stock quantity was one (or the quantity for one car or one job).
- We used a very simplified version of forecasting to set stock quantities for the most popular items. It was not necessary to stock more than one unit or set unless the item was selling more than about 12-15 times per year in that store. We made an exception and stocked more "out front" chemicals and accessories to show "full" shelves to customers. In our typical store with about 18,000 items, only about 2,000 items had a stock quantity greater than one.
- There were ongoing modifications, but many of these item stock levels stood from one annual classification to the next.

The process was simply to replenish the store up to the stock quantity levels each day.

The inventory manager spent time establishing all the stock flags and stock quantities, but then did not even review the daily replenishment order.

Our store computer generated this daily replenishment order and transmitted it to the distribution center. The distribution center processed the order that same day, and the order was delivered overnight to the store.

Our computer system had the capability to transmit an Advance Ship Notice (electronic packing list), back to the store system. The store computer had the capability to automatically post the ASN to the store's inventory the next morning when the shipment was put away at the store.

So, our inventory manager spent almost all of his time maintaining the database and setting the desired inventory for each store. He spent almost no time on the replenishment process, and no one had to review the daily replenishment orders. This was a very efficient system.

Daily Replenishment

In fact, the sales potential of most items was low enough that every item in a store did not have to be replenished daily. However, even our largest stores could only afford to stock items that covered about 85% of total demand. Every store had lots of one item special orders every day. These items were "presold" and the customers expected them the next day. So, our delivery trucks ran routes that covered every store every night.

There would have been some efficiency at both the distribution center and the store from processing a replenishment order once or twice a week rather than every day. Some of our competitors did this. We were reluctant to do it, mostly from tradition, not economic justification.

Pete's Principle of Lost Sales

It works out that the number of lost sale chances is almost the same across a wide range of auto parts store sizes. A lost sale chance is a demand for an item not in the store's inventory. It might be converted to a sale as a special order, but usually at extra cost or lost margin. I call this Pete's Principle of Lost Sales. Here it is:

"Your auto parts store should have 40-45 lost sale chances per day."

This is true, regardless of the size of your store, as long as:

- **Your inventory is appropriate and balanced.**
- **You are not turning away customers.**

Here is a table to illustrate this:

Store Size	Monthly Sales	Line Items per Day	Typical Inventory	Part Numbers Stocked	Approximate Coverage	Lost Sale Chances Per Day
Very Small	50,000	125	175,000	10,000	65%	44
Medium	75,000	175	250,000	15,000	75%	44
Large	125,000	300	400,000	25,000	85%	45
Very Large	200,000	500	750,000	35,000	91%	45

Ch 19 Fig 1. Pete's Principle of Lost Sale Chances

As you can see, the coverage each store can afford gives them about 45 lost sale chances per day on the average number of line items they process.

I have tried this out on more than 100 auto parts store inventory managers, and they acknowledge that it is reasonably true for many types of stores in the automotive aftermarket.

There are two corollaries to Pete's Principle:

First Corollary to Pete's Principle:
- If you are getting MORE than 40-45 lost sale chances per day, something may be wrong:
  - You may not have enough inventory for your size.
  - Your inventory may not have the right items in stock.
  - Either way, your coverage may not be as good as the table shows.

Second Corollary to Pete's Principle:
- If you are getting LESS than 40-45 lost sale chances per day, something may also be wrong:
  - You may have too much inventory for the sales volume of the store.
  - You may be turning away customers without logging the lost sale or getting the chance to special order items for them.

I'm sure these numbers would be different in other industries, so don' t use this unless you're in auto parts, or develop your own benchmarks. If you carefully log lost sales at your stores, this can be a quick test to validate the overall inventory management of each store.

Other Daily Processes

Because we replenished each store daily, with our own delivery trucks, we could do several other things every day to help the store inventory management.

Daily Returns

The auto parts aftermarket has a much higher rate of merchandise returns than many other merchandise categories. There are many factors. In some cases where the vendor changes parts mid-year, we can't determine the exact right part for an application, and we must deliver two or three items so the customer can pick the right one and send back the rest. In some cases the repair shop orders in advance all the items they might need for a job, uses what is actually needed after they complete the diagnosis, and returns the rest of the unused items. In some cases the customer orders the wrong item, or we deliver the wrong item. All of those are in addition to the general tendency of customers to return some percentage of what they purchase.

Our store computer swept the inventory every day, and generated a daily return to the distribution center that included all "overstock" with some exceptions. This return included:

- Special order items not in the store's regular inventory that were never sold or sold and returned.
- Regular stock items where the quantity on hand was over the stock level for that store. When a customer returned an item, it was often after the store had replenished their inventory, so that return became an overstock item at that store.
- We excluded the very most popular items, small items like fasteners where the investment was small, and items sold by the distribution center in cases or rolls where the store could not return a partial case or roll.

We did not send warranty and core (used parts exchanged for remanufactured units) items from the store back to the distribution center every day. These were usually processed once or twice a week. This balanced the need to process them quickly with the workload at the DC.

Automated Stock Adjustments

There will be more on the stock adjustment process in a couple of chapters. This is just to show how it tied in to our daily process.

The basic process of doing a store stock adjustment was to reset the item stock quantities. This was really all that was necessary because:

- The automatic daily replenishment picked up items where the stock quantity had increased, and automatically ordered them on the next daily replenishment order.

- The daily return sweep caught items that now were "overstocked" because the stock quantity had been lowered, and put them on the daily return list to be sent back.

So the daily replenishment and returns also handled the stock adjustment items.

Backorders

The distribution center held a "backorder" for any items not shipped to a store on the daily replenishment order. The store showed the item on backorder, and did not reorder it daily. These backorders had first priority when the distribution center was back in stock, and the systems handled the order at the DC and the receipt at the store.

Automatic New Numbers

Each store could post an inventory profile, which showed their basic stock level on each product line and category.

When a new item was added to the distribution center inventory, it received an initial classification code.

An automatic backorder for one unit (or set) was placed in the system for every store where that new item's classification fell with their stock level. This allowed the DC to routinely order additional quantity to fulfill these backorders.

When the item arrived at the store, the "stock" flag was turned on and the stock level was set to one unit (or one set) at that store.

This gave the DC buyer a good count of the "pipeline" requirement for a new item, and automatically handled the data maintenance process at the store.

Since filling a backorder was a transaction that did not count as DC demand, it also correctly eliminated these pipeline transactions from the DC demand history.

Delayed Replenishment

Our auto parts stores had a significant rate of return of new merchandise from customers. This came from all the reasons outlined in Chapter 4 on Defining Demand.

Our system reacted so quickly to replenish the stores that most of these returns came back after the store was replenished, and created overstock on those items at those stores. Our automatic returns software then promptly returned those same items to the DC. In some cases, the DC had ordered replenishment inventory, too, and this created overstock at the DC by the time the return arrived and was processed.

In effect, our system reacted so quickly that we were churning some merchandise, with lots of extra handling cost and the creation of some extra inventory.

The only solution was to delay the replenishment at the store on items in the lowest (or two lowest) popularity codes that store stocked. The probability of another independent sale for these items in the next few days was very low at a single store, so there was little risk to our service level. The reward was that we would not replenish items that had been sold and promptly returned.

This was a "band-aid" at best, but it did reduce our rate of return from the stores to the DC. At best, we would have visibility into the service dealer's operation, to see if the item was really installed on a vehicle. Then we would know that it was "sold" clear through the channel. There is more on this in the chapter on Supply Chain Considerations.

Chapter Summary

In our auto parts business, we used store demand to "pull" inventory from our DCs to stores daily.

We also used a technique to "sweep" the store inventories for some kinds of overstock and return it to the DC daily.

In the case of our stores, we did not need to do any detailed review of either the daily replenishment order or the daily return sweep.

Daily replenishment simplifies all the inventory management tasks and maximizes service level.

Next, we can move on to replenishment of the DCs, a more complicated process.

Pete Kornafel

Chapter 20. Replenishment Purchasing for Distribution Centers

At last. You have now done all of the preparatory work needed to place an intelligent distribution center or DC replenishment order. You have completed all the detailed building blocks of a good system. You have:

- Selected the items to be stocked and replenished.
- Forecast Demand for each item, using the best forecasting model for each item.
- Established a Lead Time Forecast and Lead Time Variability for the product line and for each item.
- Established a Service Level Goal so you can compute a Safety Stock for each item.
- Defined items ordered individually, and assigned all others to product line categories to be ordered as a group.
- Established the EOQ frequency for each item ordered individually.
- Established the best frequency for regular replenishment orders for each group of items.
- Established a Schedule and budget for all lines.

If you haven't done all that, go back and do it. Otherwise, you will spend your company's money without a clue about whether it is an optimum way to do it, and you will probably have to modify a lot of items on every suggested order.

The formulas to use for replenishment purchasing depend on how the items are ordered. This chapter considers four different situations:

1) Individual Items. Items are reviewed individually every day, and each item can be ordered as needed.
2) Groups of Items or Product Lines—with no order time or size requirements. A group of items or product line is ordered together on one purchase order. Orders can be placed at any time in any size, but are generally placed at the best-computed order frequency.
3) Groups of Items or Product Lines—with fixed dates or ordering intervals. A group of items or product line must be ordered on a specific date or at a specific interval, such as a specific day of the week or month.

4) Groups of Items or Product Lines—with required or optimum order sizes. A group of items or a product line where there is a required or beneficial order size, such as an exact trailer load or container.

Each of these requires slightly different formulas and procedures to establish the best replenishment order.

These replenishment techniques were used in IBM's INVEN packages and at our company for 20 years. They are discussed here with IBM's permission.

Individual Item Order Formula

The simplest case is an order for individual items. You can examine the inventory data every day to determine if an item needs to be ordered.

If an individual item is not ordered today, it can be ordered tomorrow, and the quantity ordered at that time will be available one lead time after that. In addition, you need some Safety Stock, as computed for that item. Therefore, the Suggested Order Point for an individual item is:

$$OrderPointInUnits = Usage\ over\ Needed\ Time$$

Where *Usage* converts the time in days to units according to the item forecast, and *Needed Time = Lead Time + Safety Stock (in Days) + 1 (for 1 day Review Time)*

Order the item whenever the Balance is below the Order Point:

$$Balance = QuantityOnHand + QuantityOnOrder—$$
$$QuantityOwedOnBackorder$$

The quantity on order should only be included if that quantity is scheduled to arrive within the needed time. The Quantity Owed on Backorder is deducted from the Balance, as these units should be shipped to customers promptly after receipt of the next order, and will not be available to satisfy future demands.

Once an item reaches its order point, the quantity to order is an Economic Order Quantity in units. It may have to be adjusted for a vendor minimum order or rounded to vendor case lots. This Economic Order Quantity will consider any vendor discounts or savings for specific order sizes.

This is where all that preparation pays off. You have established a demand forecast, a lead-time forecast, a safety stock requirement, and an economic order quantity for each item. If you approved each of those details, you should be confident that the item would be ordered just as it is needed and in the best quantity.

Converting Days to Units—(Usage)

The item forecast is used to convert the needed time span to units. This is straightforward for regular items, but must also use seasonal or trend factors if present.

The formula for Usage is:

$$UsageOverTime = \frac{ForecastUnitsPerPeriod * Periodicity * TimeInDays}{NumberOfDaysPerYearUsedInForecasts(364)}$$

For example, an item with a forecast of 50 units per month, (and therefore periodicity of 12), and a needed time of 21 days has an expected usage of:

$$UsageOver21Days = \frac{50*12*21}{364} = 35Units$$

If the item has a trend or seasonal forecast, these must be considered in the usage. The strength of seasonal forecasting is to look ahead at the coming seasonal indexes to compute the usage. Here is an example showing this item's forecast usage with no seasonal index, and then at two different dates. Use the index for that month and the number of days you need to cover in that period, and "look ahead" the total required number of days.

	Period	Average Units Per Month	Seasonal Index	Seasonal Forecast for That Month	Days to Cover in That Month	Forecast Usage in Units
Not Seasonal		50/month		50 this month	21 days	35 units
Seasonal Item	1	50/month	1.2	60 this month	10 days	20 units
at 20th of a	2	50/month	1.4	70 this month	11 days	25 units
month	Total				21 days	45 units
Same Item at	1	50/month	0.7	35 this month	15 days	17 units
15th of another	2	50/month	0.8	40 this month	6 days	8 units
month	Total				21 days	25 units

Ch 20 Fig 1. Computing Usage over Forecast Time on Seasonal Item

Pete Kornafel

That's the whole story for individual items. Review all items every day, and order each one when the order point falls below the available balance. Order it in the EOQ quantity, adjusted if necessary for vendor minimum or case requirements.

Group and Product Line Orders—Do You Need to Place an Order Today?

Before you place an order for a group of items or a full product line, the first question is whether you need to place an order today. This is not as simple as it was for a single item. The best process is to forecast the expected overall service goal for the entire product line. You do not need to place an order if the expected lost sales on the entire product line are within the overall service goal for the required coming time period. This is discussed first, as it applies to all of the product line ordering situations.

When you place an order, the goods will arrive and be ready for sale one lead-time later.

Before you place that order, you should forecast what your overall service level will be on the entire product line assuming you do NOT place an order today. You can use the forecasts to estimate when each item will run out of stock, and when you will begin to incur lost sales on each item. These can be aggregated, day-by-day, into the future, and used to estimate the overall service level for the line. At some point, enough items will run out of stock that the aggregate forecast lost sales will exceed the lost sales permitted over a review time, based on the aggregate service level goal for all items in the line. That is the day your next replenishment order should be available for sale. Those goods should arrive "just in time" to maintain your overall service level for the entire line. If that date is more than one lead-time from now, you do not need to place a full replenishment order today. Even though some items might run out, you will still deliver your overall service level goal for the full line.

Here is an example of a category where you can order whenever you wish, and order each item as required without having to hit an order total size:

Forecast Sales in $ Per Day	Days from Today													
	1	2	3	4	5	6	7	8	9	10	11	12	13	14
Item 27	26	26	26	26	26	26	26							
Item 34	11	11	11	11	11									
Item 43	47	47	47	47	47	47	47	47	47	47	47	47	47	
Item 62	35	35	35	35	35	35	35	35	35	35	35			
Item 114	15	15	15	15	15	15	15	15	15	15				
All Other Items	505	505	505	505	505	505	505	505	505	505	505	505	505	505
Daily Expected Actual Sales	639	639	639	639	639	628	628	602	602	602	587	552	552	505
Forecast Daily Lost Sales	-	-	-	-	-	(11)	(11)	(37)	(37)	(37)	(52)	(87)	(87)	(134)
Daily Forecast Service Level	100%	100%	100%	100%	100%	98.3%	98.3%	**94.2%**	**94.2%**	**94.2%**	**91.9%**	86.4%	86.4%	79.0%
Daily Acceptable Lost Sales	(26)	(26)	(26)	(26)	(26)	(26)	(26)	(26)	(26)	(26)	(26)	(26)	(26)	(26)
Acceptable Lost Sales over RT	(182)	(182)	(182)	(182)	(182)	(182)	(182)	(182)	(182)	(182)	(182)	(182)	(182)	(182)
Forecast Cumulative Lost Sales						(11)	(22)	(59)	(96)	(133)	**(185)**	(272)	(359)	(493)
Date Needed for Order	OK To Delay			Order	<=========== Lead Time ==========>						Need			

Ch 20 Fig 2. Delay Order Based on Forecast Future Service Level

This line has a review time of 7 days, and a lead-time of 7 days. The forecast sales for all items in the line are $639 per day. Five items are forecast to run out of stock soon. All other items have at least two weeks supply on hand.

Item 27 has a forecast sales of $26 per day, and has seven days supply on hand. This item is likely to run out of stock at that time, and you will begin losing that $26 per day. Item 34 is forecast to run out 5 days from now, and you will begin losing $11 per day at that point. Item 43 has 13 days supply, and then you will begin losing $47 sales per day when that item runs out of stock. The quantity used is the "on hand" quantity plus any on order quantity that is forecast to arrive during this time.

The flowed total service level goal for all the items in the line is 96%. Therefore, you will tolerate a lost sales amount of $26 per day, or an aggregate amount of $182 over the 7-day review time.

On a daily basis, the line will fall below 96% service level 8 days from now. However, the forecast aggregate total lost sales will not exceed $182 until 11 days from now. So, you could delay this order for up to three days, and the overall line will still not fall below its target service level, even though a few items will run out of stock, and the line will fall below its target service level for the last few days before this order arrives. Over the total time span, you will achieve the 96% service level.

If this is a category that must be ordered on a fixed interval imposed by the vendor, then you have to decide whether you can skip this order completely, and delay one full review time, until the next scheduled order date.

On the other hand, if you have the ability to place orders whenever you want, then you can decide to delay an order for a few days and still meet your service goals.

Silver[29] shows similar formulas for computing the acceptable shortages per replenishment cycle as a way to determine if you can delay the full order.

Items never sell smoothly and exactly on their forecast rates, so you need to run this calculation every day to on all lines where the order schedule is in your control to decide which product lines you need to order today.

Lines Ordered Infrequently

Computing a suggested order and the possible delay is a great way to determine when it is time to order lines that are ordered infrequently. When you compute a suggested order, you should see three things:

1. Whether you can delay a full replenishment order, or need to place an order now to meet your service level goal for the entire line.
2. How large a suggested full replenishment order would be based on each item's regular reorder status (and how close that is to vendor minimums or other size requirements).
3. Items that should be considered for an expedited fill in order.

Based on those three things, you can decide whether to place a fill in order, a full replenishment order, or no order for this line today.

Our system computed every line every day. Ideally, a system should show a full, suggested order for every line that is due today on a fixed schedule and every line where you need an order for service level. It should also show suggested fill in order items on all other lines.

That's the last hurdle. Now, finally, we can discuss how to compute and work with a suggested replenishment order for groups of items or for a product line.

Orders for Groups of Items or Product Lines with No Order Size Requirements

Consider product lines where you order all the items in a group or product line, where you can place an order whenever you want, and

---

[29] Pg. 440. Edward Silver, David Pyke, Rein Peterson, Inventory Management And Production Planning and Scheduling, Third Edition, 1998, John Wiley and Sons.

where there is no total order size requirement. The formulas for this are different than the one for ordering individual items, because you will not be able to place an order for each item exactly on the day it is needed.

Even though you can place an order any time you want, the Order Frequency computation shows the best ordering interval for a group of items or a product line. You should place orders for the full line, including all items that need to be ordered, at about that frequency. This interval is called the Review Time for the product line.

If you intend to place an order today, but do not order a specific item, then the next time that item can be reordered is one Review Time from now. The quantity ordered on that order would not be available until one Lead Time after that. That, plus the Safety Stock requirement, sets the time span that must be covered for each item. In this case, the formula computes a quantity to be ordered. The Suggested Order Quantity is:

SuggestedOrderQuantity = UsageOverNeededTime—Balance
> Where:
> Usage is in units, derived from the item forecast, as shown above.
> Needed Time is the larger of:
>> *ReviewTime + LeadTime + SafetyStockInDays,* or
>> *EconomicOrderQuantityInDays + LeadTime + SafetyStockInDays,* and
> *Balance = OnHandQuantity + OnOrderQuantity—QuantityOwedOnBackorders*
> (Only count the On Order quantity if these goods are expected to arrive during the needed time span).

For fast moving items with EOQs less than the review time, this system acts like an Order-Up-To-Level system, and is likely to order these items up to the proper level on every order. For items with EOQs longer than the review time, this system acts like an Order Point system, and orders approximately an EOQ quantity. These items may not be on every order. Silver[30] confirms this system is likely to have the lowest total costs of replenishment.

The order quantity of each item might have to be increased to an item minimum, or rounded to a multiple of the case lot quantity. See more on this below.

---

[30] Pg. 241. Edward Silver, David Pyke, Rein Peterson, Inventory Management And Production Planning and Scheduling, Third Edition, 1998, John Wiley and Sons.

The next order might be placed a few days earlier or later than one Review Time from now, based on the service level requirements, but the overall Review Time should be used to compute item level quantities.

You decide when to place a full replenishment order based on the delay technique to maintain the overall service level for the group. The delay computation shows whether you need to order the line today to maintain the overall service level.

Since there are no order size requirements, you can place an order whenever it is needed to maintain the service level. Place an order as soon as the delay computation shows you should not wait longer. There is no need to consider expedited special orders in this situation, since there is no required size for the group order.

Here again, if you have faith in all the detailed forecasts, you shouldn't have to make many changes to the suggested order.

Group or Product Line orders with Required Order Dates or Intervals

The next level of complexity is on product lines where you must order on specific dates or at fixed intervals. Usually, the vendor requires these dates, but the vendor will permit any size order on the scheduled date. In these cases, order dates are fixed by a schedule. This requires two changes to the math used just above.

The first change is in the delay computation. If you do not order today, you must wait until the next permitted date. You cannot delay the order for a few days. You can skip the order completely if the delay computation shows you can wait a full interval to the next order and still not fall below the overall service level for the product line. That is rare in a well-managed inventory.

The second change is to consider expedited fill in orders for key needed items if the vendor will permit them. Even if these have a penalty in freight or discount, that might cost less than the lost sales if you have to wait until the next scheduled date to order critical items. See more on Fill-in Orders in a section later in this chapter.

The proper item formula is the same as the suggested order quantity for groups with no restrictions, except that the Review Time is fixed by the arrangement with the vendor.

Groups of Items or Product Lines with Required Order Sizes

The most complex orders are those where you want to or have to place an order for a specific size, in dollars, weight, or cube. In some cases the vendor requires this (for example, if you have to exactly fill a trailer load or container). In other cases, this is at the distributor's discretion, but the Order Frequency analysis shows that a specific size order is more profitable. This might be based on the overall carrying and handling costs, or on extra discounts or savings that can be achieved at specific order sizes.

So, in these situations, you need to place orders of a required size, but you can place an order whenever you want, and the interval between orders can vary somewhat.

Here again, use the Delay technique to determine whether an order is required today to meet the service level targets for the entire line. If an order is not required, then the buyer might consider whether an expedited fill in order is needed.

It is not unusual that when the delay computation shows that a full order is needed for service the suggested order is not quite the required size.

The buyer must then decide on a course of action:

1. If the suggested order is reasonably close to the required size, the best course of action is to recompute all items and place an order for the required size. This is discussed below.
2. If the suggested order is much smaller than the required size, then the best course of action is to place an expedited fill in order for the critical items.

How to Meet an Exact Order Size

First, take the case where the suggested order is smaller than the required size. The proper way to increase the order is to add additional days to the Suggested Order Quantity formula, recompute every item's need, and get a total for the entire line. Add one day at a time to the time supply for every item in the line until the order reaches the required size.

This will increase the quantity of items already on the suggested order. It could also add other items as the order quantities required to cover the added time exceed their available balance.

This is proper. If you have to add several days supply to the suggested order quantity formula to make an order meet the size requirement today, then it follows that you are pushing the next order beyond one normal review time from now. If that is the result, then you need to order every item in sufficient quantity to cover that extra time.

In rare cases, the suggested order might be larger than the required size. This is unlikely if you compute a suggested order for the line every day. You would have to have a very large single day of business if an order was not needed at all yesterday, but today the suggested order is larger than the required size. If this does happen, then the proper thing to do is to scale the order down by removing one day at a time from the time span and recomputing the order for all the items in the line. This will reduce the quantity to be ordered on most items, and it might remove some items from the order. That is proper, too. Your next order will probably be needed a few days ahead of the normal review time.

In both of these cases the goal is to place the best balanced order today so that your next order will also make sense.

Before we could easily recompute an order with added or subtracted days supply on all items, we balanced an order by adding or subtracting just the most popular items. That always made this order fit the requirement, but it also increased the imbalance in our inventory for the next order. It was not the best way to go.

Computing Integer Values for Slow Movers

Converting the time span to units is likely to give fractional values on slow moving items. An ideal system would not simply round this value to an integer. It should go back through the safety stock and service level goal math, to establish the optimum integer value for the suggested order quantity. Ideally, the math used in the Service Level Goal chapter for slow moving parts should be incorporated into the review program, so that the most profitable suggested order quantity is selected.

This is important in our auto parts inventory, with tens of thousands of slow moving items. Letting the system round many of those items up even by one unit would add a substantial amount of inventory, probably for a very small gain in gross margin dollars from better service levels.

Special and Fill-in Orders

Some critical items might run out of stock before the next order is placed, processed and received. While these items might not be individually large enough to bring an entire product line's service level below its goal, they could be items that are much needed. These items should be brought to a buyer's attention every day. If there is no required order size, the buyer can order whatever items are needed. If there is a required size, then the buyer has to decide whether to place an expedited fill in order for just a few items, or order the entire line, even if it is a few days early. The economics of the cost of lost sales apply here, too. You can compute the expected arrival date of an expedited order placed today versus the expected arrival date of the next shipment, if it is ordered when it comes due. You can also compute the cost of lost sales that would be saved by early delivery of these expedited items versus waiting for a stock order. If that savings exceeds the cost of ordering and paying expedited freight charges for a fill-in order, then the fill in order should be placed.

You have to be careful with this, however. If you take it too far, you will place a lot of expedited fill in orders as different items get close to running out of stock, and never accumulate enough for a regular, full line replenishment order. In general, if the most popular items are about to run out and it would take a pretty large fill in order, it is probably wiser to go ahead and order the full line. If some of the middle items or some critical slow movers are the items about to run out of stock, then it might make sense to do a fill in order on just those items.

Delaying an order might also disrupt the schedule in the receiving department. That might cost more than the savings in inventory carrying cost by delaying the order for a day or two. That is another possible variable cost that should be used in determining the best overall frequency of orders for the product line.

Booking, Blanket, or Long Lead Time Orders

Some vendors offer incentives or require long lead-time orders for a variety of reasons. Several auto parts vendors of seasonal lines like air conditioning parts and batteries required "pre-season" orders well before the season. They used these pre-season commitments to help schedule production, and the orders were not shipped until just before the start of the season.

The regular formulas can be used to compute these orders, with the necessary longer lead-time. If you have to add a lot of time, it will test the accuracy of your item forecasts. That makes it even more important that you have seasonal and other unusual items correctly identified and forecast.

The quantity on order should not be included in the available balance for subsequent regular replenishment orders. The booked order may not be received during the next few regular order cycles, and must not be included in the available Balance when computing those regular orders. The booking order quantity should only be included in the balance when those goods are scheduled to arrive during the next order time span.

Here is an example. We had to place a pre-season order of air conditioning parts in January, for delivery at the end of April. This one order was based on a demand forecast from the date of the order until about the middle of June. We still had to place regular replenishment orders in February through May. We had to ignore the pre-season quantity on order when we computed those regular replenishment orders. We only added the pre-season quantity to the available balance when its expected arrival fell within the next replenishment cycle. That was the first time we could include those items in our available balance, since they would be received during the upcoming order cycle.

This same condition applies to some imported goods. A distributor might have the option of ordering large quantities for direct import, with very long lead time and low cost. They might also have the option of filling in with short lead-time and higher cost from a U.S. vendor inventory. If the distributor does some of both, then the long lead-time order quantities cannot be considered when placing short lead-time fill in orders.

It applies to items when you have a vendor who sells at different prices with different quantity and lead time requirements. For example, one of our suppliers offered a significant discount for a large order, and a smaller discount for small "fill-in" orders. The fill-in orders arrived quickly from a regional distribution center, and the big orders took more time to come from the factory. We needed to exclude the on-order quantity from the large order when computing fill-in orders that would arrive ahead of the large one.

This might also apply to blanket order situations, where a distributor has to commit to a total quantity over a long time period, and then issues "releases" against the blanket order. If the distributor can modify items and quantities on each release, then the blanket order quantity should not count, and the regular formula can be used for each release order. If the distributor cannot modify the items or quantities, then each fixed release quantity should be entered into the on order value one lead time in front of the anticipated delivery. In either case, the distributor has to keep score to make sure the blanket requirements are satisfied.

Rounding Item Quantities to Cases or Pallets

Vendors may require that some items be ordered in a minimum quantity, or in exact case, pallet layer, or pallet quantities. If required, these should be part of the item data, and every suggested order quantity should be rounded up to the next required size.

Where the distributor has the option to order any quantity, the item level Economic Order Quantity math can evaluate savings in handling or purchase cost from ordering items in the vendor's case lots, pallet quantities, or other measurements.

However, as you can see, the Suggested Order Quantity formula for product lines does not use the EOQ, but computes a specific quantity to be ordered, and it probably will not be exactly the EOQ amount.

An ideal system would incorporate the math from the EOQ formula, along with the variable costs and potential savings based on the type of order, and decide whether to round the quantity to a buying increment. This should weigh the added carrying cost of ordering that extra quantity early against the savings in handling or purchase cost from ordering in a full case or pallet lot. It is important to carefully establish the true variable costs in these situations.

An ideal system could also understand all overpack quantities—for cases and pallets of a single item for example. Each quantity should have a flag to show whether it is required or optional, and data to show the item level costs and savings if the item is ordered in that quantity.

In our auto parts business, we did not have this full software, and generally rounded up items where the exact quantity needed was more than about half of a case lot, even if the only savings was in handling a case versus individual items. We called this "convenience rounding".

Once the order quantity was more than the first standard pack size, we always rounded up to an exact number of packs. If you need 40 of an item, and cases are 24, you almost always should order 48 rather than handle partial cases.

Logistics

There can be further advantages to arranging shipments through an internal or third party system. Schneider Logistics is an example of a third party company. They work with a distribution center to map and compute the typical inbound shipments from key vendors. Most auto parts vendors will give the distributor an allowance for freight costs if the distributor will pick up the shipment. Schneider has software to help schedule trucks to aggregate multiple shipments into full truckloads. The freight savings can be significant for the distributor. This can also reduce lead-time variability, by imposing a schedule on both the distributor and vendor. It does require that the distributor use the technique for replenishing vendors on a fixed cycle. Overall, this can be a plus.

What the Buyer Should Review

It is recommended that the buyer see everything where a decision is required, but with only the minimum of detail needed to make the decision. The best systems will show just the necessary information, and let the buyer drill deeper if necessary for more details.

In our auto parts company, one buyer could handle all the purchasing for one distribution center. We stocked about 100,000 items, and ordered most lines once a week. There are 144,000 seconds in a 40-hour workweek, so there is not a lot of time for a buyer to study each item. Here are some tips based on our experience:

Show a summary report first, with all the lines that are on today's required schedule, all the lines where an order is suggested to meet service requirements, any suggested fill in orders, and any items ordered individually that have hit their order point.

The summary should show the total size of the suggested order, the number of items, the order requirements for interval or size, and the budget or normal order amount.

If the buyer has properly worked their schedule and budget, the first job is to look at whether each suggested order is reasonable. Suppose a buyer orders a line every week, and expects the average order to be $10,000. If the buyer knows that today is the right day, and the suggested order is $9,400, then it is likely that few items will need modification. If the suggested order is not close to the expected size, then the buyer should review that order in detail.

Again, this is where all that preparation should pay off. If every item demand forecast, lead-time forecast, and safety stock goal has been maintained, and if all the details of costs and deals have been analyzed to determine order frequencies, then the suggested orders should be completely acceptable.

If the buyer makes a change to an item in a suggested order, it means the buyer has some new information or has changed a decision rule about how to purchase that item.

Every time a buyer changes an item on a suggested order, they should also change the underlying data. If they do not, they won't agree with the next suggested order for that item, either.

In our auto parts company, our buyers spent more than 75% of their time on all the preliminary steps—maintaining forecasts, analyzing deals to determine order frequency, setting the schedule and budget, and performing other data base maintenance functions. Less than 25% of their time was spent reviewing suggested orders. Many orders with reasonable totals were issued with no item level changes. It was not unusual for a buyer to make no changes on an entire day's suggested orders.

Chapter Summary

This chapter presents several slightly different formulas for replenishment orders, depending on the requirements for order sizes or schedules.

If the buyer must order on a schedule or frequency established by the vendor, then the replenishment order must be sufficient to cover expected demand until the next replenishment order can be received.

If the buyer can order at any time, then the buyer can wait until an order is needed by forecasting the expected lost sales versus the service goal for the entire line. If this disrupts the routine in the receiving department, those additional costs must be included.

If the buyer must hit a defined order size (such as a full truckload), a suggested order based only on item level values can be scaled up or down by adding or subtracting additional day's supply from every item's stock lelve in the line, and recomputing the total order. This should be done one day at a time to home in on the exact required size.

If all of the underlying data has been carefully maintained, then the suggested replenishment orders are likely to be very accurate, and require very few item level changes.

A proper replenishment order this time will keep the entire product line in balance for the next order as well.

Chapter 21. Forward Buying

Forward buying refers to the opportunity to make extra profit when a vendor offers temporary special terms, or when a cost increase is about to become effective. In these situations the wholesaler can take advantage of the situation by buying more than the usual amount. The financial gain can be measured against the incremental costs of temporarily carrying more inventory. This can be a significant source of incremental profit for wholesalers.

First, this needs some definition. ALL of these conditions must be true for a purchase to qualify as a Forward Buy:

- This must be an offer not likely to be repeated soon (if the incentives are repeated regularly, use the "Order Frequency" math to decide whether to take advantage of them all the time).
- For special deals, discounts or dating from vendors, the wholesaler does not pass the special terms on to customers. If the terms are passed on to customers, this is a Promotion, not a Forward Buy.
- For cost increases, the wholesaler will implement a matching selling price increase concurrently with the cost increase, so that the amount of the price increase is captured as additional margin on goods ordered just before the increase goes into effect. (If the wholesaler does not raise selling prices promptly, it is another form of Promotion).
- Cash and warehouse space are available to handle extra inventory, and the cost of those will be included in the calculations.
- The wholesaler has the flexibility to decide how much to buy now, and this will not impact future availability.

Types of Vendor Offers

Here are some types of Forward Buying opportunities.

- **Cost Increases:** Placing an order just before a cost increase can be viewed as getting a corresponding discount off the new cost. A 4% price increase gives the opportunity to buy goods for 1.000 that will cost 1.040 just after the increase. 4% is equivalent to .04/1.04 or a 3.85% discount off the new cost.

- **Extra Discount:** When a vendor offers an extra discount for a limited time.

- **Free Goods:** If the vendor offers free goods, that can be converted into an equivalent discount. For example, a "baker's dozen" is one free with twelve. You get 13 units for the price of 12. The equivalent discount is 1/13, or 7.69%.

- **Deferred Payment Terms:** Some vendors occasionally offer deferred or extended payment terms on single orders. It is tempting, but not accurate, to just view the interest savings as a discount on the order. The value of the terms depends on the distributor's situation and the size of the order.

- **Combinations of Deals:** Sometimes a vendor offers several elements at one time—such as an extra discount combined with extended terms. These combinations can be very valuable Forward Buying opportunities.

An Example of a Cost Increase Opportunity

Here is one example item with a pending cost increase. The item costs $10, and the wholesaler has steady demand for 2,600 units per year. A receipt of the item in a reasonable quantity incurs $2 in variable handling cost. This uses a high inventory carrying cost of 40% per year to bias against holding extra inventory.

The vendor has announced a price increase of 4%, effective tomorrow. The wholesaler has one last opportunity to buy at $10.00. This is effectively the same as a one time 3.85% discount off the new cost of $10.40. The wholesaler plans to raise selling price immediately, so any gain on this order will be captured as profit for the wholesaler.

The wholesaler can buy this item at any time, and normally buys this item according to the EOQ formula. Here is the regular EOQ formula for this item with the new $10.40 purchase cost.

$$EOQUnits = \sqrt{\frac{2 * AnnualUsageInUnits * OrderCostInDollars}{AnnualCarryingCostPerUnit}}$$

$$EOQUnits = \sqrt{\frac{2 * 2600 * 2}{10.40 * .40}} = 50 Units = 7 DaysSupply$$

So, the normal procedure would be to place an order every 7 days for 50 units.

Assume the item is at its order point, so the wholesaler is ready to place a regular order for 50 units. The wholesaler has the flexibility to order any number of units at the $10.00 cost today. The wholesaler will raise its selling price tomorrow, too, so the savings of $.40 per unit on items purchased today will be captured as additional margin when they are sold.

Here is a table showing costs and savings for various order quantities.

Units On Price Increase Order	Days Covered by This Order	Handling Cost		Carrying Cost		Savings on This Quantity	Annual Total Cost Minus Savings	Extra Profit vs. EOQ Order
		This Order	Rest of Year	This Order	Rest of Year			
Normal	7	-	104.00		104.00	-	208.00	-
50	7	2.00	102.00	1.92	102.00	20.00	187.92	20.08
100	14	2.00	100.00	7.69	100.00	40.00	169.69	38.31
200	28	2.00	96.00	30.77	96.00	80.00	144.77	63.23
300	42	2.00	92.00	69.23	92.00	120.00	135.23	72.77
312	**43.68**	**2.00**	**91.52**	**74.88**	**91.52**	**124.80**	**135.12**	**72.88**
350	49	2.00	90.00	94.23	90.00	140.00	136.23	71.77
400	56	2.00	88.00	123.08	88.00	160.00	141.08	66.92
500	70	2.00	84.00	192.31	84.00	200.00	162.31	45.69
600	84	2.00	80.00	276.92	80.00	240.00	198.92	9.08

Ch 21 Fig 1. Forward Buying Table of Costs and Savings for Price Increase

The Normal row shows the regular costs for a year, with the new $10.40 cost. There are normally 52 orders per year, at $2 each, so annual handling cost is $104.00. The average cycle inventory is 25 units (1/2 the regular order for 50). The annual carrying cost is 25 units times $10.40 cost each times 40% carrying cost, or $104.00. The total handling and carrying cost is $208.00 per year.

If the wholesaler places only a regular order for 50 units today, there will still be a $20.00 gain by getting the $.40 savings from new cost on these 50 units. There is also a tiny gain on carrying cost, as these 50 units cost .40 less than the new ongoing price.

Now consider what happens if the wholesaler orders 100 units, or 2 weeks supply. The wholesaler will incur $2.00 handling cost for the order of 100. For the remainder of the year, 50 more orders will be required, for $100. By ordering 100 units on one order, the wholesaler skips one future order and saves one $2 order handling cost.

The carrying cost of the 100 units is computed as the average inventory (1/2 the quantity purchased) times the unit cost times the carrying rate times the duration of the quantity purchased on the special.

$$CarryCostDuringDeal_{100UnitBuy} = 50Units * \$10 * .40Rate * \frac{14}{364}Days = \$7.69$$

Note that this cost increases rapidly as the size of the purchase increases. There is both a larger average cycle inventory and the quantity lasts longer.

The carrying cost for the rest of the year is the regular cost times the fraction of the year not covered by this order quantity.

The savings are $.40 per unit on all units ordered today.

The optimum purchase is 312 units. This is just over six weeks supply, or five weeks of extra inventory. This produces an incremental gain of $72.88 versus the baseline, and a gain of more than $50 versus placing a normal size order in front of the price increase. The wholesaler captures about $125 by saving the $.40 on 312 units, but spends about $50 in additional carrying cost to carry this extra inventory over the six week span.

Here is a graph of the incremental profit from various quantities ordered:

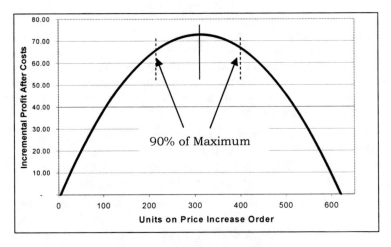

**Ch 21 Fig 2. Graph of Forward Buying Profit for
Price Increase Example**

This shows the amount of profit is fairly flat around the optimum quantity of 312 units. At least 90% of the optimum can be obtained with any purchase from 215 to 410 units.

In our auto parts business, there were a few years that had zero or negative cost changes, but most years had annual cost increases of 3-4%. There were a few years in the early '80's with more than 10%

inflation. We were able to use these Forward Buying techniques for almost every price increase. They boosted our pretax income by about $100,000 per year in years that had about 4% overall increases.

Formula for Extra Discounts and Cost Increases

Software is available from JDA that includes formulas to directly compute the optimum quantity to order.

Deferred or Extended Payment Terms

The value of deferred or extended payment terms depends on what you do with the funds saved, and the duration depends on this order size versus regular orders and payment terms.

Please review the section on the Value of Deferred Terms in Chapter 17 on Order Frequency.

Here is the same sample item. Rather than a price increase, assume you have a one-time opportunity to place an order with 30 days additional terms. The parameters for this example are:

Item Cost	$10.00 Each	Interest Rate	8% Per Year
Annual Usage	2,600 Units	Normal Order	50 Units
Carrying Cost		Normal Order	
Rate	40% Per Year	Cycle	7 Days

For this example, assume that the distributor normally borrows working capital at 8%, and that the saving from deferred terms is the interest saved on the deferred amount for the term of the savings, compared to the normal payment terms on the regular weekly orders.

Here is a table of the interest saved on various order quantities:

Order Quantity	Quantity with Deferred Terms	Days of Interest Saved	Interest Saved on That Quantity	Total Interest Saved
50	First 50	30	3.30	3.30
100	Second 50	23	2.53	5.82
150	Third 50	16	1.76	7.58
200	Fourth 50	9	0.99	8.57

Ch 21 Fig 3. Interest Saved On Sample Item with 30 Days Deferred Payment

The interest saved on the first 50 units is for the full 30 days of deferred payment. This is $10 x 50 units x .08 rate x 30/364 duration = $3.30.

Note the amount saved on the first 50 units is based on 30 days deferred. The amount saved on the next 50 units is based on 23 days deferred. These units would normally be ordered one week from now.

If the order quantity were greater than the quantity used over the span of the deferred terms, there would be an interest cost penalty, as some of the amount for the total order would be paid sooner than normal.

If the distributor is not borrowing funds, but investing surplus cash, then the "alternate investment rate" (the return obtained on the surplus cash) should be used to compute the savings.

If the distributor is not borrowing funds, and is not investing surplus cash, then there is no value to the deferred terms.

A table of the handling costs, carrying costs, and interest savings can be computed for various order quantities.

Units On Dating Order	Days Covered by Dating Order	Handling Cost		Carrying Cost		Savings on Dating Quantity	Annual Total Cost Minus Savings	Extra Profit vs. EOQ Order
		Dating Order	Rest of Year	Dating Order	Rest of Year			
Normal	7	-	104.00		100.00	-	204.00	-
50	7	2.00	102.00	1.54	98.08	3.30	200.32	3.68
100	14	2.00	100.00	6.15	96.15	5.82	198.48	5.52
150	21	2.00	98.00	13.85	94.23	7.58	200.49	3.51
181	25.34	2.00	96.76	20.16	93.04	7.98	203.98	0.02
200	28	2.00	96.00	24.62	92.31	8.57	206.35	(2.35)

Ch 21 Fig 4. Forward Buying Costs and Savings with Deferred Terms

The optimum profit order is 100 units, or one extra week's supply. The incremental profit is $5.52 versus the normal EOQ ordering. For this chart, the carrying cost of the quantity ordered on deferred terms is the regular inventory carrying cost rate (40%) minus the interest rate (8%), to show that these units do not have a financial carrying cost.

Compare this incremental $5 profit for 30 days deferred terms to the $72 profit opportunity from the 4% price increase example in Figure 1.

Most distributors feel extended terms are worth a lot, but in fact, they are not worth as much as reasonable size additional discounts or price increase buying opportunities. Don't turn them down, but don't overdo the orders to go with the extra terms, either.

This charts the incremental profit from the 30 day extra terms opportunity.

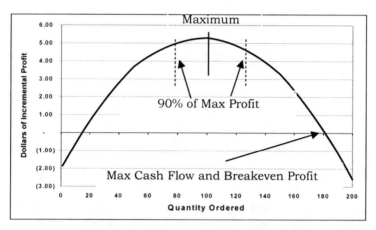

Ch 21 Fig 5. Chart of Forward Buying Profit For Deferred Payment Example

This shows that the optimum order for incremental profit is 100 units, or one extra week's supply.

It also shows that a distributor who needs cash could place an order for 181 units, or about 3-1/2 weeks supply, and not lose profit versus normal ordering.

JDA's software includes formulas to compute the optimum Forward Buy in situations where the vendor offers extended terms.

Promotions and Forward Buying Opportunities

Promotions are a special case where the distributor might be able to order enough for the promotion sales, and also order an additional quantity as a forward buy just as the promotion ends. It is necessary to forecast demand during the promotion. A promotion might accelerate some future demand, so it is also necessary to forecast demand after the promotion until sales return to normal.

Pete Kornafel

Here is another example of a single item:

Annual Demand	1,200 Units	Carrying Cost	25% / year
Regular Cost	$15.00	Normal EOQ Units	100 Units
Regular Sell Price	$20.00	Normal Order Frequency	Monthly
Handling Cost	$15.00	Pretax Income per unit	10% of sell

This item will have a two-month promotion with a 4% discount. The distributor will pass this through for two-months. Here is a forecast for the next five months:

	Months				
	1	2	3	4	5
Unit Forecast - During and After Promotion	150	150	75	100	100

Ch 21 Fig 6. Promotion Item Example Forecast

Suppose that the optimum forward buy is 90 days. If the distributor can only place one order, the most logical order is for a 90-day supply. Including the promotion forecast, this would be for 375 units. The 90 days would cover the two months of the promotion, and one extra month's supply as a Forward Buy. The distributor will keep the 4% savings on units purchased in excess of that as a Forward Buy savings.

If the distributor can place multiple orders during the promotion and one just as the promotion ends, then the distributor could order 300 units during the promotion on one or more orders, and place a full 90 day Forward Buy of 275 units just at the end of the promotion.

Here is a table of the costs and profits for these two strategies:

Units On Deal Order	Units on Each Order	Days Covered by Each Order	Handling Cost Deal Order	Handling Cost Rest of Year	Carrying Cost Deal Order	Carrying Cost Rest of Year	Profit On Extra Promotion Units	Savings on Deal Quantity	Annual Total Cost Minus Savings	Extra Profit vs. EOQ Order
Normal 100	100	30	-	180.00		187.50		-	367.50	-
One Order	375	90	15.00	166.50	173.85	141.14	192.00	45.00	259.49	108.01
Two Orders										
Promotion Order	300	60	15.00		92.72		192.00			
Forward Buy	275	90	15.00		127.49			165.00		
Rest of Year		214		105.82		110.23				
Total for Two Orders		364	30.00	105.82	220.21	110.23	192.00	165.00	109.27	258.23

Ch 21 Fig 7. Forward Buying Costs and Profits for Promotion Item Example

The first line shows the normal costs for this item, with one order each month. The distributor will sell 300 units through to customers with a 4% lower cost and 4% lower selling price during the two months of the promotion.

The second line shows the costs and profits for one order of 375 units. The handling and carrying costs are computed based on the item's 4% deal discount, and the forecast that the 375 units will cover three month's supply. The extra promotion profit is based on a pretax income of 10% of the item's selling price, $19.20 on promotion, and the 100 incremental units sold during the promotion. The savings on the deal quantity is based on the $.60 per unit (4% of $15 cost) saved on the 75 units in the forward buy. The net of all this is an incremental profit of $108 versus no promotion at all.

The third block shows what will happen if the distributor can place two orders. The first order is 300 units, to be sold in the two months of the promotion. The distributor will make the same extra profit on the 100 incremental units sold during the promotion. The next row shows the 275 units, 3 month, Forward Buy. The net here is $258 better than no promotion at all.

The ability to place more than one order is also much safer. The distributor can examine the actual on hand quantity near the end of the promotion, and revise the forecast for the next few periods if necessary. The result will be a much more accurate Forward Buy.

Our auto parts experience was that it was very difficult to forecast the promotion and its after effect accurately, so we were very reluctant to place an order for both the promotion and forward buying quantities. We were much more comfortable when we could place more than one order on the promotional terms.

Real World Considerations

All of the above techniques give the amount to buy for the maximum incremental profit under ideal conditions. Before this is done, the distributor must evaluate their own situation. It should be noted that every condition that is not "ideal" would cause the distributor to buy LESS than the optimum quantity.

- **Pass On Impact:** The examples assume the distributor will not pass any of the extra discounts or terms on to their customers. If the distributor does pass the savings on to their customers, or delays implementation of a selling price increase when cost increases, these are promotions, not forward buys. An exception is one Forward Buy order at the end of the promotion where the terms will not be passed on.

- **Time of Next Deal:** Very large discounts or special terms could cause a distributor to want to order a lot of additional inventory, of as much as six month's supply or more under some conditions. The distributor must judge when the next deal will be available, and should not buy more than the quantity needed to get to that time.

In our auto parts business, a good example was the product line of sealed beam headlamps and automotive light bulbs. If you've ever seen a light bulb factory, you know that they must run the furnaces and the production lines 24 hours a day, 365 days a year. They just can't turn off the furnace for a while—all that molten glass would solidify. The finished goods inventory takes up a huge amount of space. So, light bulb vendors will do almost anything to sell their full production quickly, at almost any price. We never paid the regular price for a sealed beam headlamp in our 25+ years as an automotive distributor. One vendor or another was always running some special deal, and our regular vendor would almost always match it.

The discounts could be huge, and we could order up to six month's supply of bulbs in some cases. We never bought more than about a sixty-day supply, as we knew there would be another deal whenever we needed it.

- **Forecast Accuracy:** It is important to have a lot of confidence in item forecasts over the full duration of the special order to take full advantage of Forward Buying. If there is uncertainty about the accuracy of the forecasts, the distributor should buy less than the optimum amount.

Another difficult situation can be with new items. Vendors often offer special terms as an incentive for the distributors to stock up on new items. However, these are generally the most unreliable forecasts, so a distributor must be cautious, and buy less than the optimum.

- **Product Line Balance:** If the Forward Buying opportunity is only on a few items within a full product line, it is important to consider what a forward buy of these items will do to the overall balance of the inventory. Any strategy erodes the Forward Buying profit.

- o   If you place a full forward buy on just the key items, you might have to delay the next regular replenishment order. You might not be able to make the vendor's minimum or prepaid freight for some time. This could cause stock outs and lost sales on the other items in the line.
- o   If you buy extra quantities on the other items in the line, too, to avoid stock outs on those items, it means you will have additional carrying costs on the rest of the line, where there are no special deals or terms.
- o   In either case, you should buy less than the optimum. We used 60-90% of the optimum amounts as a conservative way to take advantage of each deal that was offered.

- **Handling Costs:** The examples assume the handling cost for the forward buy order is the same as for a regular order. That might not be true in the real world, especially for large forward buys. It may take additional handling cost to store and move the extra goods several times, if the quantity ordered will not fit in the regular stock location. These extra handling costs will erode the forward buying profit, and you should buy less than the optimum.

Other Formulas

Silver[31] presents a formula for computing Forward Buy quantities.

Buy Some of Each Deal

Look again at the graphs in Figure 2 and Figure 5. Each graph is pretty flat around the optimum quantity. In these cases, buying two thirds of the optimum amount will still yield 85-90% of the maximum incremental profit. This is true for most forward buying situations.

In our auto parts business, we typically purchased about 2/3 of the optimum quantity for each Forward Buying opportunity.

It is a much better strategy to buy a little bit of every Forward Buying deal than to buy heavily on some deals and skip others completely.

---

[31] Pg. 177. Edward Silver, David Pyke, Rein Peterson, Inventory Management And Production Planning and Scheduling, Third Edition, 1998, John Wiley and Sons.

Distress Inventory Purchases

It's not exactly a "Forward Buy", but there were always some large batches of auto parts inventory from companies going out of business, from vendor overstocks, and from changeovers (some vendors "lifted" the competitive inventory on new accounts and then tried to sell it as a batch at a marked down price).

The prices on these depended on the "quality" of the batch. This usually meant the mix of popular items in the inventory.

Our company never purchased these distressed batches of inventory.

First, we knew that these inventories were on the market because they were someone else's overstock. All we would do is make someone else's problem our own.

Second, this would erode our position when we negotiated stock adjustment returns with our vendors. Because we did not buy distress inventory, we could assure our vendors we weren't trying to dump someone else's problem back on them, or make a profit on the return.

Third, the mix of popular items was very seldom good enough to even consider making an offer on the batch.

Some of our competitors made a business of buying some of this merchandise, because it was attractively priced. They felt they could get their vendors to handle the additional overstock returns, so there was little obsolescence risk to them.

Our best vendors actively purchased any batches of their own brands, just to get them off the market. They knew that if a distributor bought it, they were likely to be asked to handle a stock adjustment return anyway. At least by buying it themselves they were in control of their product and the price they offered.

Chapter Summary

Cost increases, special offers from vendors which are not passed on to customers, and orders at the end of vendor promotions offer the opportunity to increase profits by buying more than the regular amount at the lower cost.

These savings are offset by higher carrying costs for the extra inventory.

A number of examples are presented to show the optimum forward buy for a variety of situations.

Real world considerations such as imprecise forecasts can also reduce the potential increased profits.

Good Forward Buying can significantly improve profits for a distributor.

Software that incorporates these Forward Buying techniques and handles a number of more complex situations is available from JDA.

Pete Kornafel

Chapter 22. Alternate and Superseded Items

All distributors have some overlapping product coverage and products that are superseded to newer items. These are complicated to handle. The customer service system should help the customer choose between alternate items, and help sell out superseded items. Here are some techniques to deal with these kinds of items:

Alternate or "Can Use" items

Overlapping product coverage falls into three types:

1. **Equal items:** If a distributor carries full coverage from several vendors, there are likely to be some nearly identical items in more than one product line. For example, in our auto parts inventory thermostat gaskets were supplied by our vendor of thermostats, and also by our vendor of gaskets. We carried the full line from both vendors, so we had a series of items that were nearly equal and readily interchangeable. Each item had an alternate that fit the same applications, functioned the same way, was the same quality, and almost the same cost. We intended to maintain both product lines, and carried the duplicated items. We were indifferent which one the customer ordered. We maintained an interchange file of these items. Any time we were out of one item, we would suggest that the customer buy the other comparable item. It saved the sale and satisfied the customer. These were "Can use" items. Our order entry systems would give the customer a message that said: "You ordered CTH60415, and we are out of that item, but you CAN USE GSK30251 and we have it in stock". It is important to note that this file needs to have records in both directions as long as the interchange works both ways. In the example case, you can use the GSK item in place of the CTH item, and vice versa. There are some cases where the interchange may only work in one direction. We maintained data with the alternate item and a code that it was fully interchangeable with the original one.

2. **Not quite equal items**: In many lines we carried items with different quality grades and price points. For example, we carried both remanufactured and new brake master cylinders, and good, better, and best grades of disc brake pads. In these cases, we always wanted to give the customer full information so they could choose the best item for that vehicle. We referred to these as "Can use—But..." items. In these cases, our order entry

system would give the customer a message like this: "You ordered BPR1251. You can use BRK71628, but it is a new master cylinder. We have both in stock." Or, "You ordered CFI85515. You can use CFI85515MP, but it is a master pack of 12 for a quantity savings. We have both in stock". Or, "You ordered ECSG421. We are out of stock. You can use ECSG17, but it is a universal fit part. We have it in stock." We would present the prices for both items, and let the customer make his choice. Our data included the alternate and the comment. Here again, you have to determine if the interchange goes both ways, or only in one direction. In the case of the EC items, the universal part could be used to replace several exact fit items. So if a customer ordered one of the exact fit items, he could use the universal one. If he ordered the universal item, we were not sure which one of the exact fit items to suggest, and did not show any of them as alternates for it.

3. **Items we wanted to push**: In some cases, we favored one item over another. An item might have better value for the customer, or be more suitable for a specific application, or have better margins for us. In these cases, we wanted to push customers toward the item we preferred. The message to the customer was: "You ordered FRIBD52. We have it in stock. You SHOULD USE FRIBMD52, because that vehicle requires semi-metallic brake pads". Or, "You ordered CRC2150. We have it in stock. You SHOULD USE CCM1150, because it is comparable and costs less". These were one-way interchanges. We did not show the less preferred item as an alternate to the preferred item.

In all these cases, we let the customer decide which items they want to order. If we had both items in stock, we posted the demand to the item that was ordered and shipped. If we were out of the original item, we posted the demand to the item ordered, even if the customer accepted and we shipped a substitute item. We wanted our inventory system to support what the customers wanted to buy from us.

Superseded Items

Vendors frequently announce new items that replace existing ones. In the simplest case, the vendor starts shipping the new item under an existing part number. In this case, all you have to do is rotate inventories to sell out the older product, and coordinate the timing of a price change if it goes with the replacement.

In more complex cases, the vendor discontinues an existing item and announces a new item to replace it. These supersessions fall into two types: "Recalls" are supersessions where the vendor will accept returns of the old item. "Sell out and reorder" are supersessions where the vendor expects the distributor to sell out the old item.

1. **Recalls:** There are a variety of situations where the vendor wants the entire channel to stop selling an existing item and start selling a replacement item quickly. In these cases, the vendor will recall the existing part and introduce the new item. Ideally, the vendor will be ready with enough inventory to fill the entire pipeline and handle ongoing demand. The process is reasonably straightforward. You should discontinue the recall item, stop ordering it, and move the sales history and forecasts to the new item. A good inventory system will see the full forecast and zero available, and order enough for the distributor's inventory and demand. An ideal system would also know which stores stock the item, and order enough to replace their inventories, too. This should happen quickly, so you and your stores do not lose sales while the inventories are being shuffled. If the vendor is superseding more than one existing item into one new item, then you should add all the demand histories together and do a new forecast for the new item based on that composite history.

2. **"Sell out and reorder":** A more common situation is when a vendor announces a new part, but asks the distributors to sell out the old part first. This is the most difficult situation to manage correctly. We never got this perfect in our auto parts system, but we learned what was needed, and we learned that doing something was a lot better than doing nothing. So, here is an ideal system for "sell out and reorder" situations. It is a step by step process:

   a. Load records on the distribution center inventory database, with flags to indicate how the old and new parts should be handled to sell out the old item and reorder the new one. Stop ordering the old item immediately at the distribution centers. Load the record, but do not order the new item. Don't tell your store customers about the new item at this time. They need to keep selling and ordering the old item to flush the pipeline.

   b. At the distribution center, compute an order for the new item based on the forecast with the old and new item ongoing demand combined, but place that order quantity for the new item. You might want to gradually move the demand history and stock levels over to the new item, so that you build up an inventory of the new item as you sell down the old one.

c. As each store continues to sell the old item, they will continue to reorder the old item, because they don't know about the replacement. This will help flush the distribution center inventory.

d. When an individual store orders the old item and the distribution center has sold out of it, ship the new item to that one store and advise that store of the replacement. At that store, discontinue the old item, move the demand history to the new item, set a forecast and stock level for the new part, and post the receipt of the new item. That one store has completed the "sell out and reorder" process. That store will now begin selling and reordering the new item. The distribution center will be ready (in step b) with some inventory of the new part to handle these orders.

e. Repeat the above step with each store as they sell out their old inventory.

f. Some stores may hear about this and return their old items to the distribution center. The system should still work. The distribution center will have other stores buying the old part, so it should be able to completely sell out the old part.

g. Over a period of time, stores will help sell out the old inventory.

h. When a distribution center runs out of the old item, look at the global inventory position in all stores. At some point, it is appropriate to advise the remaining stores of the replacement, and recall any residual inventory to return it to the vendor.

i. Ideally, this system would completely sell out the old item at the distribution center and all stores. That almost never worked perfectly in our auto parts business, but it was a lot better than doing nothing, and having the entire old inventory on hand.

j. As you can see, the key is to not tell all the stores about the supersession initially. You need some stores to continue to buy the old item until that entire inventory is sold out.

k. Another key is to have an ongoing global view of the inventory position and current demand for both the old and new parts in all locations so that you can manage the process of selling out the old part while maintaining full availability of a mixture of old and new parts in every location.

Summary

You can improve order fill and customer service by offering a variety of choices to customers whenever you have more than one item for a specific application. If you are out of one item, offer the alternate, and include a comment describing any differences if they are not quite the same. If you prefer one item over another, offer the preferred item to the customer each time they order the other part, and include a comment to help them decide which to buy.

When vendors introduce a new item to replace an existing one, you need to manage the process carefully to continue to fill demand and handle the transition in all inventories. The most complex event is when the vendor asks the customers to sell out the old item and replace it with a new one. There is an eleven-step process to correctly handle this event.

Pete Kornafel

Chapter 23. Stock Adjustment Process

Before we discuss how to select items for stock adjustments, here is a suggested procedure.

Establish a Calendar

Your goal, at a minimum, should be to review the coverage in each product line once a year. In some categories of goods you might need to do it more frequently than that. Once a year worked adequately for most product lines in our auto parts business.

We built a calendar with a target date for each product line. This was the date to start the process. As you'll see, the entire process took about 90 days on each line. We used these criteria to pick the dates for each line.

1. If the line was seasonal, we wanted to have the stock adjustment process completed just before the beginning of the peak season. This would freshen our coverage going into the strongest selling months.
2. If the vendor had an established time when they announced new items or published a new catalog, we wanted to start our process soon after that information was available to us.
3. If the vendor required that we make our stock adjustment on a line in a specific month, that established a deadline. We would start the process in time to end before their deadline. This was our least favorite reason for assigning a line to our calendar.
4. We balanced the workload throughout the year by assigning other lines that did not have any particular "best time" for their review and adjustment.

The Regular Process

1. **Refresh and Validate your Data Base:** If the vendor has announced new items, make sure they are loaded on your system with all the required data, make your inventory management decisions about whether to stock them, and establish an initial stock level or forecast. We allowed one week for this task.

2. **Reclassify the Inventory:** At this point, we reclassified all the items in a product line, using the methods in Chapter 4 on Classification. This was primarily used to drive store inventories,

so this gave us a very fresh set of data for our stores to use for their inventory updates and stock adjustments.

3. **Distinguish New Items from Dying Items:** Both may show very few sales and a slow moving classification code. It is important NOT to stock adjust new items out of inventories just because they haven't started to sell. You'll just buy them back later.

4. **Publish all Data Base Updates:** In our company, we downloaded data from our DC master files to computer systems in each store location. We also published some data on paper for our sales force and customers who did not have our computer system. We allowed one week for classifying the inventory and publishing the results.

5. **Manage the Store Inventories:** We asked each store to update their inventory on a product line at this time. We gave them our most current information, and we wanted to get their returns back to our DCs before we submitted our return request to our vendor. See the next chapter for more detail. We allowed four weeks for this task.
    a. We also had a process with some stores to do this on an ongoing basis. See below. These stores were kept up to date continuously on most items.

6. **Do a Physical Inventory at the DC:** We did a physical inventory of each product line at our DCs at least once a year, but we did each line at this time, not all lines at once near year-end. This gave us the most accurate inventory balances just after the store returns had been processed, but before we ran our DC overstock reports. After all, if we had something we wanted to return and missed it here, it would have to sit for another full year. We did cycle counts of some possible problem items throughout the year. Our auditors tested our inventories each year-end, and we always passed, so they certified our financial statements without a full year-end physical inventory. We allowed two weeks for this step.

7. **Run the DC Overstock Reports and Request a Stock Adjustment:** Most of our vendors required that we submit a stock adjustment request for their approval. This let them check the amount against our eligibility, and make sure all the items we wanted to return were OK. We allowed one week for submitting the return and two weeks to get the vendor approval.

8. **Pull and Ship the Return:** Once we had the approval, we pulled and shipped the DC return. We allowed one week for this process.

So, this entire process took 12 weeks. At any one time we had 15-20 product lines in various steps of this process. A person in our inventory management department was responsible for tracking each line, and keeping it on schedule. Our worst situation was when some stores were late, and we received their stock adjustments just after we had submitted our request to the vendor. We also had to chase many vendors for approval of our requests.

Timing of Offsetting Orders

Some vendors required offsetting orders for returns. If you use the above process, you place your order for new items at the end of Step 2, when all the data is loaded in your system and you have made the item level stocking decisions for DCs and stores. You do not even request the return until Step 7. It is necessary to have an agreement with the vendor that the initial order for new items counts as the offsetting order for the return about two months later.

Immediate Return of Items Recalled or Going Obsolete

Vendors issued recall bulletins for mispackaged or potential defective items. These were always handled quickly. Our item level transaction history file (we would have called it a data warehouse, but the term hadn't been invented yet) let us track the movement of individual items. In a few cases, we paid a customer to let us remove and replace a possible defective part from their vehicle.

Good vendors issued "final recall" bulletins for items about to go obsolete, where we had one last chance to return them for credit. If this did not fit our calendar, we processed these promptly as individual, separate returns so we would not miss their deadlines.

Bad vendors simply dropped items out of their price lists without notification. Our software that loaded price updates also looked for all items with on hand balances where the item was not in the new price list. It printed an automatic return request with our quantity and most recent cost. We tried to get the vendor to take these returns immediately, and credit us at the most recent cost. Most vendors allowed this. I feel there were very few distributors who figured this out.

Daily Returns from Stores

Our store computer system had the capability to sweep the store inventory daily, and suggest the return of overstock above an item's normal stocking level on stocked items, and any non-stock items in inventory. If a customer returned an item, it was usually after the store had been replenished, so the customer's return item became overstock. If it was a special order item that was never sold or sold and returned, that was overstock, too. We kept the store inventories "clean" all the time by doing this process daily.

We made some exceptions. We did not want a store to return overstock on very popular items. We did not want the store to return very low price items. It was simpler to deal with all of them as part of an annual adjustment, and they didn't tie up much capital.

The annual stock adjustment was small for stores using this system, as it only picked up any inventory accuracy errors if the store did a physical, or items which had just changed in classification and store stock levels. We did this for our company owned stores. We did not have the courage to let our independently owned store customers use this software. We wanted to use the annual calendar and clean up each line on our schedule to evaluate the size of their returns. We knew we had the obligation to protect their inventory investment, but we wanted some intervention and approval of major returns during this process.

Chapter Summary

This chapter presents a logical process for updating the entire inventory database, using that information to reset store inventories, and then stock-adjusting the distribution centers once the slowest movers have been retrieved from the stores.

The entire process took about 12 weeks in our automotive business.

We established an annual calendar that considered seasonal peaks, vendor requirements, and overall workload balance to cover every line once a year.

The next chapter discusses how to select individual items that need to be removed from store or DC inventories.

Chapter 24. Overstock Identification and Stock Adjustments

Most people are familiar with the two main accounting conventions for inventory—FIFO and LIFO. They stand for First-In, First-Out, and Last-In, First-Out. A few people are familiar with FISH (First-In, Still Here). Not many people are aware of a special system for fruit and vegetable produce distributors. It is SISI, and it stands for Sell It or Smell It.

Gordon Graham cites three rules for overstock. [32]

- The first rule of managing overstock inventory is to prevent it.
- The second rule is to identify it.
- The third rule is to do something about it.

Produce distributors have SISI as a very easy way to identify overstock inventory. Other distributors can't just use their noses, but all distributors are likely to have plenty of inventory that "smells", too. Overstock is simply having too much of the wrong stuff. Some studies have shown that at least 15% of the inventory is overstock even in well-run companies. Without ongoing attention, all inventory will eventually begin to smell.

Prevention

Graham points out that little overstock inventory comes from items that were once great sellers, but have declined in popularity. Most overstock inventory comes from items that were "dogs" from the very beginning. That is most likely to be true for distributors who are not responsible for inventory farther down the channel in their own stores or their customer locations.

In our auto parts business, we gave our customers permission to send just about anything back to us, and charged a restocking or handling charge only on the most popular items. With two distribution centers and over 100 store customers, there was much more inventory in the field than in our DCs. In our case, prevention really had four elements:

---

[32] Gordon Graham, Distribution Inventory Management. Inventory Management Press, 1987, Chapter 15.

1. Don't buy bad stuff in the first place. Be careful how much you purchase on new items, and be VERY careful what you recommend for store inventories.
2. Once an item has established demand history, make sure you don't buy too much of it. All of the previous chapters on forecasting and replenishment buying should help.
3. Try to spot the early signs an item is declining in popularity, and begin to reduce the inventory before it dies completely. Remember the "Turtle" shaped curve for the life cycle of an item? It is much easier to sell inventory down while it still has some sales potential than to try to move it to customers or vendors after it becomes truly dead stock.
4. Phase the item out of stores inventories when it starts to decline, but still has some sales. A regular part might have an inventory of 10 units or so in each of our DCs, but it would also be stocked in more than 100 stores they supplied. We tried to withdraw the item first from smaller stores and then from all stores as it began to decline in popularity. If we got the timing right, we could still sell these as special orders from our DCs. If we did not reduce our pipeline inventory, we would have had much more overstock when we finally decided we did not want to continue stocking that item.

Tony Wild[33] also cites several good areas for review:

1. Be careful with promotions. You could wind up with a huge supply if you continue to buy as though the promotion sets a new level of demand.
2. Have a plan to deal with items that are replaced by newer ones.
3. Be careful with items that appear in sale catalogs or other "one time" programs.
4. Be careful with the initial order for a new line or new items.

Store Overstock

Refer to Chapter 5 and 6 on Classification and Selecting Items for Store Inventories. Inventory classification data is the primary information to establish store inventories.

Each store established an inventory stock depth profile, with their normal stocking level on each product line and category. For example, a store might set their normal depth at Code 5 on a product line. That meant they would generally stock all items

---

[33] Tony Wild. Best Practice in Inventory Management. John Wiley and Sons, 1997

classed Code 5 or better, and generally not stock items classed Code 6 or worse.

Our stores maintained an on hand quantity of one (or one vehicle quantity) of almost all stocking items, as their inventory was replenished daily. About 2,000 of the 20,000 items stocked in typical stores moved well enough to require two or more units in stock. So, the real investment decision was whether to stock an item or not.

Here are the rules we used for keeping items in stores, adding items to the stores, and returning items from stores to DCs.

- Keeping and Adding Items:
  - o Keep or Add every item within the stock depth profile for that line in that store whether or not it has sold in the past year.
  - o Keep or Add items below the stock depth profile that have sold twice or more in that store in the past year.
  - o Remember units per car, units per job, or case quantities.

- Returning Items
  - o Return items within the stock depth profile that have been stocked but not sold in that store in two years, or items also covered in another product line, or if the coverage is clearly wrong for that store's local market.
  - o Return all items below the stock depth profile that have sold less than twice in the past year.
  - o Remember to use the units per car, units per job, or case quantities.

Our store computer systems had "Move-In" and "Move-Out" reports that identified items that met the above criteria. These reports aggregated the cost of suggested additions to inventory and suggested stock adjustments. They were very useful to understand the financial impact of the stock depth and these rules on each store's inventory.

The "Move-In" report, with any changes, became an order for the store, and the "Move-Out" report, with any changes, became the stock adjustment from the store to our DC.

Identification of Overstock at the Distribution Centers

Here are several methods of identifying overstock inventory at the Distribution Centers.

Pete Kornafel

- **99% cutoff:** Graham recommends classifying all items with no recent sales and all items in the bottom 1% of sales as dead inventory and overstock.

- **Months Supply:** Charles Bodenstab recommends ranking items by month's supply of inventory as a way to identify overstock.[34]

- **Inventory with Very Low Sales:** Activant's ADIS system generates a special report that shows how much inventory is in a distribution center in items with five sales or less over the prior two years.[35]

Cooperative Computing, Inc. A-DIS INV098 Inventory Return Analysis		Run Date 30-Apr-02 at 12:51 PM CARQUEST Distribution Center			
Report Total		**Inventory For 1 Selling Increment**		**On Hand > 1 Selling Increment**	
Unit Sales Category	Part Count	$	% of Total Inventory	$	% of Total Inventory
YTD + LYR < 1	12,007	242,649	3.3%	270,607	3.7%
YTD + LYR = 1	5,588	118,516	1.6%	76,013	1.0%
YTD + LYR = 2	4,836	104,308	1.4%	70,403	1.0%
YTD + LYR = 3	4,102	86,078	1.2%	58,638	0.8%
YTD + LYR = 4	3,545	70,612	1.0%	60,500	0.8%
YTD + LYR = 5	2,794	55,619	0.8%	60,434	0.8%
Total	32,872	677,782	9.2%	596,595	8.1%

Ch 24 Fig 1. Activant's Overstock Report—Items with Very Low Sales

This report shows the number of items with very small sales over the past two years. There are 12,007 SKUs with one or more units on hand, but zero or negative sales over the past two years. The next column shows that it would take $242,649 in inventory to keep one selling increment (each, set, case, roll, etc.) of each of those items, and that is 3.3% of the total inventory value. The final columns show that there is another $270,607 inventory in those items in excess of one selling increment, which is another 3.7% of the inventory. So, this distribution center has 7% of its inventory in items with no net sales in the past two years. The next rows show items with exactly one sale over the past two years, exactly two sales, etc. In total, there is over $1.25 million in 32,872 SKUs that have had sales of five or less over two years, and that is 17% of this DC's inventory. Everything on this report

[34] Charles Bodenstab, A New Era in Inventory Management, Hilta Press
[35] Activant Solutions. ADIS Program INV098.

with the possible exception of one increment of items with some sales over the past two years could go away and not be missed. That is about $1 million of overstock in a well-run DC with about $7 million total inventory.

- **Carrying Cost of Overstock:** Each of the above methods uses an item's sales potential, and that is important. However, inventory is an investment, and the author feels the best way to look for overstock is to determine the cost of carrying that investment. Every item has an Order Level (Usage over Review Time plus Lead Time plus Safety Stock). In the case of items with zero sales and a zero forecast, any on hand inventory is overstock. In the case of items with a forecast, everything over the Order Level is overstock. You can use the forecast to determine how long it will take to sell out the overstock, and use the carrying cost of inventory over that time period to determine how much it costs to carry the overstock for each item. If you rank all these items in descending order by that cost, it shows the items that will cost the most at the top of the list. Here is an example:

Item Cost $30
Forecast = .5 units per month
Inventory Carrying Cost = 25%
On Hand Quantity = 15
Order Level = 1
Overstock = 14 units

The 14 units of overstock will last 28 months at the current forecast rate. The average inventory investment during that period is ½ the quantity times the cost times the carrying rate times the duration.

$$OverstockCarryCost = \frac{OverstockQuantity}{2} * UnitCost * CarryRate * \frac{DurationMonths}{12}$$

$$OverstockCost = \frac{14}{2} * 30 * .25 * \frac{28}{12} = 122.50$$

If you rank all overstock items by the carrying cost of overstock in descending order, the top of the list will be items you should return or dispose of first.

You should use a long time span (we used 999 months) for items with a zero forecast. This will push all of them to the top of the list. It is proper that they be the most important items to get out of your inventory.

Pete Kornafel

You might feel that you should use the present value of the costs for future periods. This would decrease the aggregate cost for items where it will take a very long time to sell off the overstock. It would push the ranking in the wrong direction for those items.

Here is a sample report ranking some items by the carrying cost of their overstock:

Item Number	Overstock Quantity	Unit Cost	Forecast Units Per Month	Overstock Duration Months	Inventory Investment	Overstock Carrying Cost
62	2	75.42	-	999.9	150.84	1,571.09
75	3	30.50	-	999.9	91.50	953.03
42	4	10.25	-	999.9	41.00	427.04
89	70	14.50	2.00	35.0	1,015.00	370.05
8	14	30.00	0.50	28.0	420.00	122.50
97	12	18.25	0.25	48.0	219.00	109.50
37	34	21.30	3.00	11.3	724.20	85.50
81	3	150.00	0.20	15.0	450.00	70.31
54	125	5.75	15.00	8.3	718.75	62.39
17	3	51.75	0.10	30.0	155.25	48.52
19	8	32.00	0.75	10.7	256.00	28.44
92	2	49.50	0.10	20.0	99.00	20.63
Totals					4,340.54	3,869.00

Ch 24 Fig 2. Table of Overstock Items Ranked by Carrying Cost

We used 999.9 months supply for items with a zero demand forecast, to assure these items floated to the top. For items with some movement but overstock, as you can see, this does not quite follow the months supply or dollar investment for the ranking. Item 97 ranks above item 37, even though it has a lower inventory investment, because it will take longer to sell it off. Item 54 ranks higher than item 17, even though it has fewer months supply, because the investment and carrying costs are higher.

Exclude New Items and Forward Buys: In any of these methods, it is important to exclude new items, where their forecasts might not be accurate, and forward buys, where you intentionally bought extra inventory to take advantage of some deal.

In our auto parts inventory, it took several years for some items to begin to sell. Items like brake master cylinders and exhaust parts were not likely to fail and require replacement until the vehicle was 5-8 years old.

It was important to distinguish these items from dying items. If you don't, you might try to sell off or return items that haven't started to sell, and you'll certainly buy them back later.

Disposition

Graham's book has an excellent checklist of ways to dispose of overstock. Not all methods will work in each channel, but there should be several ways that are appropriate for any particular line of merchandise.

His ranking is in a sequence that tries to recover the most value for the overstock. It ranges from a sales push at regular selling prices through closeouts at various discounts to write-offs. He even includes praying for a fire or flood, but only if you do not instigate them yourself.

Not many of his methods worked for our auto parts overstock. Markdowns, closeouts, clearance sales, and flea markets just don't work for application specific items. A Hudson water pump won't fit any vehicle except a Hudson. No one wants one at any price unless they are the very rare person who owns that vehicle.

So, our disposition efforts in our auto parts business had three main thrusts. First, we tried to sell down the inventory while it still had some sales potential. Second, we tried to manage the number of locations that stocked each very slow moving item, and transferred inventory to locations where it was still selling. Third, we tried to get our vendors to accept it on stock adjustments.

Sell Down

If you have accurate forecasts, review and lead times, and safety stock goals, you will have an accurate Order Level. Your replenishment system will not buy the item while your on hand balance is greater than this.

The key is accurate forecasts. You have to filter out false demands, such as repeated orders from stores not on your backorder systems, etc.

The demand for most auto parts declined gently over several years once they past their peak. Other industries may not have this much time. You may need to flag items with a Tracking Signal that shows the last several actual demands have been below the forecast. You could apply a downward trend to scale down the computed Order Level for future periods.

Transfers

If you have a way to move inventory between branch locations quickly, and without a huge handling or freight cost, transfers can be a good way to reduce overstock internally.

Some extra math in your replenishment ordering system could "look around" your network of locations to see if you could transfer an overstock item from a different location rather than buy another one from your vendor. One auto parts chain uses their data warehouse for this purpose. They call it their "virtual DC". It has significantly reduced their inventory and stock adjustment requirements.

We did not have this full capability in our company. We did have a program to look for items with overstock in one location and recommend transfers to a different location if the forecasts indicated it would sell more quickly in the other building. We used this to transfer some inventory each time we ran a "shuttle" truck between our distribution centers.

Stock Adjustments to Vendors

Our next to last resort for eliminating overstock was to try to return it to our vendors. (Our last resort was the dump).

Most of our vendors permitted some annual or semi-annual stock return. The policies varied from vendor to vendor. One of our vendors had the view that they really owned all inventory in the channel. They just loaned some of it to the distributors. They said the distributors could display the parts. Some would sell, but the rest would be returned to the vendor.[36]

Here is a list of the best policies a vendor can have to protect the distributor from obsolescence costs:

- Do not charge a handling or restocking fee for returns below an allowed percent of purchases. Most of our vendors allowed an annual return of up to 5% of the previous year's purchases with no handling charges.
- Allow returns in excess of the limit, even if there is a handling or restocking charge. The handling charge might cost less than anything else you can do to dispose of the extra overstock inventory.

---

[36] Jesse Hermann, referring to his experience at General Automotive Specialty Company.

- Do not count items that are superseded against the return eligibility. Vendors consolidate inventory by making one item fit more than one application, and supersede existing items to that one. We tried to sell out the old items, but they quickly became dead inventory. Good vendors allowed us to return the original items and did not count this against our eligibility, as it was their action that made the item obsolete.
- Do not drop items without notification. See the previous chapter.
- Give at least one-year advance notice of items that will become obsolete and not eligible for return.
- Establish a company wide return eligibility, and permit returns in any amount from any locations up to the company wide limit. Some vendors give bonuses to sales representatives based on their territory sales, net of returns. They use this as an excuse to try to enforce return limits building by building. A good vendor will give you a company wide eligibility and compensate their own employees properly.
- Allow "pick to keep" changes from the authorized request to the actual return. You might show four of an item in stock in your inventory system, and decide you want to keep one unit in inventory. You submit a request to return three. When you actually pull the return, you discover five on hand. You would like to "pick to keep" the one unit you want, and send back all the rest. If you cannot change the authorized quantity, then you can't keep what you want in stock.
- Not require an offsetting order. If your replenishment system is working right, all this does is build some future potential overstock. If you follow the stock adjustment process of the previous chapter, you turned in the new item order a couple of months before the stock adjustment request.

You will not have much obsolescence if vendors will do all that for you.

Priorities for Returns to Vendors

You may not be able to return everything on your overstock list. If that is the case, here is a suggested ranking of items to return:

1. Items on Final Recall or about to go Obsolete. If you have items that you can return now for credit, but will not be able to return for any credit in the future, now is the time. These items should be your highest priority to return.
2. Items not on your stock list. If you have concluded that you do not want to stock an item at all in the future, and you have a

chance to return any existing inventory, now is the time for this, too. This category should be your second priority. At a minimum, you would like to have enough eligibility to get rid of the entire inventory in these first two categories.

3. Excess Inventory on other items. If you still have eligibility to return more, you could start at the top (worst) of your ranked list of overstock items, and work your way down the list until you hit your eligibility or your own stopping point. If your vendor is supportive, and if your inventory is well managed, you might be able to go a long way into this list. You should establish your own sensible cutoff point based on that product line and vendor. In our auto parts business, we would generally stop when we got to items that had some consistent sales and where we had less than about six month's supply in overstock. We would submit a return for less than our eligibility and remind the vendors later that we had not used all our eligibility in the past. Only a few vendors would let us "bank" this eligibility for future use.

When You Need More Return Eligibility

Even with a cooperative vendor, there will still be occasions when you will need to return more than your allowable limit. Here is my "top 10" list of things you can say to a vendor to get him to give you extra return privileges.

10.	PLEASE authorize this extra return.
9.	We support your entire product line. We deserve extra return eligibility more than other customers who just cherry pick your fastest moving items.
8.	This is a "once in a lifetime" problem for us. If you will handle this return, we promise we'll never ask again.
7.	We will take on some other products you sell that we have not been stocking if you will accept this return.
6.	We will let you issue the credit over a period of time.
5.	We will agree to give you an offsetting order.
4.	We will agree to an extra handling charge if you will accept this return.
3.	We will accept a smaller return limit next year if you will authorize the extra return this year.
2.	Company X has not used all their return eligibilty. We'll sell this stuff to him and let him return it to you. He'll charge us a fee, but it's worth it.
1.	Your competitor will do this, even if you won't. We will change vendors for this category if that is what it takes to get this return handled.

Ch 24 Fig 4. Top 10 List—Ways to Ask for Extra Return Eligibility

208

These are roughly in order, from the easiest on your company to the most difficult.

I particularly like Number 8, the "Once in a lifetime" request. The reason I like it is that this really refers to the lifetime of the vendor's Sales Manager, not the lifetime of your company. Most vendors have a new Sales Manager every couple of years. You can use this once on every new person in that job. Sales Managers don't usually leave good records or have long memories, so you might be able to use it more than once with some of them.

Carrying Cost Rate

Remember that the cost of obsolescence is part of the overall inventory carrying cost. If you have good vendors who work with you on returns, you will have a lower carrying cost, and that will justify carrying more inventory, to give better service.

I was once (and only once) invited by a vendor to speak about inventory management to their distributors in Mexico. The vendor's sales manager told me their policies in Mexico were not the same as in the U.S. I quickly discovered that one of the vendor's problems was that the distributors would not stock very much inventory. I also quickly discovered that one of the distributors' problems was that the vendor would not allow any stock adjustments, so all their overstock became obsolete and a write-off. It was no wonder the distributors were reluctant to stock much inventory. Every purchasing mistake became a total loss.

So, as part of my talk to the distributors, I suggested they make their case to the vendor that a little bit of stock adjustment return privilege would go a long way to help them justify carrying more inventory. I told them this vendor permitted some stock adjustments in the U.S. I could see the vendor's sales manager holding his head in his hands in the back of the meeting room. I doubt that vendor changed their policy in Mexico, and I know those distributors have a very high carrying cost rate for that product line. I also know that vendor will never invite me back.

Tracking Overstock Trends

You should run whatever report you use to identify overstock regularly, and track the total amount in your inventory. If you have a way to do it, you should also track the value of items that came off the list (because you disposed of them somehow), and the value of items that are new on the list (so you can diagnose what caused them to make the list).

We could not track the changes in detail, but we kept a file of the total overstock reports to see if were gaining or losing ground. About the best we could do was keep even. Inventory was turning into overstock just as quickly as we could get rid of it.

Whose Inventory Is It?

An ideal inventory system would log an "owner" and a reason for each receipt of inventory. You may think you only have one buyer, but that's just not true. Here are some people who "own", or are responsible for buying inventory. A single item might have many of these contribute to its on hand quantity.

- A Buyer bought this quantity of this item on a regular replenishment order. (Hopefully, no overstock comes from this)
- A Buyer (or someone else) authorized this extra quantity for a promotion or a forward buy.
- A quantity came in a return from a customer.
- A vendor suggested items and quantities to stock, and we ordered accordingly, so the vendor really "owns" this inventory.
- Someone bought this from a diverter or as a "distress" buy. (This is a great cause of overstock. After all, it was someone else's bad inventory before you bought it.)
- The Sales Manager made us do it... He knew he had a prospect, and he made us put the inventory in just in case he made the sale.

If you could isolate the sources of inventory, you would have a better chance of preventing more overstock. You could also evaluate buyers much more fairly if you only judged them on the inventory they bought.

The Vendor Claim File

Getting a stock adjustment return authorized, picked and shipped is only half the battle. Every distributor should maintain a complete claim file, with a log of every amount due from any vendor.

All transactions should go into this file. Overstock returns, warranty returns, claims for co-op advertising, etc. should all be logged. If you don't currently do this, the total will astound you. In our $35 million sales auto parts business, it was not unusual for the vendor claim file to be $500,000. We "aged" these claims like any other accounts receivable, and chased vendors to issue credits promptly.

We audited each credit against the claim amount, just as we measured receipts against vendor invoices. Even when the vendor authorized a return, some items might not be on the credit memo, or might not have the right prices. You also have to check to see that the proper handling charge was applied, if you agreed to one.

This job is not complete until the overstock is turned into cash, and you have to get and use the credit memo from the vendor to accomplish that.

Chapter Summary

Prevention is the best way to avoid overstock.
A good way to rank items to remove is based on the carrying cost of overstock.

An ideal vendor will help a distributor protect his investment in inventory.

It is important to track stock adjustments clear through the process until credit is received and approved. We "aged" vendor claims just as we aged accounts receivable, to track vendor credits.

An imperfect forecasting and replenishment system could cause you to have some extra inventory and extra lost sales. This might reduce the distributor's profitability, but it is seldom fatal.

Inattention to handling overstock regularly and aggressively can kill any distributor over time.

Pete Kornafel

Chapter 25. Measuring Performance

It is important to measure forecast accuracy, service level, inventory turn, and other key criteria for inventory performance. Here are some issues to think about in each category.

The goal is to determine whether the actual performance matches the goals and data you have established.

Forecast Accuracy

At the end of each month, you should review the item forecasts and the actual demand. A database would allow several views of this data, and the ability to drill down to individual items. The goal is to feel good if all your forecasts are very accurate, or to discover reasons why some are not as accurate as you would like. Here are some good ways to aggregate and view this data:

- **By Forecast Model:** One view should be to aggregate items by the forecast model used on them. This shows the overall accuracy of seasonal item forecasts, slow item forecasts, etc.

- **Modified Forecasts:** One category should be for manually adjusted forecasts (or one category for each individual inventory manager's adjustments). This lets you see if the inventory manager's intervention produced accurate forecasts. We did not keep the "before and after" data, but it would have been a big help. Then, you could see what the system would have forecast on its own, what the inventory manager forecast, and which was more accurate. Don't be surprised if the manual forecasts are just as inaccurate as what the system would have done on its own. After all, if you flag only the unusual items for manual review, these are already known to be the toughest ones to forecast, because they are not following their historical demand pattern.

- **By Product Category:** An unusually hot summer could cause a spike in our air conditioning system parts business that was beyond our forecasts. A view by product category could show this better than just looking at individual problem items.

- **By Customer or Customer Category:** It is possible that one customer, or one group of customers, have had a significant change in their purchasing patterns, so aggregating this data by customers is a way to identify if this is a cause of forecast inaccuracy.

Order Fill

At the end of each period you should build a data base of items, their inventory positions, and the demand and actual order fill. This can give you a good feeling when everything is in good order, and give you a way to find trouble spots when it is not all up to par. It may be important to develop several different measures of order fill.

- **Stockouts:** This simply counts the number of items that ran out of stock in the past month. It doesn't measure the amount of lost sales. It isn't worth much as a benchmark measurement, unless you use the Normal Distribution as your method of computing safety stocks. The normal distribution gives the probability an actual observation will exceed a specific amount, based on the mean and standard deviation of the distribution. For example, it states that the probability an actual amount will exceed two standard deviations above the mean is .02275. That does NOT mean you should expect 97.7% order fill. It does mean that there will be a stockout in a little over 2% of the periods for each item, or stockouts in a little more than 2% of the items each month that have this level of safety stock. If you use Normal Distribution formulas for safety stocks, then you may want to track this measurement, to see if actual performance correlates with the safety stock goal levels.

- **Dollar Order Fill:** A measure of dollar demand versus dollar shipments gives a view of order fill by dollars. The financial people in your company will be interested in this measure, and it is usually the one quoted when you ask a distributor a general question about their order fill.

- **Unit Fill:** This measures aggregate units ordered vs. shipped. We didn't even compute it for our auto parts inventory, as we sold everything from penny cotter pins to $5,000 pieces of equipment. They would have been all jumbled together by this measurement.

- **Line Fill:** This measures line items ordered vs. shipped. This is typically how a distributor's customer measures order fill. They see their packing list or invoice, see that they ordered 100 line items, and see that only 4 were backordered. They don't usually do the math to convert that to dollars, unless a very important item was one of the ones not shipped. If you use line fill, it is also important to determine how to handle "partial" line item shipments. We always used the "harsh" measure—that a line item must be shipped complete to count as a filled order. When a customer ordered six of an item, and we shipped four, we counted that as an unfilled line item. After all, the basic measure is your customer's satisfaction. If you don't ship the full quantity, they still have an unfilled expectation.

- **Stock vs. Non Stock items:** We had an official list of items we intended to stock. We measured order fill on those items, and also tracked lost sales on items we did not stock. We used the "harsh" measure here, too, and counted lost sales even on items we did not stock when we computed our order fill. The customer didn't care whether we had decided to stock an item or not—they just tried to buy it. If we didn't have it, they had another unfilled expectation. We used the order fill on stocking items to measure our inventory manager's performance, and used the lost sales on non-stock items as a source of data for adding them.

- **Customer Backorders:** We only counted the first lost sale when the customer did not let us hold backorders and reordered the same item in the same quantity every day.

- **"Inventory Profile Analysis":** A paper by James A Robison[37] shows that the achieved service levels correlate well with "shortages". These are item level inventory positions below the inventory position derived from all the purchasing parameters. This could be a valuable way to diagnose your actual order fill performance.

Whatever measurements you use as the most appropriate one for your business, stick with them and save all the data so you can measure changes in performance over time, and diagnose what is causing them.

A database that allows different views and "drill down" capability is best. You would like to see order fill overall, by product category, by customer or customer groups, by forecast model, by inventory position, etc.

It is also important to show your service level goal vs. actual order fill achieved, and measure that variance. The mission is to find

---

[37] James A. Robison. Inventory Profile Analysis: An Aggregation Technique for Improving Customer Service While Reducing Inventory. APICS Journal, Second Quarter, 2001.

Pete Kornafel

areas where your order fill is significantly below your goal, determine the cause, and have the ability to correct the problems.

It is possible to report conditions that contribute to the service level problems along with the goal and actual data. Here are some typical problems that lead to poor order fill by a distributor:

1. Inbound order fill or vendor backorders. If your vendor is not shipping an item to you when expected, that is very likely to cause outbound service level problems for you. These can be prioritized by the amount of sales or gross margin dollars lost on a daily basis, to let your inventory managers appeal to your current vendors or find other sources.
2. Items that do not track their demand forecasts. Demands that exceed forecasts can also cause service level issues.
3. Items that do not track their lead time forecasts. If shipments are lost, delayed, or not processed quickly, that too can cause service level issues.
4. Incorrect inventory data. If on hand or on order balances are incorrect, service level issues are bound to result.

All of these problems are likely to continue until the basic data is corrected. This review, and updating the data is an important review process for your inventory managers.

How Well Can You Fill?

If your vendors shipped everything exactly on time, and if your data and systems were perfect, you should achieve your service goals. Everything that goes wrong from that ideal level is likely to cause service level problems or excess inventory. Any overstock won't really help your fill—you were going to ship all that stuff, regardless. Any inventory below the ideal level is likely to reduce your service level below the goal.

When your vendors are shipping poorly (low 90%'s or below), your outbound order fill should be better than your inbound fill from your vendors. After all, that's the whole purpose of your "buffer" of inventory. If your vendor is shipping at 88%, and you're only shipping at 85%, the vendor's service is one issue, but you must have an inventory issue of your own, too.

Inventory Turnover

Inventory turnover is defined as:

$$InventoryTurnover = \frac{SalesValueAtCost}{InventoryAtCost}$$

The Inventory Turnover value, by itself, doesn't tell you much. However, if you can compare similar inventories at different locations, or examine the trend over time at a single location, this can tell you if you are making progress on inventory management.

Turnover can be tracked by item, categories of items, and other groupings to diagnose issues and changes. Note that your inventory can change significantly for seasonal items, so you may need to compare data to the same periods in prior years.

Lead Time (and Internal Processing Time)

In our auto parts business, when business was good, it added pressure on all our vendors. Their lead-time lengthened, their order fill went down, our forecasts were too small, and each of those contributed to pressure on our own outbound service level.

Tracking changes in lead-time is a good early warning about changing conditions at your vendors.

Profits from Better Order Fill and Inventory Turn

We judged that an unfilled order cost our company the entire gross margin on that sale. Review the Chapter on Setting Service Goals for the explanation. With that definition, better service levels contribute hugely to profits. Here is a simple chart showing the incremental profit from improved order fill for several levels of contribution to profit.

% Increase in Order Fill	Incremental Contribution Margin			
	20%	22%	24%	26%
1%	0.20%	0.22%	0.24%	0.26%
2%	0.40%	0.44%	0.48%	0.52%
3%	0.60%	0.66%	0.72%	0.78%
5%	1.00%	1.10%	1.20%	1.30%
10%	2.00%	2.20%	2.40%	2.60%

Ch 25 Fig 1. Incremental Profit from Increased Order Fill

Pete Kornafel

Our company distribution centers had about a 26% gross margin, and about 5% of sales as pretax income. Each incremental point of order fill contributed the entire gross margin, or .26% of sales. So, one point better order fill could raise our pretax income from 5 to 5.26% of sales, a 5% overall profit increase.
Increased turnover helps income, too. Here is a chart showing the relative cost of capital for various inventory carrying costs and inventory turn rates.

Turns	Annual Cost of Carrying Inventory			
	10%	15%	20%	25%
2	5.00%	7.50%	10.00%	12.50%
2.5	4.00%	6.00%	8.00%	10.00%
3	3.33%	5.00%	6.67%	8.33%
3.5	2.86%	4.29%	5.71%	7.14%
4	2.50%	3.75%	5.00%	6.25%
4.5	2.22%	3.33%	4.44%	5.56%
5	2.00%	3.00%	4.00%	5.00%
6	1.67%	2.50%	3.33%	4.17%

Ch 25 Fig 2. Cost of Capital for Various Inventory Turn Rates

These costs are not isolated on financial statements, so it is not quite as easy to see a direct connection to improved profits, but it is real. Inventory carrying costs will show up in interest expense, rent, insurance, and some payroll. If the service level doesn't go down, higher turns will improve profits. It takes some analysis to choose an appropriate carrying cost for your firm. As you improve your inventory management, this rate should go up, as a dollar invested in your inventory will generate a higher return on investment.

Gross Margin Return on Inventory

The ratio of annual gross margin dollars in a product line to the average inventory gives a slightly different measurement. This is referred to as GMROI. Bigger is better, and it shows that you'd like to have more gross margin on low turnover product lines.
I met a tobacco distributor in Washington DC. This company distributed cigarettes and cigars. They got 75 turns on their cigarette inventory (with an average 4 day supply), but only had about 3-4% gross margin, so their GMROI on cigarettes was about 250%. They got over 40% gross margin on cigars, but there were so many sizes and brands that they only got about 4 turns, and a 160%

GMROI. Their business was great. There are a LOT of cigars consumed in Washington DC. Even with that, they liked cigarettes better, because of the high GMROI.

Overstock

It is important to measure overstock, and track it over time. If possible, it would be nice to track inflows (returns from customers that create overstock, or changes in your forecasts or service goals that re-define existing inventory to be overstock). It is easier to track outflows—items returned to vendors, sold somehow, or scrapped.

This can also be viewed by categories of items, or by individual inventory manager to determine actual performance.
I'm not sure who said, "You can't manage it unless you can measure it", but this quote definitely applies to inventory management.

Impact of Duplicated Items or Product Lines

Customers love choice. Many distributors will carry more than one brand of some items. There are usually at least two quality grades of almost all items, too. This can result in a significant amount of duplicated or overlapping inventory.

If these really appeal to different customers, who would not buy the other item, then they might as well be completely different items. However, to the extent they divide the sales across two or more inventories, they directly degrade inventory turnover. Where there were legitimate different quality grades and price points, we carried all the coverage, but a big part of our marketing effort was to get all of our customers to accept one brand in each category.

In our auto parts business, we referred to these overlaps as "dual lines". This meant we had two product lines covering the same parts and applications. Our New Mexico branch manager always referred to them as "duel lines". He was right, too, as they were two product lines fighting for one set of customers.

Measuring Buyer Performance

When things go well, the sales department usually gets the credit. When things go bad, the buyer usually gets the blame. It isn't always fair.

It is all too easy to give a buyer an assignment like "make sure you get at least five turns, and do the best you can for order fill." Many distributors measure buyers on similar criteria. It is almost impossible to translate that assignment into a meaningful purchasing strategy. A buyer measured on those goals will be very reluctant to add new items, support promotions, increase stocks ahead of seasons, and other steps to achieve good service.

A better system would be to measure the buyer on the elements of their assignment:

- **Order Fill:** We always wanted to achieve our order fill goals, and felt that was more important to the success of our company than making inventory level targets. While this was an overall measure, it is also important to look at key elements that contribute to it.

  o Forecast Accuracy—and regular review of items that do not follow forecasts.
  o Ordering on schedule—late or skipped orders surely cause service problems.
  o Data base maintenance—new items, updated lead times, etc.
  o Ordering more frequently—negotiating with vendors to permit more frequent orders was a good way to help our service level (and our inventory level).
  o Chasing and resolving late or lost orders and other problem situations.

- **Inventory Levels:** We also wanted to hit target inventory levels. The single most important element here was working on overstock. If we had inventory over target it almost always implied the need for a stock adjustment with our vendor.

  An ideal system would separate the "kinds" of inventory. Forward Buys, promotions, and inventory build up for seasonal peaks can all be good decisions that reduce inventory turnover, but improve order fill and overall company profits.

  Customer returns always contributed to excess inventory, and were never in the buyer's control.

Chapter Summary

You need systems to monitor all kinds of performance measurements. This includes forecast accuracy, order fill, turnover, lead times, and buyer performance.

All of these systems should update themselves for "routine" events, and flag exceptions for review by management.

Chapter 26. Logistics of Multiple Locations

A network of distribution points offers both opportunities and challenges for inventory management.

Hub and Spoke Distribution Centers

Some networks offer the opportunity to replenish branch distribution centers from one or more master distribution centers. Here are some criteria that impact the decision to do this.

- **End User Delivery Requirement:** If the end user's delivery time demand cannot be met from a master distribution center, then deploying inventory in stores or branch distribution centers is the only answer. It will result in much more system wide inventory (see the note on safety stock, below).

- **Possible Replenishment Frequency:** If a branch can be replenished from a master distribution center much more frequently than it could order direct from suppliers, this is a positive factor for internal replenishment. The additional handling and transportation costs for picking the order at the main location and delivering it to the branch may be much less than the inventory carrying cost of larger cycle and safety stocks at each branch when they order direct. Remember that frequency beats forecasting, so frequent replenishments are likely to give higher service levels, too.

- **Vendor and Product Line Complexity:** Some vendors require very high order minimums, and one of our major vendors required case lot purchases, even on very slow moving items. We had much less total inventory by internally replenishing branches on these lines. An example was the product line of body repair items (sanding discs, sandpaper, adhesives, masking tape, and other related items). The vendor required case lot purchases on every item. A case of sandpaper was 500 or 1,000 sheets, and they offered about 10 types in about 10 grits each. Many were slow movers. We chose to buy "direct" at our main warehouse, and replenish our branches with transfers. It reduced the branch inventories by about 75%.

Hub Stores or Super Stores

In our auto parts business, most professional repair outlets required same day delivery of parts. The same hub and spoke strategy applies to stores. It is possible to have one hub store, or super store in a market, and concentrate more inventory in that location. The delivery time might become 1-2 hours, versus 30 minutes from a local store, but that is usually still good enough to get the sale. Most of these stores stocked more width (more SKUs), rather than depth (more quantity of each SKU).

Special Order Strategies

Some of our automotive product lines had thousands of very slow moving items. It was just not profitable to stock all these items at branch locations. In these cases our only option was to offer overnight special orders from our main inventory or from the vendor. Our customers tolerated the freight charges on these items, as they were very seldom available from any local distributor.

The major retail auto parts chains pushed much of this back on their vendors. Their distribution centers only stocked items to replenish their stores. Their vendors filled all special orders. Their customers were making FedEx rich, but the chains saved a huge amount of inventory investment.

These customers could not get their car repaired and returned in one day. If any of our competitors had local availability of the needed item, they were likely to get the order. If no one in the local market stocked the item, then the customer just could not get same day repair service. With the ongoing proliferation of auto parts inventory, this is likely to become more common, especially on repair jobs (maintenance jobs usually require faster moving parts that are locally available).

Safety Stocks

J. David Viale presents an interesting formula for the safety stock required in a number of distribution centers.[38]

$$SafetyStockForEachDC = \frac{SafetyStockForOneDC}{\sqrt{NumberOfDCs}}$$

His example is an item that requires 200 units of safety stock if carried in one DC, or 50 units in each of 16 locations.

$$SafetyStockForEachDC = \frac{200}{\sqrt{16}} = \frac{200}{4} = 50$$

---

[38] J. David Viale. Basics of Inventory Management. Crisp Learning. Copyright 1996.

$$SafetyStockForSystem = 50 * 16 = 800$$

He presents this formula without deriving it. It makes sense only if you presume that the deviation in demand would be much larger in each location if the total business is spread over multiple locations, and that is likely to be the case.

This is certainly not intended to be a discussion of distribution center network designs. Rather it is just a few tips for working with an existing network.

Where to put the Buyers

You can start a good debate with any multi-location distributor by asking whether they favor centralized or decentralized purchasing. There are some pros and cons to both strategies. Here are some factors that should be considered in each situation:

- Factors in Favor of Decentralized Purchasing
    - The buyer is much more likely to get valuable input from customers and other employees if they are in a branch location.
    - The buyer can easily verify inventory if they are in a branch. If there is a question about the on-hand balance, or the unit of measure, or the accuracy of a shipment, the buyer is close to the action.

- Factors in Favor of Centralized Purchasing.
    - Managers feel it is easier to manage a group if they are all in one location.
    - It is easier to cover vacations and absences. It takes more coordination if individual employees are each stationed in different branches.
    - If your buyers can handle more than one location per person, then they can't be in each branch, so they might as well be centralized.
    - If your buyers are specialized by product category or vendor, and buy that one category for all locations, then they might as well be centralized.
    - If your buyers would not have any contact with customers or employees in a branch, then they might as well be centralized.

Over time we operated our company both ways. The computer and communication technology permits either way to operate very well. I always preferred a decentralized structure for our company. I felt the contact with customers and ready access to the branch inventory was very valuable. We found ways to handle the issues of reporting to a single manager, covering vacations, etc.

Chapter Summary

Multiple locations offer both opportunities and challenges. It is clearly more of a challenge to manage and coordinate activities for multiple locations.

Multiple locations can improve customer service by using some locations as master warehouses or "hub" stores, and by offering to transfer or drop ship orders directly to customers from any available inventory.

Multiple locations may also offer economies of scale by allowing buyers to manage more than one location, and by concentrating safety stocks only where they are needed.

Chapter 27. Supplier Performance Reviews

We had an excellent tool in the aftermarket. Our trade association, the Automotive Warehouse Distributor's Association (AWDA) held an unusual but very productive annual business conference.

The conference consisted of a few general sessions with educational presentations, and about thirty 45-minute time slots for "one-on-one" meetings between a distributor and a manufacturer. Distributors and Manufacturers each submitted priority ranked lists of individual member companies they wanted to see. AWDA used priority rankings and mutual requests to arrange schedules of one-on-one appointments. Our company usually had two or three "teams", so we could meet privately with 60 to 90 manufacturers over the 3-1/2 day conference.

These were very productive sessions, as you had the decision makers from both sides in a private meeting. You can get a lot done in 45 minutes if both parties are prepared and you have the right people in the room.

This was held in the late fall, so the timing was good to get plans synchronized for the coming year.

We generally covered the following topics:

1. Recent performance—We reviewed our sales results versus prior years and versus the industry data, the vendor's order fill and lead-time, and the results of any recent promotions or programs. We reviewed recent support levels from both the vendor company and ours.
2. Overall performance of the vendor and the product line. We compared our outbound service level to their inbound service level to us. We reported our inventory position, turnover, gross margin return on investment, warranty and return rates, and asked the vendor to compare them with their other distributors.
3. Status of any inventory projects in process. We reviewed new item implementation, stock adjustments, and any other inventory coordination.
4. Status of any marketing plans in process. We compared lists of new account prospects, marketing or sales programs in process, coordination of vendor efforts and ours. We reviewed usage of marketing funds if that vendor had a program.
5. A comparison of expectations. We wanted our vendor to understand what we expected from them, and offered them a

chance to tell us what they expected of us. This was great for getting "on the same page".

6. Goals and plans for the coming year. We compared our forecast of expected volume change for this line versus our vendor's forecast and any industry data.

While it was not possible in a 45-minute meeting to get into the details of many of these topics, it was possible to reach a mutual agreement to work on specific projects, or to accomplish specific goals.

It required a lot of preparation, and an equal amount of time after the conference to follow up on 60-90 individual meetings, but it was a very focused way to meet with the top management of most of our suppliers in a productive setting.

A sample data sheet from one AWDA Distributor for a meeting with one of their vendors is in Figure 1.

Sample Performace Results Chart						
1995 - 99 PRODUCT LINE PERFORMANCE RESULTS & PROJECTIONS						
1999 AWDA FALL BUSINESS CONFERENCE PLAN - PAGE 1						
VENDOR OR BRAND	Sample Product Line			VEND CODE.SL:		
PRODUCT LINE(S)	WHEEL BEARINGS & SEALS			JBR CLASS QTR:		ANNUAL
REPRESENTED BY				BUYER	K W-D	
SALES AND INVENTORY PERIOD COVERED	1995	1996	1997	1998	1999	PROJ 00
WD $ NET SALES VOLUME INVOICED TO JOBBERS	420,529	579,712	583,525	607,278	678,201	742,630
WD NET SALES CHANGE % VS PRIOR YEAR	0.00%	37.85%	0.66%	4.07%	11.68%	10.61%
WD INVOICED GM % (MOVED TO FOI DISCS 3/26/96)	30.70%	24.10%	20.20%	23.20%	23.90%	23.50%
WD INVOICED GP $ (MOVED TO FOI DISCS 3/26/96)	129,102	139,711	117,872	140,888	162,090	174,518
WD INVENTORY $ END OF PERIOD (INCLS CORES AFT	109,522	98,080	97,220	95,500	95,916	95,000
WD INVENTORY TURNOVER RATE FOR PERIOD	2.66	4.49	4.79	4.88	5.38	5.98
WD GROSS PROF RET ON INV'Y INVEST (GPROII)	1.18	1.42	1.21	1.48	1.69	1.84
30 DAY RETURNS % TO GROSS SALES	11.30%	7.50%	9.40%	10.40%	11.40%	
CLASSIFICATION RETURNS % TO GROSS SALES	12.30%	5.30%	6.30%	6.40%	2.90%	
WARRANTY RETURNS % TO GROSS SALES	1.20%	1.40%	1.40%	1.70%	1.60%	
VENDOR / WD MANAGEMENT COMMENT 1. NEED MORE HELP ON NEW NUMBERS TO UPDATE INVENTORY AND COVERAGE						
2. NEED 2000 SALES ACTION PLAN FROM CR BY 1/31/00						
3						
4						FORM LP 63099
KEY VENDOR EXECS VISITED:		PAG EXECS:				

Ch 27 Fig 1. Sample AWDA One-on-one Supplier Review Data Sheet [39]

---

[39] With Permission from Kris Walker, Packerland Automotive Group.

At its peak, AWDA had more than 300 distributor members and more than 200 manufacturers. Most attended the conference. It was not unusual for the total conference to include over 7,000 scheduled one-on-one meetings.

Chapter Summary

It is important to have at least one major review and planning meeting with each supplier each year.

The entire range of inventory management issues should be discussed.

Pete Kornafel

Chapter 28. The Impact of Inventory Management on Margin

Most managers view good inventory management as a way to optimize investment, and maximize customer service. It is less well understood that good inventory management would also generate a huge increase in gross margin dollars. Here are some points to consider:

At the Store

There is a rough rule of thumb in auto parts stores that only about 1/3 of demands for items not in the store inventory can be converted to a special order sale. This is because the service dealer or retail customer has an immediate need for a replacement part. They are likely to try all other local sources for items they need right away, and a store with the part in stock will get the sale.

Thousands of auto parts items are very slow movers, and not likely to be in any store inventory. Even in these cases, a customer is likely to call or visit several stores before he concludes the part is not available quickly. The customer will then let the store special order the item for later delivery. The last store, not the first one, is likely to get this special order, as it would be unusual for a customer to go back to the first source. We trained our store counter people to try to close special order sales. When a part was a very slow mover, and not in the store inventory, they would tell the customer that it would not be available from any local store, and they should go ahead and special order it. This only worked occasionally, so roughly 2/3 of these sales were lost completely.

For some customers, our stores would offer to perform the inventory search of other local stores. They would buy the part for the customer if anyone had it. These "buyouts" captured the sale, but usually at very low margins.

Filling as many orders as possible from the store inventory will obviously maximize the generation of gross margin dollars. It depends on the best mix of items in the store, and consistent replenishment practices. A bad mix of inventory could easily reduce the store's order fill from inventory by 10%. Even after some orders are retained by buyouts or special orders, it could reduce sales by 6-7%, and gross margin by 2-3% of overall sales. The median auto parts store generates about 4% of sales as pretax income, so a bad inventory mix can wipe out most of the store's profit.

More margin generation can come from increasing prices for some items in the store inventory. Availability, not price, is the most important purchasing criteria for most auto parts store customers. This gives a store the opportunity to increase selling prices a bit for some items in inventory. It does not work for all items—fast movers are almost commodities. A serious auto parts customer knows the price of motor oil as well as any frequent grocery shopper knows the price of milk. However, there are thousands of items where the customer does not have a preconception of the price. There has been an opportunity to add a few percent to the selling price of these items, and get a significant improvement to gross margin and income. It should be noted that the ability to price this way has come under much more competitive pressure. More customers are subscribing to data services that give the manufacturer's suggested prices for all major brands. These customers can shop on their own, and this has reduced the store's ability to mark items up over the suggested prices.

At the Distribution Center

Good inventory management is a key to maximizing distribution center profits, too. In Chapter 16 there is an explanation of the cost of lost sales.

In our company, we assumed we lost 100% of the gross margin if we did not have an item in stock.

Order fill comparisons between companies are difficult, as there are many ways to measure fill—units, dollars, line items, etc. However, it is clear that the best auto parts distributors can fill at least 5% better than average. A well-managed distribution center can achieve 95% order fill consistently, measured in line items shipped complete. An average company probably ships about 90% on this basis. Here again, the lower order fill could reduce gross margin and profits by 1-2%. This is a significant change where the average distribution center generates about 4% of sales as pretax income.

Chapter Summary:

Stores and distribution centers lose most or the entire gross margin when they can't ship an item from inventory.

This can easily cut the pretax income of the business in half.

All of the techniques in this book will help select the right items to stock, and the best way to replenish them. It is a key to maximizing distribution center gross margin and profit.

Pete Kornafel

Chapter 29. Supply Chain Considerations

I confess most of this chapter represents wishful thinking, not techniques based on actual experience. Most of the computer systems in the automotive aftermarket were incompatible and many used proprietary data formats, so there has been little coordinated effort and sharing of information on inventory management.

Automotive Aftermarket History:

Single companies treated their own locations as one entity and practiced some primitive supply chain or demand chain techniques. Many companies shared classification and item information, but few industry standards existed for this data, so what was done was typically just between a few companies.

A data standard and network called Transnet was established in the mid 1970's for transmitting orders from automotive aftermarket distributors to manufacturers. Six manufacturers set the original data standard. I transmitted my first order to a vendor by keying it in to a Teletype machine to produce a punched paper tape. Then our machine called another Teletype machine at the vendor's location, and "played" the tape over the phone line to reprint our order on their machine. It was rocket science in 1975. Transnet quickly introduced computer-to-computer file layouts and dial-up transmission protocols. Later, the manufacturer's trade association managed this (as a "for profit" company), using GE Information Systems as the network provider. Transnet is still in use today.

There was no easy way to share information on sales, demand, inventory and forecasts.

So, it is easier to document the needs and opportunities than solutions.

Some Challenges:

The single most valuable technique is to provide visibility of all inventory and demand data to everyone in the channel. This enables all kinds of collaboration on inventory, forecasts, and planning. It requires several key things:

1. Synchronized data. It is essential to confirm that each participant uses the same identification for items, units of measure, and other data. One of our vendors experienced an

early disaster in "vendor managed inventory". This vendor was going to automatically replenish the distributor's inventory based on actual end user demand. One problem came with industrial hydraulic hose. The basic unit of sale at the vendor was a case of 10 rolls of 50 feet each. The basic unit of sale at the distributor was one roll of 50 feet. The stores cut the rolls and sold exact lengths to customers, so their basic unit of sale was one foot. So, the store sold a 5 foot long hose, transmitted the sale for "5" to the vendor, and they interpreted that as 5 cases of 10 rolls of 50 feet each, or 2,500 feet. Inventory got out of hand in a hurry.

2. Trust. It requires a lot of trust to give all your sales data to a vendor. You are exposing your entire business to them. If they do not treat this properly as very confidential information, you are putting your entire business at risk. At the same time, the vendor must trust the distributors. If they put their factory inventory on line, it opens the possibility that a distributor will see shortages and order items from another source. So, trust is required all around.

3. Data exchange: A few of the larger companies used EDI to exchange some of this information, but EDI mapping software was unavailable or expensive for most small distributors.

So, up to now, most automotive aftermarket companies have managed their inventory independently.

Each time I felt that the automotive aftermarket was way behind other industries, I found some confirmation of that, but also evidence that much of this work needs to be done everywhere. A survey across many companies and industries was performed by BearingPoint (formerly KPMG Consulting) and published in Chain Store Age in December 2002.[40] More than half the respondents operate chains with more than 100 locations, and more than half the respondents have chains with more than $500 million annual sales. Even among this set of larger companies, there is much still to be done.

- 76% cited the most frequent way they communicate with vendors is with the telephone.
- Only 50% of these companies share store level sales data with vendors.

---

[40] Inventory Management 2002: Data, Detail, and Discipline. Survey by BearingPoint, published as a supplement to Chain Store Age, December 2002.

- 15% of these companies do not maintain an individual SKU level inventory.
- 37% do not have visibility of the entire inventory in their own companies.
- 20% of these companies still use manual reordering as their principal method of replenishment.

My hope is that the Internet, XML, and some third party companies who translate and map data will make all the difference and permit much more collaboration on inventory management.

The Need and Opportunity:

It has been very clear that independent actions by businesses at each level in the distribution channel magnify fluctuations in demand as you get farther away from the end user customers and closer to the manufacturers. Scheduled orders, minimum order sizes, truckload requirements, forward buying, and "loader" promotions all move large blocks of inventory part way into the channel, with little tie to the end user demand. I've always said the distributors make waves in the channel. Silver[41] refers to it as the "bullwhip" effect. He makes the point that inventories at various points in the distribution channel are supposed to buffer the factory from variability in orders, but in actuality have the opposite effect. Distributors react to small increases in demand by increasing their inventory, and that magnifies the change when viewed by orders received at the manufacturer level. In some cases the manufacturers exacerbate the situation by offering terms for large orders, end-of-quarter loader deals, and other promotions.

In fact, an auto part isn't really "sold" until it is installed on a vehicle. One particularly cynical vendor claimed a part wasn't sold until it was installed and the warranty period had expired, but I think that's going way too far. The real demand in the automotive aftermarket takes place at more than 250,000 service stations, garages, tire stores, car dealers, and other repair outlets, at more than 40,000 stores selling parts to retail customers, and at more than 1,000,000 fleet maintenance centers. We are a long way from

---

[41] Pg. 472. Edward Silver, David Pyke, Rein Peterson, Inventory Management And Production Planning and Scheduling, Third Edition, 1998, John Wiley and Sons.

aggregating all that data in a meaningful fashion, but there is a lot we could and should be doing.

Forms of Collaboration:

Silver (Pg. 489) shows two main models for collaboration:

1. Global Access to Information, Centralized Control of all Inventory. The ultimate example of this is Vendor Managed Inventory, or VMI.
2. Global Access to Information, Decentralized Control of all Inventory. Most implementations of Distribution Requirements Planning (DRP) systems are of this type.

Global Access to Information

This is the first key element in collaboration. All levels should be able to see the end user customer demand data, and treat it as the very best forecast of actual demand. The entire difference between this level of demand and the views from each position in the channel is due to pipeline movement of inventory within the channel.

Here is one last auto parts tale. I was standing behind the counter of one of our CARQUEST stores one day. The store's biggest customer was a tire store right across the street. I was listening to one side of a phone conversation. The tire store was trying to order a set of disc brake pads for a Ford F-150 pickup. I heard our counterman ask the question "does it have four wheel drive or two wheel drive?" There was a pause, and the tire store must have replied that they had not looked at the vehicle. Then our counterman asked them what color it was. I've had lots of customers tell me what color their vehicle was, some in jest and some in ignorance, but I've NEVER asked a customer that question, so my ears perked up. Our counterman ducked under the counter, came up with a set of binoculars, and looked at all the vehicles parked in the tire store's lot. He said "OK, I see the blue one, and it's a 4X4, so I'll send you the right brake pads." This must have been routine for the counterman, as he just went about his other business at the store.

This incident made a big impression on me. I've spent a lot of time thinking about how valuable it would be to have a set of "binoculars" that could look into the repair shop and see what is really happening. You could see which parts are really getting installed, which ones are going to be returned, which ones they bought from one of our competitors, and how soon they really need the parts. It would offer us tremendous opportunities for better service and better inventory management.

Where Should the Inventory Be?

Most customers want their car repaired and ready in one day, regardless of what has to be done to it. Repair shops try to accommodate that, and we try to stock "everything" at each store to support them.

Even if the parts were readily available locally, some repair jobs just can't be completed in one day. Items for these kinds of jobs don't need to be in the shop inventory or even in the local store inventory, as long as we can get them to the shop the next morning. We could provide that service from all of our distribution centers to all of our stores, and that could take a huge amount of inventory out of our stores.

Shop owners are reluctant to take on some major jobs on a "same day" basis. They are not sure how long the job will take until they perform some of the diagnostics, and they don't want to commit a technician and a service bay until they understand the length of time the job will take. They will ask the car owner to make an appointment for a future day. If we could see that information, we would have time to get the parts that might be needed to the shop on an orderly basis. Here again, we would not have to stock these items at local stores. They could be stocked at a regional DC, and could be at any shop we serve tomorrow morning, or whenever they are needed to match the arrival of the vehicle.

The kind of part also matters. If the part is a brake rotor, for example, then the car is likely to be up in the air on a hoist at the shop, with the wheels off. That bay and hoist are completely tied up until the shop can get and install the part. If it is an underhood item like a belt or hose, the car could be pushed out of a service bay if the needed part is delayed. The shop couldn't finish that vehicle, but at least it wouldn't have to tie up a bay while they were waiting for the part. So, our customers need the fastest service on undercar items.

If we could identify the parts and part types that do not have to be delivered in 30 minutes, we could serve those demands with special orders from our DCs. We could get the parts to the shop when they really need them.

We would incur some increase in returns, as we would send parts out of the DC in anticipation they will be used. Everything not used will be returned. However, that's pretty much what happens today, anyway, so I don't think the increase would be huge. It clearly wouldn't be enough to offset the tremendous inventory savings we could achieve if we could deliver these kinds of items in one day from a DC inventory rather than 30 minutes from every store inventory.

So, visibility of the repair jobs in process and the appointment book at a repair shop could give us a huge benefit in reducing store inventories on some part types.

In the longer run, a newer technology called Telematics is just emerging with fairly widespread adoption on new vehicles. Programs like GM's OnStar can enable all kinds of communications. The vehicle occupants can get services such as directions, roadside assistance, Internet access and e-mail. The vehicle itself can communicate with other locations. One prototype system proposed by Hewlett Packard demonstrated that a vehicle could transmit fault codes, mileage, and other data to service providers, and possibly make service appointments, speed diagnosis, and even pre-order required parts.

Cleaner Forecasts

The end user demand at the shop for "Do-It-For-Me" (DIFM) items and at the store for "Do-It-Yourself" (DIY) items is the very best data to use for forecasting an item at every step in the channel. It may not be possible to get visibility into the shop, but store sales and returns are a pretty good proxy for this. Data warehouses are just now making that data available widely.

You would still have to add known pipeline activity to this forecast. For example, if we open (or close) a number of stores or add a DC, or consolidate two DCs into one, or adjust the merchandise mix, that inventory has to be supplied by or returned to the manufacturers on top of the end user demand data. However, everyone would be able to separate the real usage from the pipeline events.

In Chapter 4 on Defining Demand, there was a lot of discussion about how to recognize, eliminate or filter out pipeline transactions to try to get to a good "demand" number. End user sales data eliminates the need for most of those changes to the data, and would drive much more accurate forecasts.

Dying Items

There is lots of evidence that the distribution channel cannot withdraw inventory of dying items rationally. We tend to leave it in place too long. The result is that by the time the vendor makes the part obsolete, and gets all the final returns, there is more than a lifetime supply of the item at the vendor's location. If the vendor could see the entire inventory in the channel, and weigh that against their supply position, they could decide when to stop manufacturing an item, and we could all live on the existing inventory.

All of this is possible with visibility of inventory just within the set of our vendors, our own locations, and our customers.

Even more would be possible if we could find a way to share data throughout the industry. Category management has made a great impact in food, mass merchandise, and other categories of items. It is just getting started in the automotive aftermarket.

Avoiding Sub-Optimization

When each company makes all of its own inventory decisions without benefit of information from suppliers and customers, it can optimize its own situation, but this is usually not the optimum solution for the entire channel.

JD Edwards[42], a software provider, includes a software module to consider all costs and constraints across the entire supply chain. This can set the optimum strategy using much more information. It can consider constraints: Is adequate space and handling resources available at a warehouse?; Does the transportation system have capacity or other constraints?; What are the costs of ordering from various locations, and which is optimum?; What strategy maximizes profits?.

SCORE[43], a software package from Evant, offers other tools to maximize profits across all locations. It can allocate inventory when full desired quantities are not available. It can combine orders across multiple vendors into one coordinated shipment. This balances the inventory time supply across all affected categories. This is an excellent tool, for example, to fill a container with

---

[42] Evolving from Distribution Requirements Planning to Collaborative Supply Chain Planning. A "position paper" by JD Edwards, June, 2002.
[43] Score Distribution Replenishment—brochure. Evant Software, San Francisco, CA.

imported products from multiple overseas vendors. Ordinary inventory management tools would optimize each order, but not consider the costs and profits of a combined strategy.

Inventory Management and Purchasing Collaboration

Silver[44] refers to inventory in a managed distribution channel as "echelon" inventory.

His book has a long discussion about Vendor Managed Inventory or "push" systems. I am not going to discuss them at all. I do not believe distributors and stores in the aftermarket would accept VMI systems.

Trust is one issue. A high level of trust is needed to share all the information, but an even higher level would be needed to allow a vendor to manage distributor and store inventories. I don't think our industry could make this move in one step.

Silver also discusses what he calls the Base Stock Control System. All levels of the channel see all the information, but each level decides when to reorder based on demand from a lower echelon. The advantages here are that each level stays in control of their own decisions, but can make them with full information about the entire channel.

It permits collaboration on many levels. There can be agreements on which items are stocked at each level, for example, without any level giving up control.

Silver also makes the point that the optimum solution is to NOT duplicate safety stocks between the manufacturer and the distributor. It should be held in one location or the other, but not both. This assumes the two parties negotiate on lead times and delivery commitments. This may not work in all situations. Where it does work, this level of collaboration could offer another huge system inventory reduction. Silver presents a formula that shows that the variation in demand is smaller at the central location when compared to the sum of the lower levels. This is because higher than average demands at some locations will tend to be cancelled out by lower than average demands at others. The aggregate demand is smoother.

---

[44] Pg. 486-494. Edward Silver, David Pyke, Rein Peterson, Inventory Management And Production Planning and Scheduling, Third Edition, 1998, John Wiley and Sons.

Silver gives some fairly complicated formulas to compute order points at each level in the channel for this model of collaboration. His examples show that significant system inventory reductions are clearly possible, without degrading customer service. I'm not aware of any company in the automotive aftermarket using these techniques, but we should try them to see if they will work for auto parts.

MechanicNet is a Customer Relationship Management software company in the aftermarket. They estimate the total inventory in the automotive aftermarket in the U.S. is in excess of $40 billion.[45] They ambitiously estimate that as much as half of this is unnecessary if telematics was widely adopted, and used to streamline vehicle maintenance and repair. This includes efficiencies from order accuracy improvements (with better diagnostics of vehicle problems), shipping slow moving items from distribution centers when needed, rather than maintaining inventories at each store, removing "phantom" demand from multiple orders for one item, reducing replenishment of items that are ordered but not installed, and more efficient "just in time" delivery systems.

Chapter Summary

The automotive aftermarket is just beginning to recognize the value of collaboration between vendors and distributors.

There are many techniques that can be applied when collaboration is possible.

It requires a great deal of trust between vendors and distributors. I hope our industry implements many of these techniques in the near future. It will be critical to maintaining customer service in the face of endless proliferation of parts.

---

[45] Quoted in "What is Telematics and what Impact could it have on the Independent Repair Facility." A white paper from by MechanicNet Group for a class at Ohio State University's 2010 Advanced Management Program for the Automotive Aftermarket

Pete Kornafel

Chapter 30. Conclusion and a Checklist

It is very easy to separate the companies with good inventory management from those with very bad inventory management. In the automotive aftermarket, almost all of the bad ones have failed. Bad inventory managers cannot survive the pressure of inventory proliferation in the automotive aftermarket.

Companies with excellent inventory management practices have substantially outperformed the overall industry consistently over many years. They have been able to keep up with the proliferation, and maintain their customer service levels in the face of ever more complex inventory situations.

Here is a very brief checklist of functions that a good, complete inventory management system should provide:

1. Merchandise Planning. Deciding which items to stock at each level of distribution is the single largest financial decision in the auto parts category, with its tens of thousands of slow moving parts and high need for immediate customer service. A great system would leverage all kinds of data to help choose the merchandise assortment for each location.
2. Inventory Accuracy. A good system needs tools to help maintain very accurate inventory data in every location. Collaboration on forecasting can also help position safety stocks at the optimum locations.
3. Forecasting. A wide variety of techniques are needed for items with varying customers and sales patterns.
4. Visibility. A great system would offer all authorized users visibility of inventory in many locations, enable ordering from the most profitable source, and help everyone maximize customer service.
5. Replenishment. If all the underlying data is accurate and if all the analytical work has been done, replenishment can be largely automated.
6. Logistics. There are many constraints to deal with, and opportunities for efficiency with collaboration across all levels in the distribution channel.
7. Auditing and Payables. There are opportunities to automate much of the process of auditing shipments versus billing, and the process of paying vendors.

It is my hope that every reader of this book has found a few good ideas that they can incorporate into their own company systems.

Appendix 1. Normal Distribution Values

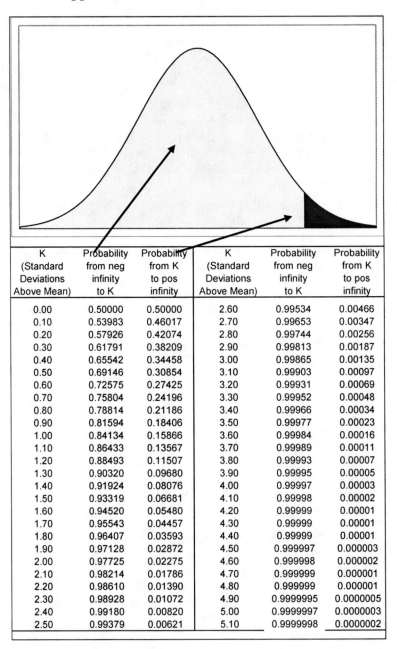

K (Standard Deviations Above Mean)	Probability from neg infinity to K	Probability from K to pos infinity	K (Standard Deviations Above Mean)	Probability from neg infinity to K	Probability from K to pos infinity
0.00	0.50000	0.50000	2.60	0.99534	0.00466
0.10	0.53983	0.46017	2.70	0.99653	0.00347
0.20	0.57926	0.42074	2.80	0.99744	0.00256
0.30	0.61791	0.38209	2.90	0.99813	0.00187
0.40	0.65542	0.34458	3.00	0.99865	0.00135
0.50	0.69146	0.30854	3.10	0.99903	0.00097
0.60	0.72575	0.27425	3.20	0.99931	0.00069
0.70	0.75804	0.24196	3.30	0.99952	0.00048
0.80	0.78814	0.21186	3.40	0.99966	0.00034
0.90	0.81594	0.18406	3.50	0.99977	0.00023
1.00	0.84134	0.15866	3.60	0.99984	0.00016
1.10	0.86433	0.13567	3.70	0.99989	0.00011
1.20	0.88493	0.11507	3.80	0.99993	0.00007
1.30	0.90320	0.09680	3.90	0.99995	0.00005
1.40	0.91924	0.08076	4.00	0.99997	0.00003
1.50	0.93319	0.06681	4.10	0.99998	0.00002
1.60	0.94520	0.05480	4.20	0.99999	0.00001
1.70	0.95543	0.04457	4.30	0.99999	0.00001
1.80	0.96407	0.03593	4.40	0.99999	0.00001
1.90	0.97128	0.02872	4.50	0.999997	0.000003
2.00	0.97725	0.02275	4.60	0.999998	0.000002
2.10	0.98214	0.01786	4.70	0.999999	0.000001
2.20	0.98610	0.01390	4.80	0.999999	0.000001
2.30	0.98928	0.01072	4.90	0.9999995	0.0000005
2.40	0.99180	0.00820	5.00	0.9999997	0.0000003
2.50	0.99379	0.00621	5.10	0.9999998	0.0000002

Bibliography

Automotive Aftermarket Industry Association (AAIA)) Aftermarket Fact Book, 2002/2003 Edition, and the AAIA Mini-Monitor. Copyright 2002, AAIA.

Automotive Service Industry Association. 1984 Edition, Automotive Wholesaling Financial Operation Analysis. ASIA, 1984.

Bearing Point. Inventory Management 2002: Data, Detail, and Discipline. Survey. Supplement to Chain Store Age, December, 2002.

Charles Bodenstab, A New Era in Inventory Management, Hilta Press 1993.

B. Jay Coleman. Determining the Correct Service Level Target. APICS Journal, First Quarter, 2000.

E3 Associates, Ltd. Seasonal Profile and Trend Forecasting. Copyright 1981 TX 696-528

E3 Associates, Ltd. Service Level Analysis. Copyright 1981. TX 663-972

J.D. Edwards. Evolving from Distribution Requirements Planning to Collaborative Supply Chain Planning. Position Paper. June 2002.

Edmunds. Model generations for various vehicles. http://www.edmunds.com/reviews/generations/articles/

Evant Software, Score Distribution Replenishment Brochure. San Francisco, CA, 2002.

Philip T. Evers. The Effect of Lead Times on Safety Stocks. APICS Journal, Second Quarter, 1999.

Gordon Graham. Distribution Inventory Management for the 1990's. Inventory Management Press, Richardson, Texas. 1987

Thomas J. Goldsby. Inventory Management Part 1. Ohio State University. 2002. http://www.cob.ohio-state.edu/~goldsby_2/classes/780/(780)05_Inventory_I.ppt

Anders Herlitz. The Economics of Forward Buying. White Paper. E3 Associates, 1982.

History of the Windsor small block. http://home.pon.net/hunnicutt/history_windsor.htm.

IBM INVEN/3, INVEN/34, INVEN/38 Program Description and Operations Manual. IBM Corporation. 1974.

Chuck LaMacchia, Sizing it Up, APICS Journal, January 2003.

MechanicNet Group. The Telematics Opportunity. White Paper. Pleasanton, CA 2001.

Alan Miller. Managing Slow Moving and Difficult Products Throughout the Supply Chain. White Paper. Mercia Software, 1999

William B. Miller and Vicki L. Schenk. All I Need to Know about Manufacturing I Learned at Joe's Garage. Bayrock Press, 2001.

Motor Equipment and Manufacturers Association. Scrapage Rates in the United States. MEMA Study, 2000

Max Muller. Essentials of Inventory Management. AMACOM, 2003.

Dave Piasecki. Optimizing Economic Order Quantity (EOQ) http://www.inventoryops.com/economic_order_quantity.htm. 2002.

REM Associates. Inventory Ownership Cost. http://www.remassoc.com/news/ownership.htm. 2002.

James A. Robison. Inventory Profile Analysis: An Aggregation Technique for Improving Customer Service While Reducing Inventory. APICS Journal, Second Quarter, 2001.

David Salsburg, The Lady Tasting Tea, Henry Holt and Company, 2002.

Jon Schreibfeder. The Mysterious Cost of Carrying Inventory. http://www.effectiveinventory.com/article35.html.

Jon Schreibfeder. Guess Right. NAW DREF. 2003.

Edward Silver, David Pyke, Rein Peterson, Inventory Management And Production Planning and Scheduling, Third Edition. John Wiley and Sons, 1998.

Bernard T. Smith. Focus Forecasting. Bookcrafters. Copyright 1997

J. David Viale, Basics of Inventory Management, Crisp Learning, Copyright 1996.

Tony Wild. Best Practice in Inventory Management. John Wiley and Sons, 1997.

Index

About the Author

Pete Kornafel and his wife Lorraine owned Hatch Grinding Company. Hatch had two distribution centers supplying a full range of auto parts to 100+ CARQUEST Auto Parts Stores, 8 company stores, and 200+ employees.

Both served as Chairman of the Automotive Warehouse Distributors Association. He received AWDA's Leader of the Year Award.

Hatch was Small Business of the Year in Denver in 1984, and he was Small Business Person of the Year in Colorado in 1985.

He has a BS in Mechanical Engineering (MIT) and an MBA (Harvard Business School).

With others, he instructs AWDA's Inventory Management Workshop, and has worked with 200+ automotive companies.

He was President of CARQUEST Corporation, and one of two founding partners of E3 Associates.

Printed in the United States
120847LV00003BA/61-81/A

9 781414 059099